WORK AND FAMILY IN AMERICA

A Reference Handbook

Other Titles in ABC-CLIO's
CONTEMPORARY
WORLD ISSUES
Series

Abortion, Second Edition, Marie Costa
Adoption, Barbara Moe
Affirmative Action, Lynne Eisaguirre
American Homelessness, Third Edition, Mary Ellen Hombs
Feminism, Judith Harlan
Human Rights, Second Edition, Lucille Whalen and
  Nina Redman
The Religious Right, Second Edition, Glenn H. Utter and
  John W. Storey
School Violence, Deborah L. Kopka
Single Parents, Karen L. Kinnear
Tax Reform, James John Jurinski
World Population, Geoffrey Gilbert

Books in the Contemporary World Issues series address vital issues in today's society such as terrorism, sexual harassment, homelessness, AIDS, gambling, animal rights, and air pollution. Written by professional writers, scholars, and nonacademic experts, these books are authoritative, clearly written, up-to-date, and objective. They provide a good starting point for research by high school and college students, scholars, and general readers, as well as by legislators, businesspeople, activists, and others.

Each book, carefully organized and easy to use, contains an overview of the subject; a detailed chronology; biographical sketches; facts and data and/or documents and other primary-source material; a directory of organizations and agencies; annotated lists of print and nonprint resources; a glossary; and an index.

Readers of books in the Contemporary World Issues series will find the information they need in order to better understand the social, political, environmental, and economic issues facing the world today.

WORK AND FAMILY IN AMERICA

A Reference Handbook

Leslie F. Stebbins

CONTEMPORARY WORLD ISSUES

A B C 🕮 C L I O

Santa Barbara, California
Denver, Colorado
Oxford, England

Library of Congress Cataloging-in-Publication Data

Stebbins, Leslie.
   Work and family in America : a reference handbook / by Leslie Stebbins.
      p. cm. — (Contemporary world issues)
Includes bibliographical references and index.
   ISBN 1-57607-224-X
   1. Work and family—United States—Handbooks, manuals, etc.
2. Work and family—Research—United States.   I. Title.   II. Series.
   HD4904.25 .S84 2001
   306.3'6'0973—dc21

                                                        2001003233

07 06 05 04 03 02 01   10 9 8 7 6 5 4 3 2 1

This book is also available on the World Wide Web as an e-book. Visit www.abc-clio.com for details.

ABC-CLIO, Inc.
130 Cremona Drive, P.O. Box 1911   ∞
Santa Barbara, California 93116-1911

This book is printed on acid-free paper   .
Manufactured in the United States of America

To Mang, Anna, and Will—
all my love

Contents

Preface

The very nature of the workplace and the home are gradually but dramatically changing, as women with children continue to move into the paid workforce and men become more involved in roles within the home. In 1998 Federal Bureau of Investigation director Louis Freeh made national headlines when he announced that he would take paid paternity leave to care for his newborn son. In 2000 Tony Blair, prime minister of England, made international headlines by discussing his reluctance to take paternity leave. In five years, perhaps, these incidents will not garner front-page headlines.

The family has changed a great deal, but the workplace has made only minor adjustments to these changes. Employees are going through increasingly difficult contortions to accommodate the demands of the workplace with the needs of their families. The price paid for these contortions—lower productivity, morale, and retention—has not been lost on the corporate world. As "family-friendly" benefits evolve, more attention will be paid to what works and what employees need, whether it is paid leave for the parent traveling to China to adopt a baby or a flexible schedule for the employee taking care of an unmarried partner's elderly mother. But corporations are not the only players in the changing relationship between work and family—the government, the community, and individuals all have important roles to play in helping place family and personal needs on equal footing with the needs of the workplace.

Work-family, first mentioned in the research literature in the 1970s, has evolved into its own multidisciplinary field of study, with thousands of articles and hundreds of scholarly and popular books. Once viewed as a "women and daycare problem," work-family now encompasses a vast and complex set of issues such as eldercare, fatherhood, telecommuting, pay equity, part-time workers, employee productivity and retention, feminism, child care and child development, youth violence, welfare, corporate benefits, nontraditional families, and family values. There are no easy answers and many divergent ideas about resolving work-family challenges. The research literature is impressive but incomplete. Though it is now beginning to surface, more research is needed on the experiences of lower-wage employees and minority and ethnic employees at all levels of the workplace.

This book is intended to provide students, researchers, human resource professionals, and activists with a balanced and detailed overview of the field of work-family. Chapter 1 consists of a detailed overview of the history and current research on work-family. The second chapter provides a chronology of work-family since 1800, a history that reflects women's increasing involvement in the workforce, the creation and evolution of child care services, the emergence of eldercare and more involved fathering, and the first and second waves of the women's movement. Chapter 3 provides a selective collection of biographies of researchers who are currently active in the field. Chapter 4 provides statistics on work-family trends, including historical, current, and international comparisons. The fifth chapter reviews legislation and cases that have had an impact on the field, with particular emphasis on employment laws affecting women—a key component of the study of work-family. The sixth chapter contains descriptions and contact information for public and private, scholarly, and activist organizations involved in work-family research and activities. The last two chapters provide annotated bibliographies of print, video, and Internet resources on work and family issues, as well as a list of important scholarly journals covering the field. A glossary of definitions of work-family terms completes the volume.

Acknowledgments

Balancing work and family implies that some equilibrium can actually be found and that one can attend adequately to the demands of work and the needs of family if only the proper mix of skills and time can be discovered. Instead, constant trade-offs must be negotiated and rethought. I would like to thank my husband Tom for the many weekends he spent with our children while I worked on this book and for his advice at every step, and my children, Anna and Will, for their acceptance and patience.

I would also like to thank my "editor of first resort," Rebecca Stebbins, and our mother, Kathryn Stebbins, who babysat while Rebecca reviewed my book. I am grateful to my father, William Stebbins, for his minimalist but sage counsel and to my sister Liz Stebbins and her husband, Jeff Osborn, for their generous support in helping me better balance work and family. In addition, I would like to thank Brandeis University Libraries for allowing me time off to work on this book and for their gradual but growing acceptance of work-family needs within the workplace. Lastly, I would like to thank my editor, Alicia Merritt, for holding my hand throughout the process of publishing this book and the other editors and assistants at ABC-CLIO for their valuable support along the way.

Leslie Stebbins

1

Introduction and Overview

This chapter outlines the major research trends in the field of work-family over the past few decades. Beginning with a broad historical view, the dynamic overlap between the work and family domains is explored. Though the roles of work and family were once completely intertwined, the Industrial Revolution and the separation of the workplace from the home led to a separation of the worlds of work and family, as well as the worlds of men and women. As women entered the workforce in greater numbers since the 1970s, the worlds of work and family collided.

Initial research on work-family from the 1970s and 1980s viewed work-family essentially as a "women's issue." Researchers investigated the effects of women's work on women's physical and psychological health and on the health of their children. As women became more prevalent in the workplace in the 1980s, issues such as employment discrimination and pay equity came to the foreground. Toward the end of the twentieth century, researchers began to include men in the work-family equation, broadening their ideas about what role men should play in child rearing and household duties. Recent research has revealed that men are experiencing significant amounts of work-family stress, as they become more involved with family life while the culture of the workplace remains largely unresponsive.

The work-family needs of lower-wage workers, workers from different minority and ethnic groups, and workers from nontraditional families are just beginning to be explored by work-family researchers. For many lower-wage employees, work-family issues present more significant challenges than for those with greater financial resources. With high demand and low retention rates for lower-wage employees, a better under-standing of the issues affecting these families is needed so that appropriate work-family supports can be developed. Little is known about work-family needs that might be unique to partic-ular minority and ethnic groups or to employees who live in non-traditional families, such as single-parent or gay and lesbian fam-ilies. In the past, organizations have tended to place diversity issues on a separate track while paying inadequate attention to the particular work-family needs of minority employees.

The role of caregiving has undergone a dramatic transfor-mation as women have entered the workforce in growing num-bers. Caregiving, both paid and unpaid, is a central issue in the work-family debate. A number of demographic trends have increased the demand for caregivers and decreased the availabil-ity of paid caregivers. Though research has proven that high-qual-ity child care does not have a negative impact on child develop-ment, there is a dearth of high-quality, affordable programs available. There is also a shortage of adequate after-school enrich-ment programs for school-age children who are not ready to be left alone. In addition, eldercare has emerged as a growing con-cern for families that are trying to balance employment demands with care for elderly relatives. Women, who are still largely responsible for meeting caregiving needs, are left with competing demands between work and family. Often women are unable to participate fully in the labor force because of caretaking demands, which leads to further inequities at work. The dissipation of neighborhood life as more women enter the workforce has further eroded the sense of community that once served as a social sup-port for children, the elderly, and the disabled, and for family life.

The roles of the various stakeholders involved with work-family issues—individuals, communities, the government, and employers—are currently under debate in the United States. The corporate world has responded to work-family tensions by creat-ing family-friendly benefits that allow employees to accommo-date some of their family responsibilities. Unfortunately, these benefits have not gained widespread acceptance within most organizations. Researchers are currently taking steps to create cultural change within organizations by relinking work and fam-ily life and demonstrating the effectiveness of work-family pro-grams in relation to productivity and worker commitment.

Social scientists and activists also call for a greater role to be played by the government and the community. Traditionally reluctant to enter the private domain of the family, the U.S. government is lagging far behind those in other industrialized nations in terms of family policy. As work-family issues fold into larger questions about the very nature of work, community, and family member roles, work-family researchers call for more broad-based solutions. The final section of this chapter discusses ways in which work can be restructured and the roles of family member, community member, and employee can be more evenly balanced for men and women.

The History of Work-Family

The history of work-family is the study of the relationship between two primary roles in American society. Work and family have undergone a transformation from being interconnected during colonial times to being viewed today as two separate and sometimes conflicting worlds. The term *housework* did not exist prior to 1841. Until that time, there was no concept that work done in the home was different from any other work done by family members (Hodson and Sullivan 1990). The gradual shift in the location of work to outside the home and the replacement of the family with the workplace as the primary economic unit heightened the tension between the two.

This section will provide a broad overview of the historical relationship between work-family roles. The history of work-family is not a distinct story, but one that varies widely by class, race, ethnicity, sexual orientation, and even by individual. It is beyond the scope of this brief overview to detail how these historical changes affected the many different players involved. Recent research has explored these different streams of history (Cott 1992; Amott and Matthaei 1996; Coontz 1999).

Work-Family in Colonial Times

The worlds of work and family were closely intertwined during colonial times in a precapitalist agrarian society in which the family was relatively self-sufficient. Though the father was the head of the household, the family functioned as a cooperative economic enterprise that competed not with other families but against the forces of nature. Economic survival was the central mission of the family; child rearing was of secondary importance

(Googins 1991). Work and family were not separate worlds; most work took place within the household or family farm. Families were large, and all members, as soon as they were old enough, contributed to the economic survival of the family. The status of women, who worked alongside men, was higher during this period than it became during the nineteenth century, and roles were less compartmentalized and dependent on gender (Barci-auskas and Hull 1989).

The colonial family took care of most of the social and phys-ical needs of its members. Birth, death, religion, politics, care and education of children, and eldercare were all functions of the family. Most families had eight or more children (Kain 1990), and the extended family played a crucial role. Marriage was an eco-nomic necessity for all but the wealthy, and children were essen-tial to running the family farm or business (Googins 1991).

The family was a patriarchal system in which women had few rights and had to submit to the authority of the male head of the household. Men were in charge of discipline and instilling values in their children, but women's agrarian duties kept them close to the home, and though their farm work took priority, they also served as the primary caretakers of the children. Larger fam-ilies often sent some of their children to work for families who had fewer children (Axinn and Levin 1982). Because work and family roles were undifferentiated, the only work and family ten-sions were those that took place within the household.

The work-family experiences of African Americans during this period were quite different. The institution of slavery prohib-ited almost any kind of family ties, though African Americans did manage to maintain some degree of connection. Jacqueline Jones (1987: 84) writes that "under slavery, blacks' attempts to maintain the integrity of family life amounted to a political act of protest."

Work-Family in the Preindustrial Era

The seeds of the split between work and family were planted in the preindustrial era between 1770 and 1880. As the town center began to grow in importance and the development of the craft and trade industries began to take shape, work began to exist as a separate world outside the family unit. From 1820 to 1860, the proportion of nonfarm workers rose from 28 percent to 41 per-cent of the total workforce (U.S. Bureau of the Census 1976).

As the family began to lose its centralized economic function, the importance of large families decreased. Also, young adults gained more independence in job seeking and marriage decisions as passing on the family farm or business became less common (Coontz 1988). The nuclear family began to rise in importance over the extended kinship system, mobility of extended family members increased, and the role of the family shifted to serve as a place for sustenance and personal fulfillment. Childhood began to be viewed as a distinct stage of life, and romantic love rather than economic issues began influencing marriage decisions (Brady 1991).

From the revolutionary period through the middle of the nineteenth century, an "ideology of domesticity" developed that placed men and women in separate spheres and made public work no longer socially acceptable for married, middle-class women (Caffrey 1991). Some scholars (Welter 1966; Bell 1981) have argued that for women, the shift from a more egalitarian division of labor on the farm to the role of running the household represented a loss of power. Stephanie Coontz (1988) and Kathryn Sklar (1973) disagree, arguing that women helped create and promote this new domesticity and that in some ways this new role for women raised their status in the family and in society. Coontz (1988) holds that women sought power and influence as mothers and through religious associations as a way to claim a distinctive space in society at a time when men were gaining access to economic and political spheres outside the home. Margaret Caffrey (1991: 232) agrees and notes that "a separate sphere for women seemed to promote democracy within the family. In theory separate spheres gave women their own autonomous realm of authority, whereas in the eighteenth century household the husband as family head claimed all authority."

This development of separate spheres represented some losses for both men and women. As wage-earning men stopped working from the home, they began to lose many of their family responsibilities, and women began taking over the moral, religious, and educational tasks (Coontz 1988). At the same time, middle-class women began to be excluded from occupations that once were open to them. Later, though still socially restricted from working, wealthier women and some middle-class women got more involved in social movements and volunteer organizations. For working-class women, work remained a central part of their lives, though many hoped to marry into a higher income bracket that would enable them to leave their jobs.

Work-Family Life during the Industrial Revolution

The Industrial Revolution completely transformed the meaning of work in American life. With the advent of factories, work became completely severed from the home, many jobs involved routine and monotonous tasks, and new roles developed within the workplace between managers and workers.

As factory towns grew in importance, people moved from largely rural farming communities to urban centers, further weakening the connections and support of extended families. For economic survival, families needed to have as many members working outside the home as possible. In 1860, 60 percent of the labor force were engaged in farming, but by 1910 less than one-third of the labor force were involved in farming (Bureau of the Census 1976). At the same time, an increase in immigration, driven in part by the need for more workers, brought about diversified communities, with members practicing many different family customs and traditions.

Prior to 1890, nepotism was widely practiced, and many early factories employed husbands, wives, and children from the same families. The family played a large role in personnel and recruitment work, though the degree to which families were able to exercise control over the workplace differed greatly by ethnic group and industry (Kanter 1977). After 1890, there was a gradual adoption of modern management systems that were designed to make the worker as productive as possible. In particular, scientific management, the application of engineering principles and techniques to maintain a high level of productivity, worked to eliminate connections between family and work and advocated antinepotism policies (Googins 1991). Management experts such as Max Weber argued that strong family influences could undermine the development of rational bureaucracies. Families began to be viewed as a threat that could hinder the success of the organization.

With the rise of capitalism and the growing importance of the workplace as a primary institution in society, industrialists sought to place work at the center of life and incorporate families more completely into serving the needs of the organization (Kanter 1977). These new organizations placed enormous stress on the family. Corporate welfare programs designed to socialize workers and improve what were seen as weaknesses in the family sprang up in an attempt to cultivate a healthy, well-behaved, and loyal workforce. These early corporate welfare programs involved building housing, schools, recreation centers, and churches and providing medical care, pension funds, and profit-sharing plans. Even some child care centers were introduced at this time, but for the most part families relied on informal arrangements with relatives or friends. Bradley Googins (1991) has argued that "welfare capitalism marked the beginning of the formal recognition of the relationship between the family and the workplace." Later, many of these programs shifted over to the public sector, and families were pushed outside the boundaries of organizational life to a large degree (Kanter 1977).

As the family ceased to be the central economic unit and as more women entered the workplace, children were no longer a necessity for economic survival. Fertility rates declined sharply (nearly 40 percent from 1855 to 1915), and divorce rates gradually increased during this time (Coontz 1988). Women's household duties continued to expand as higher standards of cleanliness and orderliness developed and as more attention was paid to the developmental needs of children, especially in wealthier households (Mintz and Kellogg 1988). Because only families from higher income levels could afford to have a wife at home, the stay-at-home wife position became one of status. Idleness went from being a sin to being a symbol of higher social standing (Barciauskas and Hull 1989). Working-class children were less supervised than those from wealthier homes, and many poor children were relegated to orphanages for care because their mothers were working outside the home. The idea of group supervision of poor children would come to have a negative influence on how society would view the development of day care programs in the latter half of the twentieth century.

During the Industrial Revolution, the family lost many of its prior functions. Welfare, health, education, and care of the poor and mentally ill were all taken over by institutions outside the household. The family changed from being an essential economic unit to more of a consumption unit. Carl Degler (1980) views the shift to an emphasis on children and personal fulfillment as a positive one that has served to democratize the family.

Work-Family during the Depression, World War II, and the 1950s

With regard to overall developments in the relationship between work and family, the Depression, World War II, and the 1950s are characterized by radical departures from the broader historical trends. Because the Depression and World War II were exceptional events and because there was a strong reaction to World War II during the 1950s, dramatic changes occurred in the work-family relationship that departed from the more steady trends of the eighteenth and nineteenth centuries.

During the Depression, women and minorities were the first to be laid off. The question of women working, especially married women, came under fire as women were accused of taking jobs from men (Sidel 1986). But women continued to work out of necessity, and they often had an easier time finding employment because they could be paid lower wages (Wandersee 1991). The devastating effects of the Depression on all segments of society spurred the government into becoming involved in the work-family relationship. The social programs initiated by the New Deal, for example, the Social Security Act of 1935 and the creation of the Federal Emergency Relief Administration, were some of the first programs aimed at helping the average American family (Wandersee 1991).

World War II shifted the view of women in the workforce from one of stigma to one of patriotic duty. As men moved to the battlefields, more than 6 million women joined the workforce for the first time, though the majority of wives and mothers remained at home (Sealander 1991). The war put extreme stress on the family, resulting in lower birthrates, fewer marriages, many "war widows," and a leap in the divorce rate, especially just after the war. Though the government did provide some child care to some working mothers, as many as 60 percent of working mothers were forced to rely on informal arrangements (Sidel 1986).

During the postwar period, returning veterans moved their families to the suburbs with help from GI loans, and a growing middle class made it possible for many families to be supported by one wage earner. By 1960, an equal number of people lived in the suburbs as lived in the cities, and 70 percent of all families consisted of a father as breadwinner and a mother who stayed home and took care of the household and children (Mintz and Kellogg 1988). The rise of the middle-class, suburban, nuclear family reinforced the notion that the worlds of work and family were discrete entities. Though some work-family strain existed, having only one wage earner per family helped ease the pressure when work responsibilities interfered with household and child-rearing responsibilities. The role of the wife was to support the wage-earner husband and the corporation who employed him. Employee benefits, which had originated during World War II, increased as the needs of the family began to be recognized by the corporation (Googins 1991).

Working-class and minority families were unable to afford the move to the suburbs. Married working-class women combined work and family as best they could, but the middle-class role of housewife became the basis for the cultural norm of separating the roles of work and family. Even if a woman worked, her primary role was still viewed as that of homemaker, and it was assumed that working men had wives at home to support them so they could dedicate themselves to their work (Kanter 1977).

Work-Family Today

Though some are nostalgic for what is viewed as a traditional family structure, the "Ozzie and Harriet" world of the 1950s with a breadwinning father and stay-at-home mother, this was a relatively short-lived phenomenon restricted for the most part to higher income groups. By the 1960s, various economic factors, including a rise in the rate of inflation, helped push women into the workforce in greater numbers. This trend, which has steadily gained momentum since 1970, completely changed the playing field in terms of work-family relationships. Women's roles changed both in the workplace and at home, and men's and children's roles changed as a result of more women, especially wives and mothers, entering the workforce.

Today most married women with children work. Almost three in four married mothers worked at some time in 1992, compared with just over half of married mothers in 1970. Thirty-seven percent of all married women worked full-time year-round in 1992, compared to 16 percent in 1970. Nearly eight in ten mothers with only school-age children worked at some time in 1992. Most women now return to work within the first six months after the birth of a child. In the 1960s, only one in eight women returned to work in less than a year, compared with two in three in the early 1980s (Taeuber 1996).

Women entering the workforce in greater numbers has dramatically affected the dynamics of the family. With no adult at home full-time to manage the household, the breaking down of household tasks by gender is gradually shifting, with men taking on an increasing load. Responsibilities such as child care, eldercare, and even food preparation that were part of the household in the past are gradually being transferred to institutions outside the family. With the loss of the one member of the household devoted solely to house and child care, there has been a decrease in leisure time and a decrease in the amount of time family members are able to spend together.

Changes in social values have also led to a higher divorce rate, more single-parent households, and an increase in alternative family arrangements, including unmarried adults living together, couples choosing not to have children, gay and lesbian couples living openly together with or without children, and people choosing to live alone. Today, less than 10 percent of all households follow the "Ozzie and Harriet" model of the breadwinning father and housewife mother (Parasuraman and Greenhaus 1997). Christopher Lasch (1979) has argued that the family is in decline and that it is failing to serve as a "haven in the heartless world," but others (Kain 1990) counter that the family is still vigorous in spite of the many changes. Rosalind Barnett (1998) argues that rather than attempt to force family relationships to return to the short-lived "traditional family," energy should be put toward supporting families during rapidly changing times.

The world of work has changed dramatically as well. The typical workplace is more often an office than a factory, the workforce as a whole is more educated, and workers have higher expectations about gaining fulfillment from work. At the same time, work is being viewed as less paramount, and family ties and leisure activities are gaining prominence. As a result of women's increased participation in the workforce, more women now hold white-collar and management positions than at any time in history. Women's workforce participation has also brought to light the challenging areas of sexual harassment and job and pay discrimination by gender.

More employees are single parents or in dual-career marriages, which creates tensions relating to household and child care that infringe on scheduled work time. Some workers still get their family needs met informally, but employees are also becoming more vocal in requests for changing policies. Personnel departments are being transformed into more prominent human resources departments as corporations are beginning to better understand how employees' personal lives impact their work performance. The following sections of this chapter will discuss many of the issues and challenges that have emerged as a result of these dramatic changes in work and family life since the 1950s.

Women and Work-Family

Early research on work and family issues centered on women. As women from higher income brackets entered the workforce, especially married women with children, concern was voiced about the effects of employment on the health and well-being of mothers and the effects of mothers' employment on their children's behavioral and social development. Initially, many people felt threatened by what was viewed as the disappearance of the traditional family and the decline in the role of the mother and wife who served as the family's moral center. In addition to entering the workforce, women were changing in other ways as well. Higher educational attainment, lower fertility, and less time spent in marriage have shifted the roles women play in society.

More and more women entering the workforce have made pay equity, the "glass ceiling," and the "mommy track" important subjects of debate. Although women's roles changed outside the home, much less has changed within the home. Responsibility for the household and the children still falls primarily on women, though men are becoming more involved. As women's wages increase and men's roles within the home grow, work-family concerns can be viewed less as a "women's issue" and more as a family and societal responsibility.

Women's Health and Well-Being

Many studies have looked at how entering the workforce has affected the psychological and physical health of women who are mothers (Moen 1992). Early studies in the 1980s focused on the negative impact of work on women's psychological health, though research had shown that men derived great psychological benefits from work (Moen 1992). These early studies found either no difference in psychological well-being or only slight differences, with some finding positive effects and some finding negative effects associated with work (Campbell 1982; Rosenfield 1989). Some researchers have suggested that women's attitudes toward working and staying at home must be taken into account. Women who follow the lifestyle they prefer show higher degrees of psychological health (Krause 1984), as do women whose husbands assist with housework and child care (Kessler and McRae 1982). Another important factor is the type of work: women engaged in jobs that have more autonomy and complexity report higher rates of satisfaction (Baruch, Barnett, and Rivers 1984).

Current research shows that work can provide women with higher self-esteem, serve as a buffer against depression, and enhance mental and physical health. Research has also shown that staying at home can lead to increased rates of depression and lower self-esteem (Waldron and Jacobs 1989; Wethington and Kessler 1989; Baruch, Barnett, and Rivers 1984). Working-class women show gains in psychological health and well-being as well (Scarr, Phillips, and McCartney 1989). Phyllis Moen (1992) theorizes that as employment becomes more common for women, especially those with young children, and as more women choose to work rather than feel pushed into working, a more positive relationship can be seen between employment and women's well-being.

But the news is not all good. Many women suffer from both role overload, which means not having enough time and energy to meet responsibilities, and role conflict, which means confronting incompatible obligations in trying to meet both work and family responsibilities (Moen 1992). Numerous studies have investigated what are referred to as "spillover" effects, defined as positive and negative feelings, attitudes, and behaviors that occur in one area of life and are carried over into another area of life (Googins 1991). For example, an employee who has a bad day at work might go home and be unpleasant to his or her children. In a review of the research, Barnett (1999) found that most studies focused on negative spillover from work to home, a few studies investigated negative spillover from home to work, but very few studies have looked at positive spillover effects. Barnett asserts that positive experiences in one domain can moderate experiences in another domain so that, for example, a supportive marriage can buffer the effects of a stressful job.

In reality, workers do not experience their home lives and work lives as truly separate experiences. Policies designed to support families will have beneficial effects on workers. As the boundaries between work and family become less clear, Barnett (1999) questions whether spillover can really be measured. In arguing for an integration of work and family life, rather than seeing work and family in conflict, Saroj Parasuraman and Jeffrey Greenhaus (1997) discuss fostering integration by enhancing positive spillover in both domains of life.

Research on the relationship between employment and physical health for women has been more consistent than studies on psychological health. Employed women are typically healthier than those not working outside the home (Baruch, Biener, and Barnett 1987; Repetti, Matthews, and Waldron 1989).

Effects of Maternal Employment on Children

As mothers from middle-income and higher socioeconomic backgrounds entered the workforce in growing numbers, there was concern about the effect that a mother's absence would have on the emotional and cognitive development of her children. In the 1960s and 1970s, numerous studies explored the possibility of a special mother-infant bond (Bowlby 1969; Ainsworth 1973). Attachment and related theories postulated that healthy psychological development depended on young children spending time bonding with their mothers. Though these theories are widely disputed among researchers today, they continue to influence public attitudes and research on the effects of maternal employment on child development (Lerner 1994).

Early studies like those cited above tried to establish a direct link between maternal employment and child development. But these studies failed to account for the numerous mediating variables that also influence child development (Lerner 1994). Current research demonstrates that the fact that a mother works outside the home does not negatively influence her child's development (Hoffman 1984; Zaslow, Rabinovich, and Suwalsky 1991; Lerner and Galambos 1986; Galinsky 1999; Harvey 1999). However, there are factors *related* to maternal employment that can affect child development. Quality of day care, degree of parental monitoring from work, quality of time spent with children, and the quality of the family environment are some of the important variables reviewed below.

Considerable research and public concern has centered on the effects of maternal employment on infants and toddlers. Early research on day care attempted to uncover differences in social and cognitive development between children who stayed home versus children who were in day care. Few differences between these two groups of children were discovered, but many of these studies focused on high-quality university-run centers, even though the majority of children are in other types of day care (Parcel 1996). Current studies have investigated links between social-structural features of day care (e.g., group size, caregiver-child ratios) and children's experiences and between those experiences and child outcomes. Studies have shown that there is a negative association between children's development and both large group size and low caregiver-child ratios (Parcel 1996).

A comprehensive study of day care centers concluded that although high-quality day care has a positive impact on children's development, language ability, self-esteem, and ability to have warm relationships with others, most day care centers do not provide the level of care that has been shown to produce these results. Most centers do not meet children's needs for health, safety, and learning. Eighty-six percent of centers surveyed were found to provide poor to mediocre care, and almost half of infants and toddlers receive care rated as less than minimal quality (Helburn and Culkin 1995). Family day care, which is less regulated than institutional care, is even more uneven in quality (Rose 1999).

Recent events such as the murder of twelve high school students by their peers in Littleton, Colorado, have focused public attention on issues related to school-age children and working parents. Studies have demonstrated that for school-age children who *are* adequately supervised, there seem to be social benefits to having a mother who is employed (Lerner 1994). Employed mothers apparently encourage healthy independence in their children as well (Hoffman 1979). For teenagers who are at home alone in the afternoon, parental monitoring has been shown to make a significant difference in outcomes for these "self-care" children. Laurence Steinberg (1986) found that when parents monitor their children from work and when children have internalized values and positive family environments, they are able to remain at home in a self-care situation without any negative consequences. Children were more likely to get into trouble if they were "hanging out" or in another home that was unsupervised.

In a groundbreaking study, Ellen Galinsky (1999) turned the tables and asked children if they were affected by having both parents in the workforce. Based on interviews with 1,000 children, Galinsky found that having an employed mother was not related to how children assessed their mothers' parenting skills. Children whose mothers were at home caring for them full-time did not rate their mothers as more supportive than children who had mothers who were employed. Galinsky also found that most children did not want more time with their parents but wanted the time spent together to be unhurried, focused, and involve shared activities. Children with employed mothers and those with mothers at home did not differ on whether they felt they had too little time with their mother. In a study of first graders, M. J. Moorehouse (1991) found that efforts made by mothers to spend time with their children greatly influenced school competence, regardless of the employment status of the mother.

Many factors related to mothers being in the workforce need further study. In addition to the issues mentioned above, maternal work hours, pay level, employment characteristics, degree of autonomy at work, and job satisfaction are also factors that seem to influence child outcomes (Rogers 1996; Lerner and Galambos 1986).

Not everyone agrees that women should be in the workplace, and this view could influence child outcomes. The Christian Coalition and other religious and conservative groups still question whether women, especially women with young children, should be in the workplace at all. A recent national survey conducted by the Kaiser Family Foundation, Harvard University, and the *Washington Post* showed a majority of people still do not fully accept working mothers. Two-thirds of Americans said that, financial needs aside, it is better if women can stay home and care for their families. Half of those polled said they respect stay-at-home mothers more than those who work while their children are young (Healy 1998).

Changes in Women's Lives

On the eve of U.S. involvement in World War II, only one in four workers was a woman; today close to half the workers in the United States are women (Spain and Bianchi 1996: 79). In past generations, women combined careers and families sequentially, taking time off to raise a family and then returning to the workforce. Today women have jobs and families at the same time, partly because women have established themselves in the labor force and postponed marriage and family and partly because single parents have to support a family. Currently, the majority of new mothers remain in the labor force, probably the most significant change for women in the labor market over the past two decades (Bachu 1993).

In addition to changes in women's labor force participation, issues relating to fertility, marriage, divorce, and educational attainment have all changed significantly. Almost one in three births took place outside marriage in 1993, compared to one in ten in 1970 (Ventura 1995a). In 1990, 24 percent of all families were single-parent households, compared with 8 percent in 1950. In 1994, the number of households maintained by women increased to 29 percent (U.S. Bureau of the Census 1995: table A). The number of single-parent black families is one of the most significant racial differences in family status. Nearly one-half of black families are single-mother households, compared with less then one-fifth of white families (Spain and Bianchi 1996). Trends toward delaying marriage and postponing remarriage and the high rate of divorce have contributed to the growth of single-parent families. In addition, women have become more educated. Three-quarters of adult women today have a high school degree, compared to one-half in 1970. In 1990, one in five women had a college degree, compared to fewer than one in ten in 1970 (Spain and Bianchi 1996).

Women at Work:
The Gender Gap in Wages

Despite increases in labor force participation and rising educational levels, the gap between earnings by gender remained relatively constant between 1950 and 1980, with women earning roughly 60 cents for every dollar men earned. Since then, the wage gap has narrowed gradually, with current estimates hovering around 71 percent of the wage rate for men (Dunn 1996).

Many theories have been put forward by researchers to account for the gap in wages by gender. Research in economics and sociology focused on the productivity-related differences between individual women and men (such as hours worked, effort expended, experience, and education). These theorists (Mincer and Polachek 1974) suggested that pay differences between the sexes are a function of voluntary choices made by women. Later research (Corcoran, Duncan, and Ponza 1984) demonstrated that this may account for possibly 50 percent or less of the wage gap as similarities between educational attainment and other variables are becoming more equal. Recent research (Fuchs 1988) has investigated the possibility of a "family gap," in other words, that mothers earn lower hourly wages than women without children. While controlling for labor force experience, Jane Waldfogel (1997) found that if a woman has children, it affects her wages negatively. In addition, she found that there is a wage penalty for being employed part-time. When she controlled for part-time work, the negative effect of having children decreased but was not eliminated.

The recent narrowing of the wage gap can be explained in part by the increase in women workers who have continuous labor force attachment. These younger women are replacing lower-paid, older women who have less employment experience because they entered the labor force after raising their families. For lower-paying jobs, the gender gap has narrowed, partly because women began working longer hours, and partly because men's wages stagnated and then declined (Spain and Bianchi 1996).

Discrimination probably accounts for a significant portion of the wage gap, but the subtle nature of this discrimination has been difficult to prove empirically. A related issue, gender segregation by occupation, seems to play a key role in explaining the current gap in wages (England 1992; Solberg and Laughlin 1995). Women and men have continued to work in occupations dominated by their own gender, and fields dominated by women are lower-paying than those dominated by men (Dunn 1996).

There is a great deal of debate about why occupations continue to be so differentiated by gender. Researchers hypothesize that women may tend to choose jobs they think will be more compatible with child rearing, they experience job discrimination in male-dominated fields, and they lack access to jobs that have strong career trajectories. In addition, lifelong socialization attracts women and men to different types of jobs (Spain and Bianchi 1996). Though it is still uncommon to see a female electrician or a male nurse, segregation by occupation is decreasing, which also explains some of the recent narrowing of the wage gap.

Some researchers point to the lower wages associated with traditional women's work as an indication that "comparable worth discrimination" is occurring. This form of discrimination takes place when the setting of wages is influenced by which gender dominates a particular field (England and Dunn 1988). Proponents of comparable worth legislation argue that experience, skill level, and other relevant issues do not currently determine wage structures. Comparable worth legislation would require that job evaluations be conducted in order to eliminate the systematic undervaluing of work usually performed by women (Dunn 1996). Opponents of comparable worth argue that raising wages for some traditionally female-dominated occupations ignores external market forces, which affect the supply of labor and the price employers must pay to attract and retain workers. Proponents counter that institutional factors have systematically subverted the market by undervaluing jobs that are characteristically held by women. Though no legislation is in place, a number of states have voluntarily adjusted state government pay scales in a more equitable way.

The "Mommy Track" and the "Glass Ceiling"

Public attitudes about women in the workforce have lagged well behind the growing numbers of women going to work. In the mid-1970s, 66 percent of Americans agreed with the statement: "It is much better for everyone involved if the man is the achiever outside the home and the woman takes care of the home and family." By the early 1990s, 40 percent of Americans agreed with this sentiment (Farley 1996). An article about working mothers by Felice Schwartz, published in the *Harvard Business Review* (1989), was quickly picked up by the media, and the phrase *mommy track* entered the popular lexicon. Schwartz proposed that some women should be able to choose a slower track during years when they had children at home, in order to keep valuable women in the labor force from dropping out completely while raising children. The media distorted Schwartz's proposal and suggested that women with children were better suited to part-time, less demanding work.

In deciding whether there should be a dual-tracking device so that women without children could compete more equally with men, researchers have investigated whether there is a difference in commitment, ability, and motivation between women who have children and women who do not. Michael Fogarty, Rhona Rapaport, and Robert Rapaport (1971) found that working women *without* children are actually less committed to work because of weaker networks of support. Moen and Ken Smith (1986) found that the most committed women workers were part-time working women who were often using part-time work as a strategy to stay in the labor force while dealing with family responsibilities. A study of women in academia also found no career disadvantage created by women being mothers (Kennedy, Carsky, and Zuckerman 1996). They concluded that women who had managed to overcome the entry barriers of this profession would be likely to give their career primary importance even if they had chosen to become mothers as well.

Deborah Swiss and Judith Walker (1993) view the mommy track as a dangerous idea because it is founded on assumptions that are determined solely by gender. Today, with a majority of mothers in the workforce, different women choose to balance their family and career decisions in different ways, and at different phases in their lives women recalibrate this balance. The equation becomes more dynamic as some fathers have greater involvement with children and housework, enabling some women to compete more effectively in the workplace as fewer demands are placed on them at home.

Many women choose jobs they hope will be compatible with raising children. Unfortunately, women often pay a high price for part-time work or for taking jobs that are less demanding. In addition to sacrificing upward mobility, earning power, job security, and occupational achievement (Moen 1992), women do not receive the psychological and physical benefits that are experienced by women who work in higher level jobs or who work full-time (Barnett 1998). Ironically, less demanding jobs or jobs that are frequently associated with women, such as the nursing profession, often provide less flexibility than higher paying positions.

Women who choose to remain on the higher powered career track after having children sometimes experience pressure from bosses and colleagues to enter a slower, mommy-track lane (Swiss and Walker 1993). In their study of more than 900 women who had graduated from professional schools at Harvard, Swiss and Walker (1993) heard repeatedly from women who had experienced the glass ceiling. The glass ceiling is described as an invisible but powerful barrier that prevents women from advancing up the career ladder due to discriminatory attitudes held by supervisors and the "old boy" networks that exist in the workplace. Swiss and Walker reported that the glass ceiling is formally buttressed by the "maternal wall," an additional barrier created by mistaken assumptions regarding a woman's ability to succeed in multiple roles. Of 400 women executives surveyed in 1992 (*Business Week*/Harris Poll 1992, as cited in Swiss and Walker 1993: 192), 70 percent said they view "the male-dominated corporate culture" as a barrier to their success. In the same survey, 57 percent of the women agreed that "the rate of progress for corporate women has slowed down or stopped altogether." Today, only 2 percent of senior executives are women, only 6 percent of law partners are women, and in the professions generally, only 10 to 15 percent of senior managers are women (Harrington 1999).

Research suggests that women are making some progress in becoming middle managers. In 1970, 18 percent of managers were women; by 1990, 40 percent were women (Reskin and Roos 1990). Some researchers are skeptical about whether this rise in women managers represents true progress for women or is a result of equal opportunity legislation that has put pressure on organizations to retitle female clerical workers as managers with little authority (e.g., changing a secretary to an executive assistant). In addition, men have left some occupations that have declined in status, thereby opening up less desirable management opportunities for women (Reskin and Roos 1990).

David Maume (1998) explored gender differences in the timing of promotions in order to understand gender inequality in the labor market. In his study, Maume was unable to determine if women were making legitimate progress into true managerial roles or were only moving into positions of "glorified secretaries." He did find that employment in female-dominated occupations slows women's progress into managerial positions and that this effect is magnified for women who held college degrees. However, men experienced a "glass escalator" rather than a glass ceiling and frequently used female-dominated jobs as a springboard into supervisory positions. Maume found that women are more likely to be promoted when they are in positions in which they work primarily with men. Employers appear to discriminate more against women in jobs held primarily by women. These jobs are evaluated as having lower skills, offering fewer training opportunities, and not linking women to jobs higher up in the organizational pyramid (Kanter 1977; Steinberg 1990). Maume (1998) is hopeful that progress will continue because the early career salaries of younger women are starting to approach the early career salaries of younger men, women's labor force attachment is longer and more continuous than it was, and women's educational experiences are converging with men's educational experiences.

Although they acknowledge that the glass ceiling is a serious issue, some researchers (Barnett and Rivers 1998) are calling attention to the "sticky floor," namely the inability of so many women to get past low-paying, monotonous jobs. Women predominantly fill these repetitive jobs, and the number of these jobs is increasing. Recent studies are finding that the type of work a woman does may have a profound impact on parenting skills, style, and ability. Children who have mothers in lower-level, repetitive, controlled work environments experience more problems both intellectually and behaviorally (Parcel and Menaghan 1990).

Women's Home and Family Responsibilities

Though married women have entered the workforce in dramatic numbers, women continue to be responsible for the majority of housework and child care activities. The total amount of time spent on housework has changed little over the past century (Schor 1991), with just the 1980s and 1990s registering a decline in the number of hours spent on housework (Spain and Bianchi 1996). The huge advances in technology for the home (e.g., washing machines, vacuum cleaners) only raised expectations and shifted the nature of the work to less strenuous but still time-consuming labor. For example, at the turn of the century, washing was done once a month, whereas today clothes are washed after being worn a single time. Juliet Schor (1991) argues that because married women were excluded from the labor force, little value was placed on their time and little effort was made to conserve their labor. Instead, inefficient and time-consuming household work was created, and businesses interested in selling products communicated to women that their homes could never be too clean.

Working mothers have two full-time jobs: paid employment and what Arlie Hochschild (1989) has called the "second shift," homemaking and child care duties. For the growing number of single mothers, the dual responsibilities are particularly challenging. That women still do the vast majority of housework and child care has been called the "stalled revolution" by Hochschild (1989). Since 1980, married mothers have experienced a significant decline in the hours they spend on housework from about thirty hours to about twenty hours per week. But married fathers have not picked up the slack. Household work by fathers has increased from about five hours a week to about 10 hours (Spain and Bianchi 1996: 169). Citing more recent research (Bond, Galinsky, and Swanberg 1998), however, James Levine and Todd Pittinsky (1998) argue that men have increased the time they spend on household work and child care substantially. In 1997 fathers were involved in 77 percent of workday time with children relative to mothers' workday time with children, an increase from 55 percent in 1977. On nonworkdays, fathers increased their time by more than an hour from 1977, spending 6.4 hours with their children, whereas mothers stayed constant, spending 7.8 hours with children. In terms of household chores, men contributed about 30 percent as much time as women in 1977, but by 1997 they contributed almost 75 percent. Ethnicity had little impact on the amount of time husbands devoted to household labor (Shelton and John 1993; Coltrane and Valdez 1993).

Household tasks continue to differ by gender, with husbands participating more in yard work, home maintenance work, and child care, while women do more cooking, cleaning, laundry, and grocery shopping (Goldscheider and Waite 1991; Coltrane 1996). In families in which the woman works outside the home, husbands perform a greater share of domestic tasks; and the higher the wife's contribution to the family income, the more equitable the division of household duties. However, women are much more likely to adjust their employment to fit their family needs. Women's family roles tend to intrude on their work, whereas men's work roles tend to intrude on their family time. When a child becomes sick, the wife is more likely to leave work, but overnight business trips, for example, are more apt to occur in the husband's job (Spain and Bianchi 1996).

As younger women and men with more similar labor force experiences replace the baby boom generation, it is expected that the division of labor in the home will become more equal. Though the unequal division of labor is a concern, many married women report that though they do the majority of the housework, they are satisfied with this situation. Daphne Spain and Suzanne Bianchi (1996) hypothesize that perceptions of fairness depend on a comparison of one's circumstances to another's. Women would be more likely to feel that the division of labor in their house was unfair if they found that more equal divisions of labor occurred in their neighbors' houses. Linda Thompson (1991) found that women who held more traditional views of gender roles were more likely to regard an unequal distribution of housework as fair.

Most women will probably continue to put the needs of the family ahead of their own jobs. Spain and Bianchi (1996) speculate that until wives contribute as much to the household income as husbands, it is unlikely husbands will devote as much time to the family as wives. For some families that time has come. Data gathered by the federal population survey from 1998 show that 30 percent of working wives of all ages are now paid more than their husbands (Goldstein 1999). These women tend to be highly educated, and their husbands do seem to be pitching in more around the house. Because of the challenges of combining full-time, year-round employment with family responsibilities, the majority of women will probably continue to work in lower-paying, female-dominated, part-time positions. Caught in a catch-22 of greater family responsibilities and lower-paying jobs, women can only become more successful at balancing work-family needs if the definition of work-family is broadened from being viewed as a woman's issue to being seen as a family and societal challenge.

Men and Work-Family

Although women have participated in a very public revolution, changes in men's lives have been more internal, invisible, and diverse. Men have largely reacted to changes in women's lives, causing some men to hold on to traditional family roles, others to abandon the family, and still others to embrace the role of the more involved "new father." Yet despite all this, workplace attitudes and cultures have seen little change. Because the workplace has remained static while many fathers are choosing to be more involved with their families, men are experiencing increasing amounts of work-family conflict and stress. As men become more comfortable in their new role of involved father, there is some evidence they will become more vocal at work, and a transformation in workplace culture may occur.

The "Quiet Revolution"

Although most recognize how women's roles changed in the twentieth century, men are viewed as having undergone little change. In fact, men are undergoing a transformation as well, but it is a more internal change. Men's private roles have shifted, but their more public roles have remained stable. Kathleen Gerson (1993) has referred to these changes as men's "quiet revolution." Researchers are just beginning to explore how men are changing in relationship to their work and their families.

During the Industrial Revolution, men began working outside the home in factories and other businesses. Their wives, denied access to the labor market, took over the running of the household. Men's sole family responsibility was transformed into that of breadwinner. In the 1920s a limited parental role emerged for men as that of mentor and friend but not as caretaker (Barnett and Rivers 1998). There was particular concern that boys were being subjected to a feminizing influence in the home, and some contact with fathers was encouraged in order to teach boys to become more masculine (Coltrane 1996).

Until a few decades ago, many researchers believed in the notion of "biology as destiny" (Barnett and Rivers 1998). In the 1950s, fathers were discouraged from interacting with young children. Research demonstrating a unique mother-infant bond, later widely disputed, reinforced the notion that men should not be involved in the role of nurturer. Talcott Parsons, an influential sociologist of that era, came up with the theory of functionalism: men were in charge of doing and women were in charge of feeling. A man's role at work was critical to whom he was as a person. Researchers have now refuted these early theories, which had been tested at a time when men were doing essentially no child care, and middle-class and upper-class women were doing little, if any, work outside the home (Barnett and Rivers 1998).

Beginning around 1970, men's role as sole economic provider for the family began to decline. Men's earnings stagnated, and families were only able to maintain their standard of living if wives entered the workforce to assist with the provider role. This sharing of the breadwinning role called into question notions about what it meant to be a man and to be a father. The collapse of men's monopoly on breadwinning had an enormous impact on the role of fathers (Griswold 1993). Although mothering referred to traditional images of nurturing and caregiving, fatherhood had a more limited definition as that of procreator and provider (Levine and Pittinsky 1998). As the economic role became more shared, options for men increased. In extensive interviews with a randomly selected group of 138 men, Gerson (1993) found that men tended to divide into three different and very diverse types:

- Breadwinning: men who are highly involved in the provider role and have little involvement in domestic work and child rearing
- Autonomous: men who are moving away from marriage and parenthood altogether, either by not having children or by not staying involved with children they have fathered
- Involved: men who, regardless of the degree to which they are involved in the provider role, are very involved in child rearing and to some extent in housework

Gerson (1993) found there was not a general trend toward all men becoming more active parents. She views the involved father as a possible model for the future and advocates for more social support to encourage men to become more involved with their families. Without such support, more men may choose to abandon family responsibilities. In fact, even as there has been an increase in involved fathers, there has also been an increase in what Gerson has called the "autonomous" man. The increases in the divorce rate, in the number of men (and women) postponing marriage, and in singlehood, combined with less social pressure for men to support their families, have all contributed to an increase in the number of men who abandon their families. Men who choose singlehood enjoy higher incomes than single women who have lower-paying jobs and whose incomes must also support children. Only 30 percent of court-ordered child support is collected (Gerson 1993). Men's abandonment of the family has contributed to a significant rise in poverty for women and children.

The "New Father"

Some men have embraced what has been called the "new father" role. Barnett (1996) has labeled this the "era of the involved father," and research and polls concur that more fathers are becoming involved parents and domestic assistants, if not equal partners. It is becoming more acceptable for fathers to act more like mothers and to view the family as central to their lives (Levine and Pittinsky 1998). Seventy-three percent of a random sample of fathers strongly agreed that their families are the most important facet of their lives; 54 percent said that "a man's most satisfying accomplishment is being a father"; and 87 percent agreed that "dad is as vital as mom in raising kids" (Peterson 1988).

Though most men have not become equal partners in parenting, there has been a significant increase in their caregiving participation. Using self-reports from married women, one study found that husbands participated in an average of just over 40 percent of the child care duties (Goldscheider and Waite 1991). In 1988, 12 percent of men were the primary caretaker for children while the mother was at work (Pleck 1993). John Snarey (1993) found U.S. Census data indicating that fathers now provide 25 percent of primary child care for preschool-age children. Men have taken a more active role in child care partly because more parents are coping with the expense of child care by having work schedules that do not overlap. In addition, men now make up 18 percent of all single-parent households (U.S. Bureau of the Census 1998).

The new father benefits a great deal from this expanded role, finding more satisfaction from family than work. A 1991 Gallup Poll found that the majority of men today derive a greater sense of satisfaction from caring for their family than from a job well done at work. Society also reaps benefits from having fathers involved in parenting. In a study by Snarey (1993), fathers who had been active in caring for their children were more likely to be connected to the larger society and its welfare and to feel a responsibility to pass on knowledge and understanding. In addition, other researchers (Cowan 1988) found involved fathers paid more attention to the needs of others and became more aware and involved in personal relationships on the job as well.

Popular culture has also reflected this change in American fathering. Media images of expressive and caring fathers have become more common, though many images of aggressive and domineering men persist. These two contradictory images reflect what Gerson views as an ongoing "diversity of paths," with no current cultural consensus on what constitutes manhood.

Although the majority of researchers have welcomed the new father as an encouraging social trend, some researchers (Blankenhorn 1994) fear that fathers are becoming less masculine and need to retreat into the role of mentor and friend, rather than nurturer and caretaker. Robert Bly, author of the popular book *Iron John*, agrees that men need to stop being "soft," and conservative Christian groups have also called on men to maintain their traditional roles as breadwinners and leave child care and housework duties to their wives.

Men as Involved Parents

The man's role as an involved parent has gained some recognition in the public sphere, with books and articles on fatherhood beginning to appear since the 1970s. But the issue of men and work-family remains largely hidden. As women entered the workforce, there was an explosion of books, articles, and entire magazines devoted to women and work-family issues. These resources sought some integration between a woman's role in the workplace and a woman's role as wife and mother. For men, the term *working father* still does not exist. The prevailing myth has been that men's work and family lives continue to be separate spheres that function independently, when, in fact, each aspect of a father's life deeply affects the other.

Though work-family is still identified by most people as a women's issue, surveys have shown that men of all socioeconomic levels experience about as much conflict with their two roles as women do (Levine and Pittinsky 1998; Bond, Galinsky, and Swanberg 1998; Barnett and Rivers 1996). A national study by Joseph Pleck found that men now "see their primary emotional, personal, and spiritual gratification from the family setting" (Pleck 1985). Other studies concur, yet men have not shown a decrease in their commitment to work (Levine and Pittinsky 1998). A majority of adults surveyed felt men should be equally responsible for day-to-day care of children, but 39 percent still felt that breadwinning should be the primary responsibility of men. Recent polls report that men value their families over their jobs, and most men say they would like to work fewer hours in order to spend more time with their families (Thornton 1989). Men also reported that they were willing to trade a bigger paycheck for more time with their families (Barnett and Rivers 1998). Clearly, some men are feeling a conflict between their status as economic provider, which is central to their self-concept, and their growing desire for more involvement with their children.

Men's Health and Well-Being

Historically, research studies on environmental influences on men's health have focused on employment. Current research is turning toward how work-family issues affect not just women's but men's physical and psychological health. Because men tend not to talk much about family life at work, many assume that men do not worry about their children while they are at work and that men have compartmentalized their two roles. Research now shows that worries about children can cause either parent to experience stress-related health problems (Barnett and Rivers 1998). A man's experience as a parent, rather than as an employee, was the strongest predictor of whether he would have stress-related physical symptoms.

In terms of mental health, the roles of worker, spouse, and parent had equal significance for men (Levine and Pittinsky 1998). In a carefully controlled study, Kirby Deater-Deckard and colleagues (1994) found that fathers experienced more anxiety than mothers did about separating from their preschoolers, though the researchers had been expecting to find the opposite effect. Supporting their research was evidence from the National Study of the Changing Workforce (Bond, Galinsky, and Swanberg 1993), which found that fathers who are more satisfied with their child care providers felt less stress at work and more satisfaction in their roles as parents and their lives in general. Pleck (1993) found that men experience their family life as much more psychologically significant than their jobs. Working fathers often feel torn both by guilt for not spending more time with their children and worry about being able to support their family (Simonetti et al. 1993).

In terms of sharing the load, Barnett (1996) found that for men, missing work when child care arrangements break down is more strongly associated with stress and diminished well-being than it is for women. However, fathers who have accepted child care as part of their role feel less stress than fathers who feel they are taking on a duty that should be the responsibility of their wife.

The Impact of the New Father on Children

Research has just begun to document the vital role that fathers play in children's lives. Information gathered from studies on women and work-family is now influencing the research done on working fathers. One major discovery in the study of working mothers was that it was not whether a mother was employed that necessarily affected her children but how she felt about her job. Research on working fathers has uncovered similar findings, with fewer behavioral problems occurring among children whose fathers are more satisfied with their work roles (Barnett and Rivers 1996). In addition, more stress in a father's job resulted in less well-behaved children, and underemployment and overemployment were shown to have negative effects on young children (Parcel and Menaghan 1994).

How fathers are treated at work also affects their parenting. Fathers who are not treated well at work have lower self-esteem and tend to be much more harsh and strict in their interactions with their children, whereas fathers with supportive supervisors demonstrate higher self-esteem and more supportive parenting styles (Grimm-Thomas and Perry-Jenkins 1994). Research has demonstrated that children are better off in terms of intelligence and social development at every stage when fathers are more involved in parenting (Levine and Pittinsky 1998).

Fathers who take on more responsibility for child care develop the more caring and emotional sides of themselves. Child care can provide men with a safe opportunity to explore more sensitive ways of relating (Coltrane 1996). When fathers care for children, they tend to develop more caring and supportive relationships with other adults around them (Snarey 1993).

Sharing Family Work

Though many men are more actively involved in child care, they still lag behind their wives in housework. Scott Coltrane (1996) feels that over time the sharing of family work will become more equal because women's bargaining power in marriage will increase due to the following trends:

- Postponement of marriage, which means prior to marriage men have experience doing housework
- Rise in the divorce rate
- Increase in the number of wives in the labor force and rise in wages as job segregation decreases
- Increase in marriage between men and women closer in age
- Lack of quality child care that increases men's involvement in care
- Increase in the number of men and women who believe in gender equality

No one theory can fully explain how household work gets divided. Often there is a mix of elements and social contexts that influence the division of labor. Coltrane (1996) found that most couples use some combination of three factors to determine how work will be divided:

1. The "theory of relative resources" holds that whoever has more "power" in the marriage or a higher income or resources will do less housework. When a wife's relative income is higher, the husband will do more housework. This simple exchange model is limited because there are many exceptions relating to feelings of entitlement and gratitude that shape the division of labor.

2. The "theory of gender ideology" assumes that people are socialized to believe that certain tasks are appropriate for men and others for women. These beliefs either inhibit or encourage the sharing of domestic tasks. Research has found that people who have more traditional gender attitudes share less (Hiller and Philliber 1986). But not all studies have found this effect. Some studies demonstrate that a husband's attitude overshadows the wife's beliefs, and others argue the opposite effect.

3. The "theory of time availability" asserts that work is assigned to the spouse with the most free time, but it does not specify how people end up with free time. Some research has found this to be true for a woman's time—the more she works, the less housework she does. In households where men and women work full-

time, the men increase their relative participation, either because they actually do more or because the women do less. But not all research has found this to be true because of what Coltrane refers to as the "economy of gratitude." Some husbands feel they are "letting" their wives work, and others feel grateful for their wives' added income. Those men who feel gratitude tend to participate more in family work.

Like Gerson (1993), Coltrane (1996) found no dominant thesis for how men are changing. Though underlying social forces are pushing toward a blending of gender and family roles and away from traditional breadwinner and homemaker roles, at the same time a backlash is occurring, with an emphasis on "family values" and calls for a return to a more traditional (if mythical) family.

The "Invisible Dilemma" of Work-Family Conflict for Men

Although women's struggles for work-family integration have been in the public eye, men have faced what Levine and Pittinsky (1998) have called the "invisible dilemma" of "daddy stress." Internally, some men want to be more involved in their children's lives, but they are reluctant to vocalize this shifting value. Some men experience conflict in trying to integrate the roles of father and breadwinner.

Work-family conflict for men has remained largely invisible for two reasons. Traditional masculine culture discourages men from admitting they are overwhelmed or acknowledging they need help. In addition, the culture of work frowns on any mention of family responsibilities (Levine and Pittinsky 1998). Men fear that they might be steered into a "daddy track" and taken less seriously if they request leave or miss work to take care of a sick child or attend a school play. A woman requesting part-time work might be acceptable to an employer (and to society), but a man requesting part-time work in order to participate in family care might be ridiculed. There is still a strong social mandate for fathers to provide financially for their families. In a recent study, college students judged fathers harshly when they sacrificed financial security for caregiving, but the same behavior by mothers received high approval ratings (Riggs 1997).

Pleck (1993) found that although men want employers to allow them more family time, the time they do take off for family responsibilities often masquerades as something else. Men take sick time or vacation time instead of paternity leave, and some men claim they have meetings to go to when they are picking their children up at day care (Levine and Pittinsky 1998). Though much about family roles has changed since women entered the workforce, workplace cultures have been slower to change. Most employers expect their employees, both men and women, to act like traditional males who have wives at home. In the current era of "downsizing," employees are expected to do more work and to work extra hours. Joan Kofodimos (1995) found that corporations tend to be run by workaholic executives who are willing to sacrifice their own family lives to gain mastery and control and find they can gain this control at work but not at home. These top executives then set the standards by which managers are judged and promoted. At such a company, a man who takes advantage of a work-family program would be jeopardizing his career.

Because men's needs for workplace changes are often invisible, they often are unacknowledged. But some researchers (Pleck 1993; Levine and Pittinsky 1998) see a shift occurring. Work-family issues are beginning to "come out of the closet" for men, with hundreds of men in large corporations turning out for work-family workshops and more men beginning to voice their need for more family-supportive employer policies. As the new father emerges as an acceptable male role, men are beginning to voice their work-family needs.

Low-Income and
Minority Groups and Work-Family

An Understudied and
Underserved Population

Most of the research conducted on work-family focuses on middle- and upper-income employees and their work. Lower-wage workers, workers from minority and ethnic groups, and workers from nontraditional families are just beginning to be studied by scholars in the field of work-family. Most work-family corporate benefit programs, often an outgrowth of research, focus on the needs of upper-level managers and salaried workers who tend to be the employees that corporations most value. Most work-family benefits are accessible to only about 20 percent of the workforce (Klein 1997). With high demand and low retention rates for lower-wage employees, a better understanding of the diversity of needs and issues affecting families from different income groups is needed so that appropriate work-family supports can be developed within the workplace, government, and community. For many lower-wage employees, work-family issues present more significant challenges than for those with greater financial resources.

In addition to lower-wage employees, little is known about work-family needs that might be unique to particular minority and ethnic groups. Organizations and researchers have tended in the past to place diversity issues on a separate track while paying inadequate attention to the unique work-family needs of minority employees. The following paragraphs provide an overview of the research that has recently been conducted on these understudied groups. Research is still greatly needed on single-parent, gay and lesbian, and other nontraditional family arrangements and the particular needs these workers might have in balancing the responsibilities of job and home.

The Working Poor and Lower-Wage Workers

In 1998, 9 million Americans worked some time during the year but fell below the official poverty level. Of these 9 million, 2 million worked full time year-round. Researchers assert that the number of workers living under extreme financial hardship is probably much higher, with many working families earning just over the $13,880 poverty level set for a family of three (Kim 2000). The majority of lower-wage employees live in families and must struggle to balance work and family responsibilities while coping with constant financial challenges. The working poor is currently the fastest growing sector of those that are poor, and their numbers are expected to increase due to changing welfare policies that require more welfare recipients to work.

The working poor are most likely to work in service, sales, or agricultural jobs or as machine operators. Many work part-time because they are unable to secure full-time work (Kim 2000). The working poor and lower-wage workers are likely to be less educated, have health constraints, and live in single-parent households. In 1998, only 30 percent of the working poor lived in married-couple families, compared with 65 percent of all workers (Kim 2000). For the working poor that are in two-parent families, choosing whether to work has never been an option for either member of the couple because financial need dictates that both parents must work. Almost half of all single parents who work and have children under six years old live in poverty. In addition, only 18 percent of the working poor are covered by health insurance through their employer or union, compared to 55 percent of all workers (Kim 2000). Women, noncitizens, blacks, and Latinos are disproportionately represented within the ranks of the working poor and lower-wage workers.

Many researchers have studied the difficult challenges middle-class workers face when balancing work and family responsibilities. Long hours on the job, lack of affordable and quality child care, public schools that release students in the middle of the afternoon, and little time for parents to attend to household responsibilities create a great deal of stress for working families. The working poor must cope with all these issues and in addition face problems such as fluctuating hours, overnight shifts, and lack of health insurance, vacation, or sick pay. Working different shifts greatly affects the ability of families to spend time together and maintain healthy relationships (Swanberg 1996). Child care is often negotiated through informal and unreliable connections with family or neighbors, and often the working poor must resort to unregulated, even unsafe conditions. In a study of lower-wage working women in Harlem, Katherine Newman (2000) found that it was common for informal arrangements for child care to be made with husbands or sisters working different shifts. The adults rarely were able to spend time together, and sometimes the adult responsible for the children needed to sleep while performing his or her caregiving shift.

Though the work-family needs of lower-wage workers clearly overlap with the needs of workers earning higher salaries, they also face unique issues that are just beginning to be touched on by researchers and corporate benefit programs. The lack of reliable child care arrangements can prevent lower-wage employees from holding on to steady employment. Newman and other researchers (Newman 2000; Lambert 1999) advocate that subsidized early childhood education, similar to what is available in Europe, be implemented in the United States. This would assist the working poor by providing them with reliable and safe child care and improve school readiness among poorer children, who frequently lag behind other children when entering the public school system.

In addition to child care issues, many of the working poor face serious day-to-day challenges such as unreliable transportation arrangements, eviction, or immigration problems that need to be dealt with in order for them to function in the workplace. One company developed an effective phone hotline providing assistance, in several languages, for any family or personal life need. Other companies have implemented full family support services, including parent education, immunizations, nutrition counseling, and referrals to community programs in order to improve the lives of their employees and improve worker retention and productivity. One researcher discovered that out of thirty-five lower-wage employees who were eligible for child care subsidies through state block grants, only one worker was receiving the subsidy. Other workers at this company were unaware of the subsidy or did not understand the application procedures (Klein 1997).

Many of the working poor are unable to take advantage of the Family and Medical Leave Act (FMLA) that provides for unpaid leave for the birth or adoption or foster placement of a child, an employee's own serious health condition, or the serious health condition of an immediate family member. Most lower-wage workers cannot afford to take any unpaid time off from their jobs, and many companies that employ lower-wage workers are too small to be covered by the FMLA. Some activists advise that the FMLA needs to provide workers with paid leave and include all employers. Owners of small businesses argue that this places excessive hardship on their ability to keep their businesses operating. Comprehensive health insurance coverage for the working poor, improved transportation options, and an increase in the minimum wage are all issues that have been debated on the national stage. These programs would improve work-family issues impacting lower wage workers, but not without some costs to businesses and the government.

Lack of job autonomy and lack of participation in work schedules have been shown to produce a great deal of stress for all workers (Swanberg 1996) and are common elements of many lower-wage workers' jobs. Research has shown that by providing more flexibility and making changes in scheduling and supervisory practices for lower-wage workers, businesses in the service sector can build loyalty and commitment among workers, reduce staff turnover and increase profits (Reichheld 1996). Jennifer Swanberg's (1996) study of a large hotel chain found that even a little flexibility in work schedules—such as allowing maids to be a few minutes late to work in order to cope with child care needs—greatly improved the ability of these employees to function at work.

The number of service jobs is increasing in the United States, and there is a growing need for workers to fill these jobs. Because the work-family needs of lower-wage workers differ from those of other workers (Lambert 1999), further investigation is needed to better understand this group of workers and provide support for them and their families.

Blacks and Work-Family

Black people in the United States have a unique work-family history that remains to be fully explored. In his groundbreaking book, *Black Working Wives*, Bart Landry (2000) suggests that in many ways black women were the pioneers of the dual-career family. Beginning at the end of the nineteenth century, the majority of black middle-class wives promoted a more egalitarian version of the family that differed sharply from the "cult of domesticity" being promulgated in white families. Unlike their white counterparts, black women were engaged much more in the public sphere—within the church and community as well as in the workforce. In 1900, only 3 percent of married white women worked outside the home, whereas 26 percent of married black women worked outside the home (Weiner 1985, as cited by Landry 2000). In some cities, the number of married black women working approached 65 percent (Pleck 1978). Though black married women, even middle-class women, worked partly for economic reasons, Landry argues that the history black women have had of fighting for racial equality influenced them in fighting for equality within the family sphere. One way they gained more equality within the family was by being engaged in the workforce.

When researchers in the 1970s first approached the study of dual-career couples, couples in which both partners were employed in professional or managerial occupations, about 14 percent of whites fell into this category, but almost one-fifth of upper-middle-class black families were headed by dual-career couples (Landry 2000). Landry argues that as early as 1940, about 14 percent of black families fit this definition. By 1980 the percentage of white dual-career couples finally overtook that of black couples, but if the definition is broadened to include dual earners (i.e., both partners in the workforce), by 1990, 89 percent of black upper-middle-class couples were dual earners, versus 78 percent of upper-middle-class whites (Landry 2000).

Very little research has been conducted on dual-career black couples, but the few studies done suggest that black upper-middle-class men have historically been more supportive of having working wives than their white counterparts and that black women have been more interested in pursuing employment than were white women. But black men are more similarly aligned with white men in their failure to share household responsibilities when their wives are employed (Landry 2000). Although the two-parent family now makes up slightly less than half of all black households, or 49 percent in 1996 (U.S. Bureau of the Census 2000), the vast majority of research on blacks in many social areas focuses on the black female-headed household. The work-family field is just beginning to study the black family and gain an understanding of the diverse work-family needs of different types of black families. Single-parent families in general have also been an understudied demographic for work-family researchers.

Other Minority Groups

Although little research is available on blacks and work-family issues, even less research has been conducted on other minority groups in the United States and their work-family issues. In recent research, Spain and Bianchi (1996) found that the roles of motherhood, marriage, and employment—all significant factors in the work-family equation—vary greatly by race and ethnicity. Numbers culled from the 1990 census indicate that white women are the most likely to be married, black women are the least likely to be married, and Latinas fall in the middle. The labor participation rate for mothers from all groups has increased, with white mothers being the most likely to work outside the home in 1990 and Latina mothers the least likely. Latinas were most likely to live in a "traditional" family arrangement with a stay-at-home wife and breadwinning husband; black women were least likely to live in this type of arrangement. The group with the largest number of workers in the family in 1990 was Asian Americans, with nearly 20 percent of Asian-American families having three or more workers employed in the workforce; Latinos ranked second for this category. Asian-American women have the highest rates of labor force participation and the highest levels of education compared to other minority groups.

The Latino population in the United States is composed of many diverse groups, including Mexican Americans, Puerto Ricans, Cuban Americans, Central Americans, and South Americans. One frequent misconception about the Latino population is that Latinas have only recently entered the paid workforce, when many have always been part of the workforce. In 1973 the U.S. Census Bureau found that 39.7 percent of Latinas were engaged in paid work, and in 1993 that number had increased to 51.9 percent, almost as high as the participation rate for all women during that year. Though many Latinos embrace more traditional attitudes about gender roles—that women need to attend more to family responsibilities and men need to be the primary breadwinners—these beliefs have not unduly influenced women's participation in the labor force. Latinas who are better educated are more likely to be employed, though financial necessity is also a factor for many working women in the Latino community. A recent study of white blue-collar couples who work alternative work shifts in order to share child care indicates that couples can hold on to traditional ideas while behaving in nontraditional ways. The study found that these couples continued to embrace traditional gender role ideologies while living nontraditional lives, by holding on strongly to their beliefs that the father remained the primary breadwinner, the mother only worked because of economic need, and the mother remained the primary parent (Deutsch and Saxon 1998).

Very little research has been conducted about the work-family needs of the diverse groups that make up the Asian-American community, American Indians, and other minority and ethnic groups. In addition, few studies have been conducted on the needs of single parents coping with balancing work and family and the work-family needs of gay, lesbian, and other nontraditional families. Though a few recent studies have been conducted on single mothers, many of these studies have focused on upper-income women who were single mothers by choice (Hertz and Fergusen 1997, 1998; Foster, Jones, and Hoffman 1998), a growing but still tiny minority of the population of single mothers overall. The few studies done on lower-income single mothers have found that single mothers who work are less stressed and depressed than their nonworking counterparts (Jackson et al. 1998) and that workplace supports are the most important factor in enabling welfare mothers to succeed in the workforce (Parker 1994). A recent study on lesbian coparents found that household, child care, and paid labor responsibilities were most likely to be shared equally, but for a minority of these couples the model of primary breadwinner and primary caregiver prevailed, often based on one parent's relative income and the extent that a partner wanted a stronger sense of family (Sullivan 1996).

As work-family researchers broaden their scope to include the needs of lower-wage workers, minority and ethnic groups, and nontraditional families, the workplace will be better able to accommodate the needs of these workers and measure the impact new programs have on worker productivity and retention. Although many researchers acknowledge that the needs of lower-wage workers must be even more acute than the needs of middle- and upper-income workers, more corporate interest needs to be generated in order to support and respond to new research in this area.

Caregiving

Caregiving is broadly defined to include both those who provide unpaid informal care to family members and employees who are hired to provide services to children, the elderly, or disabled adults. The issue of caregiving is central to the work-family debate. Because of a number of demographic trends detailed below, there is an increase in the need for caregivers and a decrease in their availability. The dual responsibilities of employment and caregiving are taking a toll on women who are employed outside the home but still must provide the majority of caregiving within the home. Informal caregivers, for the most part women who are in the workforce, experience stress and other negative psychological consequences from their double burden, and the workforce suffers from losses in productivity.

Though studies have found that high-quality child care does not affect children adversely, many child care situations are less than ideal. The interrelated problems of quality, affordability, and availability are discussed below. For school-age children

who are not quite ready to be left unsupervised, there is a shortage of after-school programs or acceptable alternatives. For
elderly people, there is also a shortage of affordable, available,
high-quality community and home care services. As demographics change, eldercare has emerged as a growing concern to families trying to meet employment demands while caring for elderly
relatives and adults with disabilities.

Child care, eldercare, and family care depended in the past
on the unpaid labor of women at home. As more women entered
the paid workforce, no cohesive system was developed to replace
this full-time caretaking work in the United States (Harrington
1999). Because women remain largely responsible for caregiving,
they are unable to fully participate in the labor force, and issues
such as job discrimination and pay equity remain uncorrected. At
the same time, serious social issues are developing because of a
shortage of high-quality or even adequate caregiving situations.
The decline in women's participation in many volunteer community activities such as work in the schools, churches, and hos-
pitals further hampers the availability and quality of services
(Harrington 1999).

The Crisis in Caregiving

Current social, demographic, and economic trends are increasing
the need for family caregivers and decreasing the availability of
these caregivers. Scientific and technological advancements have
increased longevity in the United States. Over time, an increasing
proportion of the population will be elderly. In 1990 one in eight
people were over sixty-five; the projected ratio for 2030 is one in
five. The most rapidly growing sector of the population, those
age 85 and older, are also the most likely to need care (Vierck
1990).

For the first time in history, families will soon spend more
time caring for elderly parents than for children (Harrington
1999). In 1900, the number of 40-year-olds with at least one surviving parent was 70 percent; today, it is more than 95 percent
(Cordtz 1990). In addition to the elderly who need care, there are
a greater number of adults with permanent disabilities. Medical
and technological advances have led to an increase in the number of people who survive what were once fatal accidents. At the
same time that care needs for the elderly and disabled are growing, the need for child care, especially care for very young chil-

dren, is increasing as more women with infants and toddlers remain in the labor force.

Although the need for caregivers has increased, there has been a decrease in the availability of informal caregivers due to several factors. The decline in fertility means that there are fewer adults to care for the growing elderly population. Because of a rise in the divorce rate and an increase in "blended families," there is sometimes only one adult to care for more than two parents. Because of declining birthrates, there are fewer siblings to share the burden of caring. And because more families are single-parent families, the adult caring for an elderly parent sometimes does not have support or assistance from a spouse. The most significant trend, however, is that more women are working outside the home. Sixty percent of women were working in 1998, with women making up almost 50 percent of all workers (Smith and Bachu 1999: 6), yet it is women who are often expected to be responsible for the care of elderly parents or parents-in-law.

Because women are marrying later, there is also an increasing likelihood that they will be part of the "sandwich generation"—women who are responsible for the care of both young children and elderly parents at the same time. Of women caring for elderly relatives, nearly 40 percent are still raising children of their own (England 1989). As women have entered the workforce, there has been a rise in the number of families needing child care services and assistance with elderly parents and a decrease in the number of people able to provide quality services. Grandmothers, aunts, and older daughters, relied on by baby boomer women as they went off to work, are also more likely to be in the labor force and thus unavailable for even informal dependent care arrangements (Presser 1989).

Work and Caregiving Conflict

Eldercare, child care, and care for adults who are disabled place a significant amount of stress on working adults, particularly women who provide the majority of dependent caregiving (U.S. House of Representatives 1987). Surveys of employees have found that 25 percent of those responding were currently involved in providing care to an older person and 45 percent of those responding were parents of children under the age of eighteen who were living at home (Emlen and Koren 1984). Employees with children have trouble locating quality child care options and after-school programs. Some communities provide no after-school programs. A recent study indicated that for parents who have day care and backup arrangements, nearly one-third experience breakdowns in their arrangements over a three-month period (Parasuraman and Greenhaus 1997).

Employees responsible for elderly parents are being hit harder by changes in health care regulations that put more emphasis on community-based or home care and less emphasis on institutional care. Families now provide 80 percent of the in-home care to elderly relatives who have chronic illnesses, even when some formal services are used (Leutz et al. 1992; U.S. Senate 1992).

An expanding body of research has found that caregiving responsibilities are having a negative impact on productivity. Work absences, tardiness, stress, and use of work hours to deal with caregiving concerns (e.g., by excessive use of the phone) have been attributed to employees trying to cope with caregiving issues (Ehrlich 1988; Scharlach and Boyd 1989; Warshaw 1986). In addition, Michael Creedon (1987) found that employees themselves were aware that caregiving was affecting their performance at work.

Some caregivers end up leaving the workforce altogether in order to care for family members. A study by Ellen Galinsky, James Bond, and Dana Friedman (1993) found that 25 percent of caregivers changed jobs, 22 percent considered quitting their jobs, and 14 percent actually quit because of caregiving responsibilities. LouEllen Crawford (1990) found similar results. Elaine Brody and colleagues (1987) found that 28 percent of caregiving women had to quit their jobs to look after a parent.

Child Care Issues: Quality, Affordability, and Availability

Child care has come to be accepted as a normal part of life. According to the National Survey of America's Families in 1997, 75 percent of children under five were in some type of child care (Capizzano, Adams, and Sonenstein 2000a). Of this group, about one-third were cared for in their own home by parents working different shifts, nannies, relatives, or babysitters; one-third were cared for in the home of a relative, neighbor, or home day care provider; and one-third were cared for in a center or preschool (Hofferth 1999). Low-income families are more likely to rely on a mother working half-time or working a night shift (Helburn 1999). Low-income children under the age of five are less likely than higher-income children to be in some sort of formal center or preschool. Nearly 40 percent of children under age five are in two or more nonparental caregiving arrangements, with low-income children no more likely to be in multiple arrangements than children from higher-income families. Three- and four-year-olds were much more likely to be in three or more caregiving arrangements in any given week (Capizzano, Adams, and Sonenstein 2000b).

In most industrialized countries except the United States, child care is either free or affordable because of government subsidies, similar to subsidies provided for public schooling (Helburn 1999). In the United States, families must rely on the private sector for the most part, with some subsidies and private charities giving assistance to families with very low or no income. Leaving child care responsibilities to the private sector without any public support creates problems relating to quality, affordability, and availability.

A number of studies in the past few years have documented the prevalence of low-quality child care centers (for a review, see Morris 1999). Studies on home providers, who are subject to less regulation or none depending on state law and the number of children cared for, found even lower-quality services than the services provided by centers (Kontos et al. 1995). A 1994 study by the Family and Work Institute found only 9 percent of home care arrangements they surveyed could be rated "good," 56 percent were rated "adequate" or merely "custodial," and 35 percent were rated "poor" or "disadvantageous" (Galinsky et al. 1994). Forty percent of centers are operated for profit, and this number appears to be increasing (Harrington 1999). For-profit centers have the potential to have quality issues because making money may conflict with providing high-quality care (Harrington 1999). For low-income families who cannot afford centers or home providers, older siblings who have limited or inadequate child-rearing skills provide care (Dodson 1998).

Providing high-quality child care is expensive because it requires small group sizes, high teacher-child ratios, skilled and trained staff, and low staff turnover (Harrington 1999). Because most parents cannot afford centers that provide this type of care, many centers have lowered their standards in order to be affordable. Parents purchase these services because they have little choice. Even parents who can afford quality services often have trouble identifying high-quality care (Morris 1999). When parents cannot afford high-quality centers, they accept lower-quality arrangements.

Availability of care is also a problem because of staff shortages. Wage levels for staff remain low, which creates a staff with few skills, little incentive to improve those skills, and a propensity to leave for better-paying jobs. The turnover rate for day care providers is about 30 percent a year nationwide (Harrington 1999). It takes parents an average of seven weeks to locate acceptable child care, with a more serious shortage in urban areas and very rural areas and a shortage in care for infants, sick children, or children needing care at night (Witte and Queralt 1997; Fuller et al. 1997).

Researchers argue that high-quality child care is essential because a large part of early development and learning occurs while a child is in care (Helburn 1999). Not surprisingly, researchers have found a link between quality of child care and children's development (Burchinal 1999). High-quality child care has a positive effect on children's cognitive and social development, regardless of the child's home environment. For infants, often the age group subject to the lowest quality of care, research has demonstrated that daily experiences are vital for actually increasing brain capacity (Cryer 1999). Experiences in the first three years of life determine how the brain develops, with neural circuits getting stronger with use and atrophying with disuse. In a review of the research literature, Debby Cryer (1999) found that high-quality care was linked with later school success, and there is an assumption that later school success is linked to productive citizenship.

After-School Care for Older Children

School-age children are less likely to be in formal after-school programs than their preschool counterparts. In 1991, of the 36 million children between the ages of five and fourteen, about 24 million were in families with employed parents, but only 2 million were enrolled in formal after-school programs. About one-third of children of working parents are "latchkey" children who come home to empty houses while their parents are still at work (Seppanen, DeVries, and Seligson 1993). Sandra Hofferth reported that in 1990, 3.5 million school-age children regularly spent after-school time unsupervised by adults or older teenagers (1991).

Some parents have expressed interest in more after-school options. Recent school shootings such as the tragedy in Littleton, Colorado, provide support for this request. Geographic mobility has reduced the availability of relatives to watch over children while parents are at work, and smaller families limit the availability of babysitting by older siblings. Some neighborhoods have become less friendly and in some cases dangerous places for children to play unsupervised because many adults in the neighborhood are at work during the day.

The general perception of latchkey children is that they are neglected and that they do less well in school. Research has produced mixed results regarding these children. Some studies found problems; other studies found little difference between supervised and unsupervised children; and some studies found poorer outcomes for children who spent after-school time with older siblings, babysitters, teachers, and even their own mothers than for children who were unsupervised (for a review, see Belle 1999). Unfortunately, most studies did not investigate the tremendous variation in self-care arrangements, and few studies looked at children over time to investigate long-term effects of different caregiving arrangements. Deborah Belle (1999) has postulated that after-school supervision may not be the most crucial variable to study but instead suggests investigating the location at which children spend unsupervised time and the amount of "distal" supervision by parents who monitor their children's activities. Steinberg (1986) found that self-care children who "hung out" at settings away from home were more susceptible to peer pressure and more likely to engage in antisocial behavior than either self-care children who spent time at their own homes or children who were supervised by adults. Later studies support Steinberg's research (Galambos and Maggs 1991).

To make up for shortcomings in earlier studies, Belle (1999) interviewed both parents and children over a four-year period. These parents and children came from dual-earner, single-parent, and joint custody households and a wide range of socioeconomic and ethnic backgrounds. Belle found that locating and sustaining acceptable after-school care was often complicated and time-consuming and required complex negotiations between family members with conflicting agendas. By age ten or eleven, many children spend some time unsupervised. Although some chil-

dren seem ready to deal responsibly with this new independence, other children are clearly unready for the challenges they
face when no adults are present. Many children would clearly
benefit from after-school programs that are currently not available to them because their parents cannot afford them or they do
not have transportation.

Although middle childhood can be a time when children
begin to exercise some self-regulation, it is important that parents
continue to exercise supervisory control. Eleanor Maccoby (1984)
reported that a parent and child can successfully "coregulate" the
child's behavior if parents effectively supervise their children
when they are together and guide and support their children
when they are not being directly supervised. Essential ingredi-
ents for success included keeping lines of communication open;
strengthening a child's ability to keep behavior within safe limits; and developing a child's awareness of when to turn to a parent for help.

Eldercare: The New Frontier

Just as child care emerged as a significant issue several decades
ago, eldercare is becoming a serious issue for families today.
There is a widely held myth that most adult children no longer
care for their elderly relatives as they did in the "good old days,"
but research indicates otherwise (Neal et al. 1993). In the mid-
1990s, an estimated 22.4 million households, or almost one in
four, were providing home care for family members or friends
over the age of 50 (Harrington 1999). More than 65 percent of disabled elderly people live at home or with relatives, with most of
their care coming from family members with minimal governmental support (Harrington 1999). An estimated 15 percent of
adult men and women bear responsibility for the care of aging
parents or other elderly relatives (Scharlach 1995).

Although very wealthy families are able to purchase high-
quality services for their relatives, and families with very low
incomes can receive institutional care, for middle-class families
there are few alternatives between informal home care and institutional care (England 1989). In the past, women who were at
home were able to take on this caretaking role. Today, most
women are in the workforce and are no longer able to address
long-term care needs for aging relatives. Though assistance for

home care is far less expensive than institutional care, little such support is available (Harrington 1999).

Most literature on eldercare focuses on the impact of caregiving on the caregiver rather than the recipient (Crawford 1996). Many variations exist, but the typical recipient of caregiving is a widowed mother or mother-in-law age 75 or older with a limited income (Anastas, Bibeau, and Larson 1990). Although informal family caregiving is a common role for women in the United States, women who have graduated from college are less likely to take on caregiving roles (Moen, Robinson, and Fields 1994). For home care, quality of care is usually less of an issue than the ability to negotiate roles between the caregiver and care recipient. The caregiver must permit the elderly parent to be dependent, and the parent must be able to be appropriately dependent. Researchers (Neal et al. 1993) hypothesize that dependent mothers feel better if they think the help given by their daughters is discretionary, not obligatory.

Eldercare is similar to child care in that meeting the dependency needs of an elderly relative can be extremely demanding both physically and psychologically. Unlike child rearing, in which the dependence of the child diminishes over time, eldercare usually involves having to meet increasing physical and psychological needs. Research has found that eldercare can be more stressful than child care. Other studies have shown that employees with eldercare responsibilities are more apt to experience anxiety, depression, insomnia, headaches, and weight changes than employees who do not have these responsibilities (Wagner, Creedon, Sasala, and Neal 1989, as cited in Neal et al. 1993). When American Express surveyed its employees' off-work burdens, they found that eldercare ranked higher than alcoholism, drugs, and divorce as a primary concern for these employees (Perham 1987).

Roughly one-third of caregivers to the elderly are employed, but this figure approaches 50 percent if spousal caregivers, who are more likely to be retired, are excluded (Singleton 1998). Roberta Spalter-Roth and Heidi Hartmann (1990) estimate that $4.8 billion are lost annually to employees' caregiving responsibilities. This estimate includes unpaid labor, lost wages, and missed opportunities. According to a recent study by the National Center on Women and Aging (1999), caregivers who take time off sacrifice on average more than $600,000 in lost wages, lost Social

Security and pension contributions, and reduced opportunities for promotions. Among caregivers in the labor force, five in six are forced to quit, retire early, cut back work hours, or take sick or vacation leave in order to provide caregiving.

Eldercare issues are the most acute for women in the so-called sandwich generation, those with both eldercare and child care responsibilities occurring at the same time. Elaine Brody (1985) found that though these women accomplish a lot, many are frustrated and feel they do not do enough. Many employees use vacation, personal, and sick leave extensively for eldercare purposes. Phoebe Liebig (1993) found that two-thirds of employees did this, whereas Phyllis Mutschler (1994) found that different occupational groups adapt work roles to eldercare demands in different ways. Production workers, for example, are more likely to take unpaid leave and less likely to rearrange their schedules. Eldercare issues are just beginning to be acknowledged in the workplace. For example, child care assistance is now offered by 85 percent of employers surveyed, but eldercare assistance reached only 26 percent in 1995, although that figure had more than doubled from 12 percent in 1990 (Hewitt 1995).

Caregiving: Personal or Societal Responsibility?

Changing demographics, such as the increase in women in the labor market, have created a crisis in caregiving. Women who once took care of elderly relatives and neighbors, looked out for the well-being of teenagers in the neighborhood, took care of babies and school-age children, and volunteered in schools, churches, and other community service points are no longer available to fill these needs. The privatization of caregiving has not proven to be a satisfactory alternative to the unpaid work women previously provided because high-quality services are too expensive for the majority of families.

Liberals advocate for government subsidies for caregivers in order to provide high-quality, affordable caregiving arrangements, especially to low-income families. Ensuring the availability of high-quality caregiving arrangements would support women's full participation in the labor force as well. Liberals argue that caregiving is a societal issue rather than a women's issue. However, social conservatives argue that caregiving should remain primarily a women's issue. They argue that money should be spent to encourage women to stay home with their children or with relatives in need of care (Olsen 1997). They feel that children benefit most from being at home with their mothers. For those parents who cannot afford to be at home, social conservatives argue that most parents are satisfied with the quality of caregiving arrangements and dispute studies that indicate that a great deal of child care is substandard. Though most other economically advanced countries provide subsidized care for young children and recognize it as an essential public investment, the United States does not appear to be ready to provide this type of support in the near future.

Some families have adopted a different approach by focusing on caregiving first and adapting work to fit their caregiving needs rather than the more typical arrangement of fitting caregiving needs around employment demands. Rosanna Hertz (1999) studied couples who were placing priority on family needs over work and found that some dual-earner families carefully planned schedules and nontraditional career paths in order to meet family needs, whereas others reluctantly coparent because of underemployment. Single mothers in professional occupations negotiate contract work, whereas lower-income single mothers needed regular employment in order to receive benefits. A recent but growing movement, led by organizations such as the Third Path Institute in Philadelphia, supports the idea of "shared care," in which parents put a high priority on being the primary caretakers of their children while staying actively engaged with work. Different families achieve shared care in different ways—some rely on extended families or limited day care, some telecommute or work back-to-back shifts, and some reduce work hours or job share.

Strategies for Resolving Work-Family Conflict

Debate about what role the individual, community, government, and employer should play in lessening work-family tensions is currently underway in the field of work-family. Although the government has been reluctant to enter the domain of private family life, the corporate world has responded as work-family pressures mount. As family-friendly benefits proliferate, their underutilization raises questions about their ability to truly resolve work-family tensions. As these issues fold into larger questions about the very nature of work, community, and family roles, work-family takes on an ethical dimension. Researchers and policymakers need to address the questions of how work should be defined and what kind of support should be provided to nourish and sustain the community and the family.

Stakeholders in the Work-Family Debate

The family, government, employer, and community all have a stake in work-family issues, but until now these issues have largely been left to the family to solve. Federal, state, and local governments, as well as local communities, have been reluctant to become involved in what is viewed as a private responsibility. Many employers have added family-friendly programs to their benefits packages, but work conditions have changed little since the 1950s. Employees continue to be treated as if they had wives at home to cope with family and household responsibilities (Barnett and Rivers 1998).

One popular cultural assumption is that having children is an individual choice and has nothing to do with business or society (Bailyn 1997). Some in society feel that women who choose to have children should stay home, whereas others feel that if some women choose to take on multiple roles, then it is their responsibility to deal with any work-family issues that arise. But because working mothers' salaries are often essential to maintaining a reasonable standard of living, staying home is no longer a viable option for many. In addition, many feel that women, who are now a permanent fixture in the workplace, should not have to make a trade-off between working and having a family when men do not have to make a similar trade-off. With more women in the workplace, husbands are also beginning to experience work and family conflict as they are required to take on more family and household responsibilities.

The Role of Government

The awareness of work-family issues is growing, but the U.S. government has been slow to respond. Despite strong rhetoric on family values, there has been a noticeable absence of formal policy with regard to families and little articulation about the role that individuals, employers, and the government should play.

The passage of the Family and Medical Leave Act (FMLA) in 1993 after more than a decade of delays was a major accomplishment. Today the FMLA provides for unpaid leave for the birth, adoption, or foster placement of a child; an employees' own serious health condition; or the serious health condition of an immediate family member. But the FMLA covers only 11 percent of U.S. employers (those with 50 or more employees), leaving 41 percent of all workers ineligible (Drake 1997). The act does not provide leave to members of less traditional family arrangements such as gay and lesbian couples or people in common-law marriages. In addition, because the leave is unpaid, it discriminates against low-income workers who cannot afford to live without a paycheck for any length of time. A recent study on the FMLA (Gerstle and McGonagle 1999) reported that many people who feel they need the FMLA are unable to take advantage of it because it is unpaid. This study also showed that married women who have employed husbands are more likely to use the leave. Recent efforts have been made by about a dozen states to provide paid family leave benefits through the expansion of unemployment or disability insurance.

International Comparisons

Many industrialized countries have taken a different approach to policymaking in the area of work-family. In researching government responses in other countries, Suzan Lewis (1997) found that social policy has been influenced by both state ideology regarding the family as either an individual or collective responsibility and economic factors such as the need for women's labor. In the United States and the United Kingdom, the family is viewed as an individual responsibility, and the government provides minimal support. In other industrialized countries, especially in Europe, policy is supported by a larger sense of communal responsibility for families, and a more proactive role is taken by the state on issues such as child care.

Giele (1994) argues that women's actual experiences with balancing work and family, rather than attitudes and ideology, have been a key factor in shaping social policy. In countries such as France and Finland, where there is less of a tradition of wives who stay home, more supportive work-family policies have been promulgated. Lewis (1997) found that to the degree that there is acceptance of dual-earner families as the norm, government support for child care and related issues is seen as essential, and many countries encourage women in their role as breadwinner and support men in their increasing involvement with family matters. In industrialized countries where there is a more traditional view of women, such as in India, Israel, and Spain, the government's focus is on helping women balance their new roles rather than diverging from traditional gender roles.

In many Asian countries, the extended family plays a significant role in helping with child care so that mothers can work, but eldercare has increasingly become a problem. Though many women are involved in market work, daughters and daughters-in-law are still expected to be the primary caretakers for aging relatives (Lewis 1997). Unlike the United States, all European countries currently have legally mandated paid maternity leave, though the length and percentage of pay varies. The majority of European countries provide some form of parental leave, though men have underutilized this benefit (Lewis 1997). Parental leave of three months has been annexed to the 1992 Treaty of the European Union, but the United Kingdom has not agreed to this aspect of the treaty. The European Union has not been able to reach agreement that part-time workers should have equal employment rights, a policy adopted by many of its member countries. Some countries, such as the Netherlands, are working toward fully valued part-time work that would include equal pay, benefits, and rights.

In countries in which legislation has addressed some work-family needs, corporations have gone a step further in order to attract workers, offering solutions such as flexible work arrangements. These corporations are far different from those in the United States, where there has been little government attention to work-family issues and corporations' need to address basic issues. At a time when the labor market is highly competitive and corporations are engaged in downsizing and trying to "do more with less," many see work-family benefits as a way to recruit and retain valuable workers who are desperately seeking help in meeting the conflicting demands of work and family.

The Corporate Response: Family-Friendly Programs

Historically, companies have only become involved in family issues during national emergencies. For example, during World War II, companies assisted the government in providing child care, as more women were needed in the workplace (Bankert and Lobel 1997). Since the 1980s, as competitive pressures mounted in the increasingly global economy, employers have become more concerned with productivity. At the same time, workplace demographics have shifted as the pool of workers began to include more women, minorities, and older workers. As corporations downsized their workforce, there was also concern about both morale and the need to support the remaining workers, who were expected to carry a heavier load. A new focus on the needs of people within the organization, designed to improve productivity as well as recruit and retain valuable workers, has led to a proliferation of family-friendly policies and programs.

Originally, these work-family programs focused on child care issues. Early efforts were centered in the human resources or personnel departments. These initial attempts were seen not as relevant to business concerns but rather as a way to respond to women in the workforce who were asking for help (Rapaport and Bailyn 1996). The programs focused on the needs of women with young children, but often women using these benefits were viewed as less committed to their jobs. On-site child care centers were one of the first major programs to emerge, but they were expensive and difficult to manage, and some employees preferred at-home care. As corporations grew more aware of other competing personal needs and faced concerns about equity and as the more inclusive term *work-life* began to replace the term *work-family*, they began to offer broader programs such as flexible work arrangements and eldercare benefits.

What started as a low-key response to some requests from working mothers has grown to be viewed as a vital benefit by many organizations and employees. Findings from the National Study for a Changing Workforce (Bond, Galinsky, and Swanberg 1993) found that the second most important factor considered when taking a job was the effect of the job on family life. In general, employees are motivated more by intrinsic factors than extrinsic rewards such as salaries. Today many corporations tout their family-friendly benefits and vie to be included in *Working Women* magazine's list of the 100 best companies for working mothers, as well as the more recent "Best Companies for Work and Family" in *Business Week* magazine. As executives realize that family-friendly benefits are not that expensive compared to their value as a tool for retention and recruitment, both the number of companies offering benefits and the types of benefits provided have grown substantially.

Some of the more common family-friendly benefits or programs are discussed below.

Part-Time Work or Job Sharing

Part-time work can be temporary or permanent and can include working fewer hours each day, fewer than five days a week, or fewer than twelve months a year. Employers benefit from hiring part-time workers because they can hire from a larger labor pool, retain valuable workers, and avoid paying expensive benefits. Employers can also adjust the number of workers they have to fit the amount of work available. Part-time employees benefit from being able to attend to family needs, but often part-time workers must give up valuable benefits and in some cases job security.

Job sharing involves two people sharing one full-time position. Sometimes these employees have separate but related work activities, and sometimes their work is unrelated, but they are viewed as the equivalent to hiring a full-time employee. Job sharing enables employers to retain valuable employees and allows for continuity in a job if one person leaves. Certain jobs do not lend themselves well to job sharing, and sometimes employers have trouble evaluating individuals whose jobs overlap.

Part-time work is useful to workers who want to spend more time with children or an elderly relative, but some researchers (Rapaport and Bailyn 1996; Harrington 1999) argue that part-time work has resulted in greater inequality for women, who make up the bulk of part-time workers. Because workers are often viewed as more committed and more valuable in direct relationship to their hours on the job, it has been difficult for part-time workers to gain acceptance. Part-time workers are undervalued and less likely to be promoted. Rapaport and Bailyn (1996) argue that work hours need to be restructured to make room for family time and other life needs for all workers. Doing so would remove the stigma currently associated with those who work part-time.

Leave of Absence Programs

In Europe, some form of paid parental or family leave is available to all workers. In the United States, there is no statutory guarantee for leave to care for an ill family member or take paternity leave. Women who give birth are covered under paid or unpaid disability leave policies. Under the FMLA, employees working in organizations with more than 50 employees are entitled to up to three months of unpaid leave for the birth, adoption, or foster placement of a child; an employee's own serious health condition; or the serious health condition of an immediate family member.

Even for those employees who are eligible for leave under the FMLA, use has been much lower than expected, and significantly fewer men take advantage of the FMLA than women (Commission on Family and Medical Leave 1996). Some managers discourage female employees from taking leaves because they are concerned that these employees will not return. In fact, the majority of women who take a leave of absence return to their jobs (Bond 1991). More than 50 percent of large companies have a paid or unpaid leave policy available in addition to what is required under the FMLA, with 22 percent extending this leave to fathers and 23 percent extending this leave to adoptive parents (Friedman and Johnson 1997).

Dependent Care Benefits

Though the first steps toward work-family programs were on-site child care centers, only a small proportion of employers provide this type of care. The significant cost of establishing and running a center and not being able to address all employees' needs with an on-site center led to the search for other dependent care benefits.

In 1981, dependent care became a nontaxable benefit to employees. As a result, companies offer financial assistance to employees by allowing them to pay child and eldercare services with pretax dollars. This is one of the most widely used forms of corporate support for dependent care because the government absorbs the cost. Referral networks are also a popular benefit with employers because this service assists a large number of employees in finding child care and eldercare and is inexpensive to provide. Referral networks are now broadening their scope to include finding enrichment activities for school-age children as well.

Flexible Work Arrangements or Telecommuting

Flexible work arrangements and telecommuting are among the most popular work-family benefits but are difficult to implement (Friedman and Johnson 1997). Flexible work arrangements, or "flextime," consists of any schedule that an employee works that is outside normal work hours, such as coming in early and leaving early. Many flexible work arrangements involve part-time work (see above). A recent study (Catalyst 1993) found that flexible work arrangements are much more widespread than a decade ago and that many organizations have formal policies on flexible work arrangements, but that managers and supervisors continue to be resistant to these arrangements. Many workplace cultures continue to define work and productivity as "hours on the job," which makes it difficult to accept nontraditional work schedules whose productivity needs to be measured by work accomplished rather than hours present in the workplace.

Telecommuting involves doing some or all work from home, usually keeping in contact with the workplace by telephone, fax, or email. Currently it is estimated that more than 25 million employees participate in some form of telecommuting. The advantages of telecommuting include an increased ability to balance work-family needs, less work-related stress, greater productivity, increased morale and commitment to work, lower absenteeism, fewer costs for employers, and better air quality because of fewer commuters traveling by automobile (Riley and McCloskey 1997).

But telecommuting only works well with employees who have a high degree of self-discipline and motivation. It often fails when employees try to combine telecommuting with supervising children. In addition, some employees are reluctant to telecommute because they fear it will reduce opportunities for promotion. Many successful telecommuters spend only some of their time each week working from home, with the balance of their work time spent at the office. One danger with telecommuting is that employees sometimes put in large amounts of overtime because work is so accessible. This practice can result in health problems, lower productivity, and job and family dissatisfaction (Riley and McCloskey 1997). Recent research (Golden 2000) found that access to flexible work schedules is uneven, with more men and more people in managerial and professional jobs who are working more than 50 hours a week making some use of telecommuting. This statistic suggests that telecommuting might be more of a job perk used to retain workers than a benefit that reduces work-family tensions (Riley and McCloskey 1997).

Future Trends in Family-Friendly Programs

As corporations add to their ensemble of programs, they are demonstrating a growing interest in playing a more extensive role with dependent care. The increasing need for eldercare services and referral, the need for short-term emergency child care, and the increased parental concern about quality after-school enrichment programs are leading to more involvement in this area by corporations. One entity, the American Business Collaborative, has invested more than $25 million to improve the supply and quality of dependent care in more than 40 communities (Friedman and Johnson 1997).

In addition, corporations are beginning to address the needs of low-income workers (Friedman and Johnson 1997), who are especially subject to work-family stress and have previously been neglected in terms of work-family programs. Results from the National Study for a Changing Workforce (Bond, Galinsky, and Swanberg 1993) demonstrated that low-income workers' work-family needs were largely ignored by employers and that the less pay a worker received, the less likely that work-family programs were available to that worker. With few government programs or policies to support working-class families, the need for work-family programs for these workers has become crucial to their ability to participate in the workforce.

Some researchers (Young 1999) argue that work-life programs are not meeting the needs of the majority of workers. Mary Young (1999) asserts that though many corporations have changed the names of their programs from "work-family" to "work-life," in essence these benefits remain focused on the needs of parents. Employees without children under the age of eighteen are now the predominant group in the workforce—58 percent of the workforce have no children under the age of eighteen (U.S. Bureau of the Census 1996). She argues that more research needs to be conducted on the needs of this emerging group.

With the growing number of childless adults in the workforce, a work-family backlash movement that started in the early 1990s has accelerated. Sometimes referred to as the "childfree," some employees without children claim they are expected to work additional hours and to fill in for parents who have child care needs during work hours. These employees also object to subsidizing parental benefits such as dependent health care, insurance, and in some cases child care, and they object to flexible work arrangements and unpaid leaves offered to employees who are parents. A survey by Gillian Flynn (1996) found that 81 percent of employees surveyed believed that single employees "end up carrying more of the burden than married employees." In a recent popular book titled *The Baby Boon: How Family-Friendly America Cheats the Childless* (Burkett 2000), the author calls for more attention to be paid to a growing sector of adults who are choosing not to have children and claims parents are getting "equal pay for unequal work."

Underutilization of Family-Friendly Programs

Though the variety of family-friendly programs continues to expand, many of the programs offered are underutilized (Powell 1997). Some programs are little used because of lack of awareness, and some programs do not have buy-in from all layers of the organization (Fried 1998). Many employees are reluctant to use work-family benefits because they feel doing so brands them as less committed to their jobs (Hochschild 1997). Because many programs are available at the discretion of the supervisor, buy-in from all supervisors and an underlying, sweeping culture change are essential but challenging requirements for the success of work-family programs. Many corporations feel they are responding to work-family needs by instituting programs, but many of these programs are glitter with little substance because in reality the culture of the organization discourages employees from taking advantage of them (Christensen 1997).

Mindy Fried (1998) spent a year doing extensive fieldwork at a large corporation that offered an impressive number of family-friendly benefits available to all employees. At this corporation, Fried discovered that employees were subtly discouraged from using these benefits because the corporation viewed family-friendly benefits as "taking time" away from the company rather than as "making time" for children. Time at work was viewed as being directly related to productivity. Committed employees were expected to work long hours, especially when deadlines were approaching, and any family leave time taken was interpreted negatively and was seen to interfere with long-term career goals.

Many work-family programs are viewed as being for women. Men are much less inclined to participate in parental leave programs or flexible work schedules, though informally many men do take time off but disguise the reason why they need time off (Powell 1997; Fried 1998). Many men are still trying to function as their fathers did in the role of the "ideal worker," who is always available, never mentions family responsibilities at work, and is free to travel for business at a moment's notice. But unlike their fathers, most men do not have wives who are doing all the housework and child care. In their book on working fathers, Levine and Pittinksy (1998) found that the greatest obstacle to having a father-friendly workplace, a workplace that provided support for men who needed to balance work and family demands, was corporate culture. This corporate culture is reinforced by mothers who continue to ask for time off for a sick child, for example, and by fathers who either depend on their wives to take time off or who lie about why they are staying home. A recent study found that managers' attitudes and the general work environment were even more important than actual policies in helping staff make use of work-family programs (Bond, Galinsky, and Swanberg 1998).

Though many companies have work-family benefits on the books, few have managed to weave a work-family culture into the fabric of the organization. Though many studies have shown that companies reap advantages when providing work-life balance to employees, corporations cannot reap the benefits of greater productivity and employee loyalty unless they adopt a more comprehensive strategy.

Changing the Culture of the Workplace

How managers and others within the organization view work-family benefits and how this view is communicated throughout the organization are crucial factors in the success or failure of work-family programs. One of the cultural barriers to greater acceptance of work-family benefits throughout the broader organization is the perception that conflict arises from a woman's decision to combine work with parenthood (Parasuraman and Greenhaus 1997). Instead, the corporate culture needs to view having a family as a common life event experienced by *most* employees and therefore a systemic conflict that, if addressed, can contribute to an employee's and society's well-being. Viewing work-family issues as a human issue rather than a woman's issue and as a societal responsibility rather than an individual one will help eliminate the stigma attached to those who use these benefits (Parasuraman and Greenhaus 1997).

As employers look into the personal requirements of employees and build work-family programs into their corporate paradigm, ideas about how work is accomplished will need to shift as well. Many managers adhere to the traditional notion that presence at the workplace is equal to productivity and loyalty. Research on work has not proven a relationship between "face-time" and productivity or loyalty. In fact, one recent study (Bailyn 1997) demonstrated that some people with more external constraints on their time worked in ways that were actually more productive and creative, but often their accomplishments were not noticed. By evaluating the work accomplished rather than the amount of time spent in the workplace, employers can more accurately evaluate productivity and provide employees with some flexibility in meeting family needs (Parasuraman and Greenhaus 1997).

The current trend toward self-managed teams and greater autonomy for workers lends itself to breaking away from the traditional management practice of closely monitoring workers. This trend will enable workers to make use of flexible work policies with less fear that it will disrupt their careers. As employers reorganize tasks, often using fewer workers, work-family issues need to be brought into the mix as a strategy for increasing productivity and employee loyalty. Corporations with very limited flexible time policies often experience a high incidence of disruptive and unplanned absences and tardiness. In one study (Rapaport and Bailyn 1996), a division manager made flexible time policies widely available to employees and found that many men and women chose to change their schedules to accommodate both work and family needs. As a result, the company experienced a 30 percent drop in absenteeism.

Educating managers to view work-family policies as a management tool to accomplish long-term business objectives rather than as an individual accommodation is crucial in gaining management support and increasing utilization rates. Dana Friedman and Arlene Johnson (1997) found that workers with more social support from supervisors and coworkers experience less work-family conflict and less stress and are able to more effectively cope with both work and family responsibilities. Job autonomy and worker support were also found to correlate with employee commitment to work and desire to accomplish work goals.

In their extensive study and intervention with three large companies, Rapaport and Bailyn (1996) investigated work cultures and structures in order to find ways for employees to integrate work and personal life without interfering with business goals. These researchers found that companies continue to attempt to separate work from family goals, which often undermines both work and family. They also found that traditional ideas about gender roles continue to influence corporate culture. Women are discouraged from bringing up family demands at work but are also looked on negatively if they are seen as neglecting their family; men are discouraged if they express a desire to spend more time with their families. Rapaport and Bailyn found that there is an underlying assumption in organizations that work and family are "inherently in competition with one another" and that the ideal worker is "career primary." In order to succeed at work, employees feel the need to hide family obligations, which leads to increased stress and conflict.

Rapaport and Bailyn intervened in the three companies they studied by relinking work and family at a systemic rather than a personal level. They suggested that by restructuring the way work is accomplished while attending to work and family needs, both companies and families can benefit. They talked with managers and workers about developing a new vision of the ideal worker. This new ideal would be a worker who is an "integrated individual," combining behaviors typical of both public and private spheres. Behaviors such as linear thinking, assertiveness, and rationality are considered public behaviors that are usually associated with the workplace, whereas behaviors such as working behind the scenes to smooth things over, supporting people in meetings, and communicating with other groups have traditionally been associated with the home. Rapaport and Bailyn helped employers develop ways of evaluating these often-unappreciated "relational" skills.

Other researchers (Christensen 1997) agree that having a family can enable the employee to develop useful skills and should be viewed as an opportunity for growth rather than a potential detriment to a successful career. As workplaces become more collaborative and team approaches are widely embraced, skills that women traditionally developed while raising families have become more relevant and valuable to organizations. In the long run, employers need to recognize that helping employees attend to family needs can contribute to healthier families with children who will grow up to be more productive, creative, and useful workers. In his book *The Fifth Discipline*, Peter Senge concurs with these ideas, stating that we cannot build an effective organization "on the foundation of broken homes and strained personal relationships" (cited in Christensen 1997: 28).

Rapaport and Bailyn (1996) sound the alarm that trying to separate work and family life leads to serious inequalities, with the needs of work taking precedence over all other needs. Achievement at work is viewed as the main measure of success and self-esteem, and the needs of families and communities are given less attention by government and policymakers. They state that "the goal of relinking work and family life is not simple.... It is about shifting to a more equitable society in which family and community are valued as much as paid work is valued and where men and women have equal opportunity to achieve in both spheres" (Rapaport and Bailyn 1996: 38).

The Role of the Community

Googins (1997) argues that the community has been the "forgotten stakeholder" while corporations and families try to address work-family needs. Googins and others (Parasuraman and Greenhaus 1997) argue that corporate work-family benefits should shift into the public policy domain. Because the government has been largely uninvolved in the process, corporations have gradually offered more comprehensive benefits that are beginning to resemble a social welfare system. Googins (1997) argues that corporate involvement in this area is an inadequate model for providing fully for the needs of the family because it defines work-family as a business issue rather than an issue of public policy. In addition, corporations often provide inequitable benefits by not addressing the work-family needs of the working poor or welfare recipients.

Googins also views the community as comprising both the informal and formal systems that support family life. He points out that much of the informal system has disappeared. People who traditionally provided support for children and the elderly are now in the workplace, and neighborhood life is almost nonexistent during the day. Formal systems such as schools must adapt more to working parents' schedules, and informal systems need more support and encouragement. Googins calls for a family-friendly society rather than a family-friendly corporation. Parasuraman and Greenhaus (1997) suggest that a federally funded "Work-Family Coordinating Council" be set up to review work-family needs and provide funds for community projects that assist in reducing work-family tensions. Paula Rayman and Ann Bookman (1999) argue for improving the connection between work-family research and policymaking and suggest ways of prodding the government into taking a more active role.

Faith Wohl (1997) suggests that the essential role of work-family professionals is that of community builder. The field of work-family includes both the work people do and the relationships they enjoy. People in the field need to reach beyond corporate benefit solutions and focus more on developing community and societal responsibility for the common good. Wohl calls for us to "reinvent work, renew family life, and reawaken our historic sense of community" (Wohl 1997: 22).

Addressing the Imbalance: Restructuring Work and Family Life

Work-family researchers are broadening their focus to include not just physical schedules and roles played by family members but underlying societal values. Many in the work-family field argue for better integration between work and family and a strengthening of work and family programs both at work and within the community (Googins 1997). Some researchers have gone a step further and have argued that Americans need to question the very nature of the definition of work and its place within their lives. In her call for a "new contract," Wohl (1997: 18) states: "What America needs is a new contract that redefines the critical agreements among work, family, and community.... Integrating work and family is thus ultimately an ethical issue that suggests the need for a new social balance in which work assumes its more rightful place within our lives—rather than demanding that we rearrange our lives around it."

The central conflict between work and family is both a practical one and an ethical one. Employees want to perform well at work but also want a rewarding and satisfying personal and family life. Although family-friendly benefits can be useful and need to be better integrated with workplace culture, they will not rectify the problem. The reality is that the nature of work has changed, the nature of the family has changed, and the nature of the community and its role has changed as well. Some argue (Wohl 1997; Glass 2000) that Americans need to reassess their societal values in light of these changes and restructure the roles played by business, the community, and the family.

Caregiving as a National Value

Currently many people, especially women, are caught in a bind between caretaking responsibilities and having rewarding careers. In her book *Care and Equality: Inventing a New Family Politics*, Mona Harrington (1999) investigates this dilemma. Without women's full-time unpaid caretaking labor, families must purchase care from the private market, yet most families are not able to afford adequate care. If women return home or work part-time in order to provide caretaking, they are denied equality in the workplace. Harrington postulates that the old structure cannot support both adequate care and equality and that the solution is that care needs to become a national political value. Jennifer Glass (2000) pushes this one step further to argue that job structures are unresponsive to workers' caregiving responsibilities and child care has become excessively privatized. Glass also argues that the cost of child rearing, which benefits employers and communities, has become increasingly a private rather than a community obligation and has increasingly become the responsibility of fewer people, especially fewer men. Having children has become an economic liability. Those who have children are more likely to experience poverty, have a lower job status, and have less authority at work.

Several scholars (Glass 2000; Schor 1991; Hochschild 1997) have found that work now requires longer hours and discourages family and community involvement. Hochschild (1997) argues that the rewards at work have started to replace the comforts of home, as employees spend fewer hours in the home while dishes and family problems pile up. Workers find themselves in a time bind in which limited time at home is increasingly becoming more efficiency-based, whereas time at work is becoming less efficient and more social. Men and women who want to responsibly parent their children are finding they must lower their ambitions at work and accept reduced career goals because they cannot compete with workers who can single-mindedly pursue career success. Glass (2000) calls it a "collision course" between success at work and success at child rearing, with the result being an increased marketization of caregiving ranging from more take-out dinners to more child care centers. This marketization of caregiving roles has further increased the costs of being a parent. The postponement and reduction in childbearing may be a response in part to the increasing financial cost of raising a child today.

The "Time Bind"

In her 1991 book *The Overworked American*, Schor found that since 1980 the average worker has added an extra 164 hours—a month of work—to his or her work year. Hochschild, in her 1997 book *The Time Bind*, also found that American working parents are working longer hours. She found that for workers with children under 13, only 4 percent of men and 13 percent of women worked fewer than forty hours a week. John Robinson and Geoffrey Godbey (1999) disagree with this research. They found that though Americans are not working longer hours, they are feeling more rushed. In their study Robinson and Godbey found that 38 percent of the adult public say they "always" feel rushed, an increase from 22 percent in 1971. Robinson and Godbey hypothesize that people who feel more rushed and stressed are more likely to overestimate how long they work.

Kathleen Gerson and Jerry Jacobs (1998) agree with Robinson and Godbey's finding that Americans are not actually working longer hours in the workplace than previous generations. Gerson and Jacobs found, however, that the increase in dual-earner and single-parent families combined with the decrease in unpaid caregiving and household support has resulted in men and women experiencing greater time binds, even though most are not actually putting in more hours at work. They also note a bifurcation in the workforce, with both excessively long and short workweeks becoming more common, though the average workweek has remained largely unchanged since 1970. These long workweeks are most common among professionals, with almost two in five men with a college education working 50 or more hours per week.

Unlike earlier researchers, Gerson and Jacobs (1998) supplemented their data with information on workers' preferences. They found that there is a mismatch between the hours many Americans work and the amount of time they would like to spend at work. Many workers would like to work less than they actually do, but one underemployed group would like to work more. Almost half the workers reported that their workweek was longer than their ideal, but an additional one in six said that they would prefer to work additional hours. These researchers point out that employers lower their costs by pressuring salaried workers to work as many hours as possible and also reduce the expense of benefits by hiring part-time workers. Gerson and Jacobs (1998) asserted that jobs that require long hours prevent parents from spending time with their children, inhibit gender equity because workers (often women) cannot compete at the upper levels and still meet family responsibilities, and threaten the development of community and society. They state, "The nation should see the promotion of a balance between work and the rest of life not as simply a private choice between employers and employees, but as a matter of great importance to the public interest" (456).

Hochschild (1997) notes that in the fight for balance between work and family, employers seem to be winning, as corporations define and set policy on how people meet their work and family goals. Because the need for balance is not always, in the short-run, beneficial to business interests, many feel the community and the government need to put forward ideas and legislation that can rectify this problem. Corporations ultimately have an interest in supporting work-family balance because the healthy development of children who can became productive and useful citizens is in everyone's interest.

Shortening the Workweek

Because most adults are in the workforce, they spend fewer hours at home engaged in caregiving and household duties. As a result, they spend less time with children, especially leisure time (Galinsky 1999). Partners also have less time for each other, which may result in more stress and even a higher incidence of divorce. Work-family researchers (Parasuraman and Greenhaus 1997; Gerson and Jacobs 1998) argue that it is time to move to a shorter workweek. The 40-hour workweek, which has remained unchanged for more than 50 years, was designed for the male-breadwinner family model. This type of family composition represents less than 10 percent of all families in the United States (Parasuraman and Greenhaus 1997). If a 35-hour workweek were the cultural standard, working parents would have more time to take care of children, men would have time to become more involved in parenting and household activities, and more people would be able to spend time participating in community activities and volunteerism.

The assumption that it is heroic to spend long hours in the workplace needs to be questioned, and the challenging work taking place at home and in the community needs to be better recognized and appreciated. Gerson and Jacobs (1998) call for the Fair Labor Standards Act to be extended to cover professionals and managers so that there is a federally imposed limit to the workweek for all employees. Parasuraman and Greenhaus (1997) suggest that new ways of working be explored, including asking employees to put in more time at the beginning of their careers and less time when they are involved in caregiving responsibilities. Glass (2000) suggests a utopian solution that would include a 30-hour workweek, required community service, and jobs designed with the assumption that the incumbent has caregiving responsibilities. This arrangement would guarantee that all workers support and share in the costs of raising children and ensure that no one is expected to completely dedicate his or her life to the workplace.

Schor (1991) found that most employees who work extensive hours are not very productive toward the end of long shifts, so it is possible that the workweek could be shortened without any loss in productivity. Leslie Perlow (1995) also found worker inefficiency. In her fieldwork she found that the workers engaged in very disruptive and inefficient work patterns tend to have a crisis mentality. Her research also demonstrated that more efficient ways of working were possible and could allow for more time to be spent outside work and create less stress in all areas of life. In addition, the government needs to promote an even playing field between part- and full-time work so that companies do not choose to hire part-time workers to save money on benefits. Part-time workers should receive proportional benefits.

Sharing the Wealth

Currently, the United States has the most unequal distribution of corporate profits in the industrialized world (Harrington 1999). As a result, many families do not have the resources to care for their children. Jeremy Rifkin (1995) suggests that wealth accumulated from gains in productivity from new technologies should be shared with all working people, not just upper-level managers. He argues that these corporate savings could be more equitably distributed by reducing the workweek without reducing pay and decreasing overtime work. Harrington (1999) feels that some sort of subsidy needs to be provided to allow every family enough income to adequately support themselves. The social costs of not providing families with adequate resources—costs such as increased crime and drug abuse—far outweigh the cost of providing this subsidy (Phelps 1997).

Increased Government Involvement

The United States is lagging far behind other industrialized countries in the area of family policy and support. Liberals argue that the barriers between government and family need to be broken down so that policy can address the current inequities. The United States needs to pass legislation expanding the Family and Medical Leave Act to more closely resemble parental leave policies in European countries, and steps need to be taken to provide publicly supported preschool for children ages three to five. However, conservatives define family in the more traditional form, with mothers at home providing care and fathers in the workplace. As a result, conservatives argue for tax breaks to support this more traditional notion of the family in hopes that this nostalgic view of the family might regain prominence.

Researchers in the field of work-family argue that changes need to be made in how Americans view paid work versus caregiving. The latter needs to be recognized as a highly valued and important role or occupation. More support, subsidies, and training for paid caregivers would be money well spent. Additionally, Glass (2000) argues for a "family impact statement" that would be similar to an "environmental impact statement" created for proposed legislation. The family deserves at least as much consideration as the environment when new legislative proposals are being reviewed.

The Evolution of Gender Roles

Lastly, many argue (Harrington 1999; Williams 2000) that notions of motherhood and gender roles need to continue to evolve. Americans need to question the belief that skills needed in parenting are different from skills needed for running a corporation and that women have the former set of skills and men the latter

(Harrington 1999). By changing our conceptions of motherhood and fatherhood, Americans can allow women to be viewed as equal players in the workplace and further open the door for men to become full, active participants in the home.

Achieving Integration

The nature of work and the composition of families have changed remarkably since the 1960s as well as since the 1600s. From the relocation of work outside the home during the Industrial Revolution to the movement of women into the workplace in the past 30 years, the way work-life and family life interact has become increasingly problematic. In her classic study on work-family, Rosabeth Moss Kanter first called attention to the linkages between work and family life (1977). She argued for the abandonment of the view that work and family were "separate spheres" that could be thought about and researched separately. Kanter traced the history of work-family from preindustrial and early industrial times, when work and family were integrated, to the early 1900s, when work and family became more segregated as men took on the role of breadwinner and middle- and upper-income women stayed home to manage the household. Women have now entered the workforce, and the separation between these two spheres is evaporating. Tensions between work and family are increasing. As the labor market becomes tighter, workers' expectations about being able to achieve both satisfying work and family lives are rising.

Policymakers need to acknowledge and rectify imbalances that have been created between work and family life. As men and women become more equally involved in both spheres of life, work and family, and as the role for legislating what the rules will be in these two spheres shifts to government and away from the corporate sector, greater integration can be achieved between work and family. As the balance between these two essential roles improves, the result will be healthier families, healthier workers, and more productive workplaces.

References

Ainsworth, Mary. 1973. "The Development of Infant-Mother Attachment." *Review of Child Development Research* 3: 18–36.

Amott, Teresa, and Julie A. Matthaei. 1996. *Race, Gender and Work: A Multicultural Economic History of Women in the United States.* Boston: South End Press.

Anastas, Jeane, Janice Bibeau, and Pamela Larson. 1990. "Working Families and Eldercare: A National Perspective in an Aging America." *Social Work* 35, no. 5: 405–411.

Axinn, June, and Herman Levin. 1982. *Social Welfare: A History of the American Response to Need.* New York: Longman.

Bachu, Amara. 1993. "Fertility of American Women: June 1992." U.S. Bureau of the Census, *Current Population Reports*, P20-470. Washington, DC: U.S. Government Printing Office.

Bailyn, Lotte. 1997. "The Impact of Corporate Culture on Work-Family Integration." Pp. 209–219 in *Integrating Work and Family: Challenges and Choices for a Changing World.* Edited by Saroj Parasuraman and Jeffrey H. Greenhaus. Westport, CT: Quorum.

Bankert, Ellen C., and Sharon A. Lobel. 1997. "Visioning the Future." Pp. 177–191 in *Integrating Work and Family: Challenges and Choices for a Changing World.* Edited by Saroj Parasuraman and Jeffrey H. Greenhaus. Westport, CT: Quorum.

Barciauskas, Rosemary Curran, and Debra Beery Hull. 1989. *Loving and Working: Reweaving Women's Public and Private Lives.* Bloomington, IN: Meyer-Stone Books.

Barnett, Rosalind C., and Caryl Rivers. 1998. *She Works/He Works: How Two-Income Families Are Happy, Healthy, and Thriving.* Cambridge, MA: Harvard University Press.

———. 1999. "A New Work-Life Model for the Twenty-First Century." *Annals of the American Academy of Political and Social Science* 562 (March): 143–158.

Baruch, Grace K., Rosalind C. Barnett, and Caryl Rivers. 1984. *Lifeprints: New Patterns of Love and Work for Today's Women.* New York: Signet.

Baruch, Grace K., Lois Biener, and Rosalind C. Barnett. 1987. "Women and Gender in Research on Work and Family Stress." *American Psychologist* 42: 130–136.

Bell, Donald. 1981. "Up from Patriarchy." In *Men in Difficult Times: Masculinity Today and Tomorrow* by Robert Lewis. Englewood Cliffs, NJ: Prentice-Hall.

Belle, Deborah. 1999. *The After-School Lives of Children.* Mahwah, NJ: Lawrence Erlbaum Associates.

Blankenhorn, David. 1994. *Fatherless America.* New York: Basic Books.

Bond, James T. 1991. "The Impact of Childbearing on Employment." In *Parental Leave and Productivity: Current Research*. Edited by Dana Friedman, Ellen Galinsky, and Veronica Plowden. New York: Families and Work Institute.

Bond, James T., Ellen Galinsky, and Jennifer E. Swanberg. 1993. *National Study of the Changing Workforce*. New York: Families and Work Institute.

———. 1998. *1997 National Study of the Changing Workforce*. New York: Families and Work Institute.

Bowlby, John. 1969. *Attachment*. Vol. 1, *Attachment and Loss*. New York: Basic Books.

Brady, Marilyn Dell. 1991. "The New Model Middle-Class Family (1815–1930)." Pp. 83–124 in *American Families: A Research Guide and Historical Handbook*. Edited by Joseph M. Hawes and Elizabeth Nybakken. New York: Greenwood Press.

Brody, Elaine M. 1985. "Parent Care as a Normative Family Stress." *Gerontologist* 25: 19–29.

Brody, Elaine M., Morton H. Kleban, Pauline T. Johnsen, Christine Hoffman, and Claire B. Schoonover. 1987. "Work Status and Parent Care: A Comparison of Four Groups of Women." *Gerontologist* 27: 201–208.

Burchinal, Margaret R. 1999. "Child Care Experiences and Developmental Outcomes." *The Annals of the American Academy of Political and Social Science* 563: 73–97.

Burkett, Elinor. 2000. *The Baby Boon: How Family-Friendly America Cheats the Childless*. New York: Free Press.

Caffrey, Margaret M. 1991. "Women and Families." Pp. 223–258 in *American Families: A Research Guide and Historical Handbook*. Edited by Joseph M. Hawes and Elizabeth Nybakken. New York: Greenwood Press.

Campbell, Angus. 1982. "Changes in Psychological Well-Being during the 1970s of Homemakers and Employed Wives." Pp. 291–302 in *Women's Lives: New Theory, Research and Policy*. Edited by Dorothy G. McGulgan. Ann Arbor: University of Michigan, Center for Continuing Education of Women.

Capizzano, Jeffery, Gina Adams, and Freya Sonenstein. 2000a. "Child Care Arrangements for Children under Five: Variation across States." No. B-07 in New Federalism: National Survey of America's Families. Washington, DC: Urban Institute. http://newfederalism.urban.org (cited 5 December 2001).

———. 2000b. "The Number of Child Care Arrangements Used by Children under Five: Variation across States." No. B-12 in New Federalism:

National Survey of America's Families. Washington, DC: Urban Institute. http://newfederalism.urban.org (cited 5 December 2001).

Catalyst. 1993. *Flexible Work Arrangements II: Succeeding with Part-Time Options*. New York: Catalyst.

Christensen, Perry M. 1997. "Toward a Comprehensive Work/Life Strategy." Pp. 25–37 in *Integrating Work and Family: Challenges and Choices for a Changing World*. Edited by Saroj Parasuraman and Jeffrey H. Greenhaus. Westport, CT: Quorum.

Corcoran, Mary, Greg J. Duncan, and Michael Ponza. 1984. "Work Experience, Job Segregation, and Wages." Pp. 171–191 in *Sex Segregation in the Workplace: Trends, Explanations, Remedies*. Edited by B. F. Reskin. Washington, DC: National Academic Press.

Coltrane, Scott. 1996. *Family Man: Fatherhood, Housework and Gender Equity*. New York: Oxford University Press.

Coltrane, Scott, and Elsa O. Valdez. 1993. "Reluctant Compliance: Work-Family Role Allocation in Dual-Earner Chicano Families." Pp. 151–175 in *Men, Work, and Family*. Edited by Jane C. Hood. Newbury Park, CA: Sage Publications.

Commission on Family and Medical Leave. 1996. *A Workable Balance: Report to Congress on Family and Medical Leave Policies*. Washington, DC: Commission on Leave; Women's Bureau, U.S. Department of Labor.

Coontz, Stephanie. 1988. *The Social Origins of Private Life: A History of American Families, 1600–1900*. London; New York: Verso.

Coontz, Stephanie, ed. 1999. *American Families: A Multicultural Reader*. New York: Routledge.

Cordtz, Dan. 1990. "Hire Me, Hire My family." *Financial World* 159 (September 18): 76–79.

Cott, Nancy F., ed. 1992. *History of Women in the United States*. Vol. 5, *The Intersection of Work and Family Life*. New York: Saur.

Cowan, Phillip A. 1988. "Becoming a Father: A Time of Change, an Opportunity for Development." Pp. 13–35 in *Fatherhood Today: Men's Changing Role in the Family*. Edited by Phyllis Bronstein and Carolyn Pape Cowan. New York: J. Wiley.

Crawford, LouEllen. 1990. *Dependent Care and the Employee Benefits Package*. Westport, CT: Quorum.

Creedon, Michael A. 1987. "Introduction: Employment and Eldercare." In *Issues for an Aging America: Employees and Eldercare: A Briefing Book*. Edited by Michael A. Creedon. Bridgeport, CT: University of Bridgeport, Center for the Study of Aging.

Cryer, Debby. 1999. "Defining and Assessing Early Childhood Program

Quality." *The Annals of the American Academy of Political and Social Science* 563: 39–55.

Deater-Deckard, Kirby, Sandra Scarr, Kathleen McCartney, and Marlene Eisenberg. 1994. "Paternal Separation Anxiety: Relationships with Parenting Stress, Child-rearing Attitudes, and Maternal Anxieties." *Psychological Science* 5, no. 6: 341–346.

Degler, Carl N. 1980. *At Odds: Women in the Family in America from the Revolution to the Present.* New York: Oxford University Press.

Deutsch, Francine M., and Susan E. Saxon. 1998. "Traditional Ideologies, Nontraditional Lives." *Sex Roles* 38, nos. 5–6: 331–352.

Dodson, Lisa. 1998. *Don't Call Us Out of Name: The Untold Lives of Women and Girls in Poor America.* Boston: Beacon Press.

Drake, Eileen. 1997. "A Legal Perspective on Work-Family Issues." Pp. 122–132 in *Integrating Work and Family: Challenges and Choices for a Changing World.* Edited by Saroj Parasuraman and Jeffrey H. Greenhaus. Westport, CT: Quorum.

Dunn, Dana. 1996. "Economic Aspects of Women's Labor-Force Participation." Pp. 61–63 in *Women and Work: A Handbook.* Edited by Paula J. Dubeck and Kathryn Borman. New York: Garland Publishing.

Ehrlich, Elizabeth. 1988. "For American Business, a New World of Workers." *Business Week,* September 19, 112.

Emlen, Arthur C., and P. E. Koren. 1984. *Hard to Find and Difficult to Manage: The Effects of Child Care on the Workplace.* Portland, OR: Portland State University, Regional Research Institute for Human Services.

England, Paula. 1992. *Comparable Worth: Theories and Evidence.* New York: Aldine de Gruyter.

England, Paula, and Dana Dunn. 1988. "Evaluating Work and Comparable Worth." *Annual Review of Sociology* 14: 227–248.

England, Suzanne E. 1989. "Eldercare Leaves and Employer Policies: Feminist Perspectives." Pp. 117–121 in *Proceedings of the First Annual Women's Policy Research Conference.* Washington, DC: Institute for Women's Policy Research.

Farley, Reynolds. 1996. *The New American Reality.* New York: Russell Sage Foundation.

Flynn, Gillian. 1996. "Backlash." *Personnel Journal* (September): 59–69.

Fogarty, Michael P., Rhona Rapaport, and Robert N. Rapaport. 1971. *Sex, Career and Family.* Beverly Hills: Sage.

Foster, E. Michael, Damon Jones, and Saul D. Hoffman. 1998. "The Economic Impact of Nonmarital Childbearing: How Are Older, Single Mothers Faring?" *Journal of Marriage and the Family* 60, no. 1: 163–174.

Fried, Mindy. 1998. *Taking Time: Parental Leave Policy and Corporate Culture*. Philadelphia: Temple University Press.

Friedman, Dana E., and Arlene A. Johnson. 1997. "Moving from Programs to Culture Change: The Next Stage for the Corporate Work-Family Agenda." Pp. 192–208 in *Integrating Work and Family: Challenges and Choices for a Changing World*. Edited by Saroj Parasuraman and Jeffrey H. Greenhaus. Westport, CT: Quorum.

Fuchs, Victor R. 1988. *Women's Quest for Economic Equality*. Cambridge, MA: Harvard University Press.

Fuller, Bruce, Casey Coonerty, Fran Kipnis, and Yvonne Choong. 1997. *An Unfair Head Start: California Families Face Gaps in Preschool and Child Care Availability*. Berkeley: University of California, PACE Center.

Galambos, Nancy L., and Jennifer L. Maggs. 1991. "Out-of-School Care of Young Adolescents and Self-Reported Behavior." *Developmental Psychology* 27: 644–655.

Galinsky, Ellen. 1999. *Ask the Children: What America's Children Really Think about Working Parents*. New York: William Morrow.

Galinsky, Ellen, James T. Bond, and Dana Friedman. 1993. *The Changing Workforce: Highlights of the National Study*. New York: Families and Work Institute.

Galinsky, Ellen, Carollee Lowes, Susan Kontos, and Marybeth Shinn.1994. *The Study of Children in Family Child Care and Relative Care*. New York: Families and Work Institute.

Gerson, Kathleen. 1993. *No Man's Land: Men's Changing Commitments to Family and Work*. New York: Basic Books.

Gerson, Kathleen, and Jerry A. Jacobs. 1998. "Who Are the Overworked Americans?" *Review of Social Economy* 56 (Winter): 442.

Gerstel, Naomi, and Katherine McGonagle. 1999. "Job Leaves and the Limits of the Family and Medical Leave Act." *Work and Occupations* 26, no. 4: 510.

Giele, Janet. 1994. "Women's Changing Lives and the Emergence of Family Policy." Pp. 153–168 in *Unresolved Dilemmas: Women, Work and the Family in the United States, Europe and the Former Soviet Union*. Edited by Tuula Gordon and Kaisa Kauppinen-Toropainen. Aldershot, UK: Avebury.

Glass, Jennifer. 2000. "Envisioning the Integration of Family and Work: Toward a Kinder, Gentler Workplace." *Contemporary Sociology* 29, no. 1: 129.

Golden, Lonnie. 2000. "Flexible Work Schedules—Their Distribution and Tradeoffs." Unpublished paper presented at the Midwest Economics Association Conference, Chicago, IL.

Goldscheider, Frances K., and Linda J. Waite. 1991. *New Families, No Families? The Transformation of the American Home.* Berkeley: University of California Press.

Goldstein, Amy. 1999. "Breadwinning Wives Alter Marriage Equation." *Washington Post,* 27 February 2000, A1.

Googins, Bradley K. 1991. *Work/Family Conflicts: Private Lives, Public Responses.* New York: Auburn House.

———. 1997. "Shared Responsibility for Managing Work and Family Relationships: A Community Perspective." Pp. 220–231 in *Integrating Work and Family: Challenges and Choices for a Changing World.* Edited by Saroj Parasuraman and Jeffrey H. Greenhaus. Westport, CT: Quorum.

Grimm-Thomas, Karen, and Maureen Perry-Jenkins. 1994. "All in a Day's Work: Job Experiences, Self-Esteem and Fathering in Working-Class Families." *Family Relations* 43, no. 2: 174–181.

Griswold, R. L. 1993. *Fatherhood in America: A History.* New York: Basic Books.

Harrington, Mona. 1999. *Care and Equality: Inventing a New Family Politics.* New York: Alfred A. Knopf.

Harvey, Elizabeth. 1999. "Short-Term and Long-Term Effects of Early Parental Employment on Children of the National Longitudinal Survey of Youth." *Developmental Psychology* 35, no. 2: 445–459.

Healy, Melissa. 1998. "Questions of the House Not Being a Home; Politics: Campaigning Mothers Face Uphill Battle of Rising Public Scorn." *Washington Post,* 29 June 1998, A1.

Helburn, Suzanne W. 1999. "The Silent Crisis in U.S. Child Care. Preface." *The Annals of the American Academy of Political and Social Science* 563: 8–19.

Helburn, Suzanne, and Mary L. Culkin. 1995. "Cost, Quality, and Child Outcomes in Child Care Centers: Executive Summary." Economics Department, University of Colorado. Unpublished report.

Hertz, Rosanna. 1999. "Working to Place Family at the Center of Life: Dual-Earner and Single-Parent Strategies." *The Annals of the American Academy of Political and Social Science* 562: 16–31.

Hertz, Rosanna, and Faith I. T. Ferguson. 1997. "Kinship Strategies and Self-Sufficiency among Single Mothers by Choice: Post Modern Family Ties." *Qualitative Sociology* 20, no. 2: 187–227.

———. 1998. "Only One Pair of Hands: Ways That Single Mothers Stretch Work and Family Resources." *Community, Work and Family* 1, no. 1: 13–37.

Hewitt Associates. 1995. *Work and Family Benefits Provided by Major U.S. Employers in 1995.* Lincolnshire, IL: Hewitt.

Hiller, Dana V., and William W. Philliber. 1986. "The Division of Labor in Contemporary Marriage: Expectations, Perceptions, and Performance." *Social Problems* 33: 191–201.

Hochschild, Arlie R. 1989. *The Second Shift: Working Parents and the Revolution at Home.* New York: Viking.

———. 1997. *The Time Bind: When Work Becomes Home and Home Becomes Work.* New York: Henry Holt.

Hodson, Randy, and Teresa A. Sullivan. 1990. *The Social Organization of Work.* Belmont, CA: Wadsworth.

Hofferth, Sandra L. 1991. *National Child Care Survey, 1990.* Washington, DC: Urban Institute.

———. 1999. "Child Care, Maternal Employment, and Public Policy." *The Annals of the American Academy of Political and Social Science* 563: 20–38.

Hoffman, Lois W. 1979. "Maternal Employment: 1979." *American Psychologist* 34: 859–865.

———. 1984. "Maternal Employment and the Young Child." Pp. 101–127 in *Minnesota Symposium in Child Psychology* 17. Hillsdale, NJ: Erlbaum.

Jackson, Aurora P., Phyllis Gyamfi, Jeanne Brooks-Gunn, and Mandy Blake. 1998. "Employment Status, Psychological Well-Being, Social Support, and Physical Discipline Practices of Single Black Mothers." *Journal of Marriage and the Family* 60: 894–902.

Jones, Jacqueline. 1987. "Black Women, Work, and the Family under Slavery." Pp. 84–110 in *Families and Work.* Edited by Naomi Gerstel and Harriet E. Gross. Philadelphia: Temple University Press.

Kain, Edward L. 1990. *The Myth of Family Decline: Understanding Families in a World of Rapid Social Change.* Lexington, MA: Lexington Books.

Kanter, Rosabeth Moss. 1977. Work and Family in the United States: A Critical Review and Agenda for Research and Policy. New York: Russell Sage Foundation.

Kennedy, Ellen J., Mary Carksy, and Mary Ellen Waller Zuckerman. 1996. "The 'Mommy Track': Impact of Family Life on Women in the Professoriate." Pp. 424–430 in *Women and Work: A Handbook.* Edited by Paula J. Dubeck and Kathryn Borman. New York: Garland Publishing.

Kessler, Ronald C., and James A. McRae. 1982. "The Effects of Wives' Employment on the Mental Health of Married Men and Women." *American Sociological Review* 47: 216–227.

Kim, Marlene. 2000. "Problems Facing the Working Poor." Pp. 49–57 in *Balancing Acts: Easing the Burdens and Improving the Options for Working*

Families. Edited by Eileen Appelbaum. Washington, DC: Economic Policy Institute.

Klein, Donna. "Cultural Diversity in Organizations: Implications for Work-Family Initiatives." Pp. 115–121 in *Integrating Work and Family: Challenges and Choices for a Changing World.* Edited by Saroj Parasuraman and Jeffrey H. Greenhaus. Westport, CT: Quorum.

Kofodimos, Joan R. 1995. *Beyond Work-Family Programs: Confronting and Resolving the Underlying Causes of Work-Personal Life Conflict.* Greensboro, NC: Center for Creative Leadership.

Kontos, Susan, Carollee Howes, Marybeth Shinn, and Ellen Galinsky. 1995. *Quality in Family Child Care and Relative Care.* New York: Teachers College Press.

Krause, Neal. 1984. "Employment outside the Home and Women's Psychological Well-Being." *Social Psychiatry* 19: 41–48.

Lambert, Susan J. 1999. "Lower-Wage Workers and the New Realities of Work and Family." *The Annals of the American Academy of Political and Social Science* 562 (March): 174–190.

Landry, Bart. 2000. *Black Working Wives: Pioneers of the American Family Revolution.* Berkeley: University of California Press.

Lasch, Christopher. 1979. *Haven in a Heartless World : The Family Besieged.* New York: W. W. Norton.

Lerner, Jacqueline V. 1994. *Working Women and Their Families.* Thousand Oaks, CA: Sage.

Lerner, Jacqueline, and N. L. Galambos. 1986. "Child Development and Family Change: The Influences of Maternal Employment on Infants and Toddlers." In *Advances in Infancy Research.* Edited by Lewis P. Lipsitt and Carolyn Rovee-Collier. Norwood, NJ: Ablex.

Leutz, Walter N. 1992. *Care for Frail Elders: Developing Community Solutions.* Westport, CT: Auburn House.

Levine, James A., and Todd L. Pittinsky. 1998. *Working Fathers: New Strategies for Balancing Work and Family.* San Diego: Harcourt Brace.

Lewis, Suzan. 1997. "An International Perspective on Work-Family Issues." Pp. 91–103 in *Integrating Work and Family: Challenges and Choices for a Changing World.* Edited by Saroj Parasuraman and Jeffrey H. Greenhaus. Westport, CT: Quorum.

Liebig, Phoebe S. 1993. "Factors Affecting the Development of Employer-Sponsored Eldercare Programs: Implications for Employed Caregivers." *Journal of Women and Aging* 5, no. 1: 59–78.

Maccoby, Eleanor E. 1984. "Middle Childhood in the Context of the Family." Pp. 184–239 in *Development during Middle Childhood: The Years from*

Six to Twelve. Edited by W. A. Collins. Washington, DC: National Academy.

Maume, David J. 1998. "Occupational Constraints on Women's Entry into Management." Pp. 167–182 in *Challenges for Work and Family in the Twenty-First Century.* Edited by Dana Vannoy and Paula J. Dubeck. New York: Aldine de Gruyter.

Mincer, Jacob, and Solomon Polachek. 1974. "Family Investments in Human Capital: Earnings of Women." *Journal of Political Economy* 82: 76–108.

Mintz, Steven, and Susan Kellogg. 1988. *Domestic Revolutions: A Social History of American Family Life.* New York: Free Press.

Moen, Phyllis. 1992. *Women's Two Roles: A Contemporary Dilemma.* New York: Auburn House.

Moen, Phyllis, Julie Robison, and Vivian Fields. 1994. "Women's Work and Caregiving Roles: A Life Course Approach." *The Journals of Gerontology* 49, no. 4: 176–186.

Moen, Phyllis, and Ken R. Smith. 1986. "Women at Work: Commitment and Behavior over the Life Course." *Sociological Forum* 1: 450–476.

Moorehouse, M. J. 1991. "Linking Maternal Employment Patterns to Mother-Child Activities and Children's School Competence." *Developmental Psychology* 27: 295–303.

Morris, John R. 1999. "Market Constraints on Child Care Quality." *The Annals of the American Academy of Political and Social Science* 563: 130–145.

Mutschler, Phyllis H. 1994. "From Executive Suite to Production Line: How Employees in Different Occupations Manage Elder Care Responsibilities." *Research on Aging* 16, no. 1: 7–26.

National Center on Women and Aging. 1999. "The MetLife Juggling Act Study." Waltham, MA: Metlife Mature Market Institute/National Center on Women and Aging. Unpublished report.

Neal, Margaret B., Nancy J. Chapman, Berit Ingersoll-Dayton, and Arthur C. Emlen. 1993. *Balancing Work and Caregiving for Children, Adults, and Elders.* Newbury Park, CA: Sage.

Newman, Katherine S. 2000. "On the High Wire: How the Working Poor Juggle Job and Family Responsibilities." Pp. 85–94 in *Balancing Acts: Easing the Burdens and Improving the Options for Working Families.* Edited by Eileen Appelbaum. Washington, DC: Economic Policy Institute.

Olsen, Darcy. 1997. *The Advancing Nanny State: Why the Government Should Stay out of Child Care.* Cato Policy Analysis no. 285. Washington, DC: Cato Institute.

Parasuraman, Saroj, and Jeffrey H. Greenhaus. 1997. "The Changing World of Work and Family." Pp. 3–14 in *Integrating Work and Family: Challenges and Choices for a Changing World*. Edited by Saroj Parasuraman and Jeffrey H. Greenhaus. Westport, CT: Quorum.

Parcel, Toby L. 1996. "Maternal Working Conditions, Childcare and Cognition." Pp. 413–415 in *Women and Work: A Handbook*. Edited by Paula J. Dubeck and Kathryn Borman. New York: Garland Publishing.

Parcel, Toby L., and Elizabeth G. Menaghan. 1990. "Maternal Working Conditions and Children's Verbal Facility: Studying the Intergenerational Transmission of Inequality from Mothers to Young Children." *Social Psychology Quarterly* 53, no. 2: 132–147.

———. 1994. *Parent's Jobs and Children's Lives*. New York: Aldine de Gruyter.

Parker, Louise. 1994. "The Role of Workplace Support in Facilitating Self-Sufficiency among Single Mothers on Welfare." *Family Relations* 43: 168–173.

Perham, J. 1987. "Eldercare: New Company Headache." *Dun's Business Month* 129, no. 1: 64–65.

Perlow, Leslie. 1995. "The Time Famine: An Unintended Consequence of the Way Time Is Used at Work." Ph.D. diss., Massachusetts Institute of Technology.

Peterson, Karen S. 1988. "Today's Man Loves Family, Being a Dad." *USA Today*, 24 March, 1A.

Phelps, Edmund S. 1997. *Rewarding Work: How to Restore Participation and Self-Support to Free Enterprise*. Cambridge, MA: Harvard University Press.

Pleck, E. H. 1978. "A Mother's Wages: Income Earnings among Married Italian and Black Women, 1896–1911." In *The American Family in Social-Historical Perspective*. 2nd ed. Edited by Michael Gordan. New York: St. Martin's Press.

Pleck, Joseph H. 1985. *Working Wives/Working Husbands*. Beverly Hills: Sage.

———. 1993. "Are Family-Supportive Employer Policies Relevant to Men?" Pp. 217–237 in *Men, Work, and Family*. Edited by Jane C. Hood. Newbury Park, CA: Sage.

Powell, Gary N. 1997. "The Sex Difference in Employee Inclinations Regarding Work-Family Programs: Why Does It Exist, Should We Care, and What Should Be Done about It (If Anything)?" Pp. 167–176 in *Integrating Work and Family: Challenges and Choices for a Changing World*. Edited by Saroj Parasuraman and Jeffrey H. Greenhaus. Westport, CT: Quorum.

Presser, Harriet B. 1989. "Can We Make Time for Children? The Economy, Work Schedules, and Child Care." *Demography* 26: 523–543.

Rapaport, Rhona, and Lotte Bailyn. 1996. *Relinking Life and Work: Toward a Better Future. A Report to the Ford Foundation Based on a Collaborative Research Project with Three Corporations.* New York: Ford Foundation.

Rayman, Paula A. M., and Ann Bookman. 1999. "Creating a Research and Public Policy Agenda for Work, Family and Community." *The Annals of the American Academy of Political and Social Science* 562: 191–211.

Reichheld, F. 1996. *The Loyalty Effect.* Boston: Harvard Business School Press.

Repetti, Rena, Karen A. Matthews, and Ingrid Waldron. 1989. "Effects of Paid Employment on Women's Mental and Physical Health." *American Psychologist* 44: 1394–1401.

Reskin, Barbara, and Patricia Roos. 1990. *Job Queues, Gender Queues: Explaining Women's Inroads into Male Occupations.* Philadelphia: Temple University Press.

Rifkin, Jeremy. 1995. *The End of Work: The Decline of the Global Labor Force and the Dawn of the Post-Market Era.* New York : G. P. Putnam's Sons.

Riggs, Janet Morgan. 1997. "Mandates for Mothers and Fathers: Perceptions of Breadwinners and Care Givers." *Sex Roles* 37, nos. 7–8: 565–580.

Riley, Francine, and Donna Weaver McCloskey. 1997. "Telecommuting as a Response to Helping People Balance Work and Family." Pp. 133–142 in *Integrating Work and Family: Challenges and Choices for a Changing World.* Edited by Saroj Parasuraman and Jeffrey H. Greenhaus. Westport, CT: Quorum.

Robinson, John P., and Geoffrey Godbey. 1999. *Time for Life. The Surprising Ways Americans Use Their Time.* University Park: Pennsylvania State University Press.

Rogers, Stacy J. 1996. "Maternal Working Conditions and Children's Behavior Problems." Pp. 419–421 in *Women and Work: A Handbook.* Edited by Paula J. Dubeck and Kathryn Borman. New York: Garland Publishing.

Rose, Elizabeth. 1999. *A Mother's Job. The History of Day Care, 1890–1960.* New York: Oxford University Press.

Rosenfield, Sarah. 1989. "The Effects of Women's Employment: Personal Control and Sex Differences in Mental Health." *Journal of Health and Social Behavior* 30: 77–91.

Scarr, Sandra, Deborah Phillips, and Kathleen McCartney. 1989. "Working Mothers and Their Families." *American Psychologist* 44, no. 11: 1402–1409.

Scharlach, Andrew E. 1995. *The Family and Medical Leave Act of 1993: Analysis and Appraisal.* Boston: Boston University Center on Work and Family and U.S. Bureau of Labor Statistics.

Scharlach, Andrew E., and Sandra L. Boyd. 1989. "Caregiving and Employment: Results of an Employee Survey." *The Gerontologist* 29: 382–387.

Schor, Juliet B. 1992. *The Overworked American: The Unexpected Decline of Leisure.* New York: Basic Books.

Schwartz, Felice N. 1989. "Management Women and the New Facts of Life." *Harvard Business Review* 67, no. 1: 65–76.

Sealander, Judith. 1991. "Families, World War II, and the Baby Boom (1940–1955)." Pp. 157–182 in *American Families: A Research Guide and Historical Handbook.* Edited by Joseph M. Hawes and Elizabeth Nybakken. New York: Greenwood Press.

Seppanen, Patricia. S., Diane K. DeVries, and Michelle Seligson. 1993. *National Study of Before- and After-school Programs: Executive Summary.* Washington DC: U.S. Department of Education.

Shelton, Beth Ann, and Daphne John. 1993. "Ethnicity, Race, and Difference: A Comparison of White, Black, and Hispanic Men's Household Labor Time." Pp. 131–150 in *Men, Work, and Family.* Edited by Jane C. Hood. Newbury Park, CA: Sage Publications.

Sidel, Ruth. 1986. *Women and Children Last: The Plight of Poor Women in Affluent America.* New York: Penguin Books.

Simonetti, Jack L., Nick Nykodymn, Warren R. Nielsen, and Janet M. Goralske. 1993. "Counseling Employee Guilt: A Corporate Necessity." *Employee Counseling Today* 5, no. 3: 17–23.

Singleton, Judy. 1998. "The Impact of Family Caregiving to the Elderly on the American Workplace: Who Is Affected and What Is Being Done." Pp. 201–216 in *Challenges for Work and Family in the Twenty-First Century.* Edited by Dana Vannoy and Paula J. Dubeck. New York: Aldine de Gruyter.

Sklar, Kathryn Kish. 1973. *Catharine Beecher: A Study in American Domesticity.* New Haven, CT: Yale University Press.

Smith, Kristin E., and Amara Bachu. 1999. "Women's Labor Force Attachment Patterns and Maternity Leave: A Review of the Literature." Washington, DC: U.S. Bureau of Census, Population Division Working Paper no. 32.

Snarey, John. 1993. *How Fathers Care for the Next Generation: A Four-Decade Study.* Cambridge, MA: Harvard University Press.

Solberg, Eric, and Teresa Laughlin. 1995. "The Gender Pay Gap, Fringe Benefits, and Occupational Crowding." *Industrial and Labor Relations Review* 48, no. 4: 692–708.

Spain, Daphne, and Suzanne M. Bianchi. 1996. *Balancing Act: Motherhood, Marriage, and Employment among American Women.* New York: Russell Sage Foundation.

Spalter-Roth, Roberta, and Heidi Hartmann. 1990. *Unnecessary Losses: Costs to Americans of the Lack of a Family and Medical Leave.* Washington, DC: Institute for Women's Policy Research.

Steinberg, Laurence. 1986. "Latchkey Children and Susceptibility to Peer Pressure: An Ecological Analysis." *Developmental Psychology* 22: 433–439.

Steinberg, Ronnie J. 1990. "The Social Construction of Skill." *Work and Occupations* 17: 449–482.

Sullivan, Maureen. 1996. "Rozzie and Harriet? Gender and Family Patterns of Lesbian Coparents." *Gender and Society* 10, no. 6: 747–767.

Swanberg, Jennifer E. 1996. "Job-Family Role Strain: Understanding the Experience of Lower Wage Service Employees." Ph.D. diss., Brandeis University.

Swiss, Deborah J., and Judith P. Walker. 1993. *Women and the Work-Family Dilemma: How Today's Professional Women Are Finding Solutions.* New York: John Wiley and Sons.

Taeuber, Cynthia M. 1996. *Statistical Handbook on Women in America.* Phoenix: Oryx Press.

Thompson, Linda. 1991. "Family Work: Women's Sense of Fairness." *Journal of Family Issues* 12: 181–195.

Thornton, Arland. 1989. "Changing Attitudes toward Family Issues in the United States." *Journal of Marriage and the Family* 51: 873–893.

U.S. Bureau of the Census. Various years. *Current Population Reports.* Series P-20: Population Characteristics. Census P-20. Washington, DC: U.S. Government Printing Office.

———. 1976. *Historical Statistics of the United States, Colonial Times to 1970.* Washington, DC: Government Printing Office.

———. 1997. *Current Population Survey.* Employment Characteristics of Families: 1996. Washington, DC: U.S. Government Printing Office.

U.S. House of Representatives, Subcommittee on Human Services of the Select Committee on Aging. 1987. *Exploding the Myths: Caregiving in America.* Committee Publication no. 99–611. Washington, DC: Government Printing Office.

U.S. Senate, Special Committee on Aging. 1992. *Aging America: Trends and Projections, 1990–1991.* Washington, DC: U.S. Department of Health and Human Services.

Ventura, S. J. 1995a. "Trends in Pregnancies and Pregnancy Rates: Estimates for the United States, 1980–1992." *Monthly Vital Statistics Report* 43, no. 11.

———. 1995b. "Advance Report of Final Natality Statistics, 1993." *Monthly Vital Statistics Report* 44, no. 3.

Vierck, Elizabeth. 1990. *Fact Book on Aging.* Santa Barbara, CA: ABC-CLIO.

Waldfogel, Jane. 1997. "The Effect of Children on Women's Wages." *American Sociological Review* 62: 209–217.

Waldron, Ingrid, and J. Jacobs. 1989. "Effects of Multiple Roles on Women's Health—Evidence for a National Longitudinal Study." *Women and Health* 15: 3–19.

Wandersee, Winifred D. 1991. "Families Face the Great Depression." Pp. 125–156 in *American Families: A Research Guide and Historical Handbook* Edited by Joseph M. Hawes and Elizabeth I. Nybakken.

Warshaw, Leon J. 1986. *Employer Support of Employee Caregivers.* New York: New York Business Group on Health.

Weiner, L. Y. 1985. *From Working Girl to Working Mother: The Female Labor Force in the United States, 1820–1890.* Chapel Hill: University of North Carolina Press.

Welter, Barbara. 1966. "The Cult of True Womanhood: 1800–1860." *American Quarterly* 18: 151–175.

Wethington, Elaine, and Ronald C. Kessler. 1989. "Employment, Parenting Responsibility and Psychological Distress: A Longitudinal Study of Married Women." *Journal of Family Issues* 10: 527–546.

Williams, Joan. 2000. *Unbending Gender: Why Family and Work Conflict and What to Do about It.* New York: Oxford University Press.

Witte, Ann Dryden, and Magaly Queralt. 1997. *Factors Influencing the Neighborhood Supply of Child Care in Massachusetts.* Working paper 97004. Wellesley, MA: Wellesley College.

Wohl, Faith. 1997. "A Panoramic View of Work and Family." Pp. 15–24 in *Integrating Work and Family: Challenges and Choices for a Changing World.* Edited by Saroj Parasuraman and Jeffrey H. Greenhaus. Westport, CT: Quorum.

Young, Mary. 1999. "Work-Family Backlash: Begging the Question, What's Fair?" *Annals of the American Academy of Political and Social Science* 563 (March): 32–46.

Zaslow, Martha, Beth A. Rabinovich, and Joan T. D. Suwalsky. 1991. "From Maternal Employment to Child Outcomes: Pre-Existing Group Differences and Moderating Variables." Pp. 237–282 in *Employed Mothers and Their Children*. Edited by Jacqueline V. Lerner and Nancy L. Galambos. New York: Garland.

2

Chronology

This timeline traces the emergence of work and family issues in the United States from the advent of the Industrial Revolution and the physical separation of the workplace from the home. The growing numbers of married women, and eventually women with young children, joining the labor market; the shifting attitudes regarding child care outside the home; the emergence of several waves of feminism; the evolution of welfare; and the changing role and involvement of fathers in their children's lives are traced over time.

1776–
1783
During the American Revolution many women run farms and businesses while their husbands are at war. Divorce is common during this period, with the grounds for many divorces based on desertion.

1790s
The majority of free black women in the United States work as domestic servants. For the most part, they are barred from other nonagricultural labor.

1800s
The Industrial Revolution transforms the meaning of work and its relationship to the family in American life. With the advent of factories, work becomes physically separate from the home, many jobs involve routine and monotonous tasks, and new roles develop within the workplace between managers and workers. As factory towns grow in importance, people move from largely rural farming communities to urban centers, breaking ties with extended family

1800s *cont.*	members. Farm work is performed by less than 30 percent of the labor force in 1910, down from 60 percent in 1860.
1825	The first child care center in the United States, for children ages 18 months to six years, opens at a mill in Indiana owned by Robert Owen. At age seven, the children attend a regular classroom; at age 10 they begin work in the mill.
1830s	Infant schools for working families open in Boston, New York, Hartford, Cincinnati, and Detroit. In 1835, Boston schools charge a sliding scale fee of up to 2 cents a day. Most infant schools are supported by wealthy patrons.
1840s	The "cult of domesticity," a nineteenth-century concept, romanticizes family life and women's roles within the home. The ideal of the female-centered, middle-class home is held up for others to emulate. Women are charged with upholding moral virtues, such as self-sacrifice and purity, for the good of society. One consequence is that women become isolated in the domestic sphere, whereas men are able to participate in the public sphere. Lower-income women are unable to conform to middle-class mores, but they pass the value of domesticity on to their daughters.
1841	Catharine Beecher writes the bestseller *A Treatise on Domestic Economy.* The book attempts to apply scientific principles to housework. Beecher believes that women belong in the home, but she tries to emphasize the importance of domestic duties. Her book provides information on plumbing, building, gardening, child care, and other domestic issues. The term *housework* is first recorded to be in use. Prior to this time, there was no need to make a distinction between work done inside the home and other work done by family members in a largely agricultural economy, where work and family were usually not separated by physical location.

1845   The first female trade union leader in the United States, Sarah Bagley, lobbies for a ten-hour day and better working conditions for women in the cotton mills in Lowell, Massachusetts. The first U.S. government investigation of labor conditions takes place at the mills but rules against a ten-hour limit to the workday for women.

1854   The Nursery for the Children of Poor Women is founded in New York City, and other major cities quickly follow suit. Leaving children in day nurseries is considered a last resort for poor women, when they cannot take in work at home or find friends or relatives to care for their children.

1868   Susan B. Anthony assists in establishing the Working Women's Association to obtain the credentials she needs to attend the 1868 convention of the National Labor Union. Though it lasts only one year, it is an important first step in uniting women who work outside the home in a challenge to male-dominated labor unions and employers.

1873   In *Bradwell v. State of Illinois*, the state refuses to grant Myra Bradwell a license to practice law because she is a married woman. The Supreme Court concurs with the state and rules against Bradwell's right to practice law. The Court finds that the right to practice law is not a right of citizenship under the Fourteenth Amendment and holds that married women have no legal existence apart from their husbands.

1875   Increasing numbers of immigrants enter the United States, and charities work to set up additional day nurseries to keep families together. The staff is untrained, and the quality of care is poor.

1890   Nineteen percent of all women are in the labor force; 5 percent of married women are in the labor force.

        Pauline Agassiz Shaw establishes the North Bennett Street Day Nursery in Boston. It differs from earlier

1890 *cont.*	nurseries because it emphasizes education and allows children of non-wage-earning mothers to attend in order to benefit from the programs offered. This blend of care and education leads to the kindergarten movement in the United States, influenced by the development of kindergarten programs in Germany. Management experts such as Max Weber argue that strong family influences could undermine the development of rational bureaucracies. Employers begin to view families as a threat that could hinder the success of organizations.
1891	Thirty-two free kindergartens are established in California by the Golden Gate Kindergarten Association, which receives funds from the San Francisco Produce Exchange. This is one of the first examples of business involvement in child care assistance.
1892	Charlotte Gilman publishes "The Yellow Wall-Paper" in *New England Magazine*. Today a feminist classic, it describes a housewife who goes insane because of her life of domesticity. Gilman, who divorces her husband after becoming depressed from having to perform domestic and child care chores, goes on to a career in writing and public speaking on reform of working conditions and women's equality. She argues that housework and child care should not be the solitary responsibility of the housewife and advocates for communal nurseries and kitchens so women can be engaged outside the home.
1898	The National Federation of Day Nurseries is established and headed by Josephine Jewell Dodge. The federation is criticized later for pursuing regulations but not providing support for educational activities for children and training for staff.
1900	Twenty-one percent of all women are in the labor force; 6 percent of all married women are in the labor force, 26 percent of black married women are in the labor force.

1903   The first day nursery for black children opens in New York City.

1908   The Supreme Court upholds the constitutionality of maximum hour employment laws for women in *Muller v. State of Oregon*. The Court states that the childbearing capacity of women creates a special societal need to protect them from stressful work that could interfere with their ability to bear children or with the health of their fetuses. Later, the Fair Labor Standards Act of 1938 extends protective legislation to male and female workers, including the regulation of hours.

Theodore Roosevelt states that "mothers should raise their own children" at the White House Conference on Care of Dependent Children.

1910   Founders of a day nursery in Boston close the center, claiming "it was doing more harm than good."

Twenty-five percent of all women are in the labor force; 11 percent of married women are in the labor force.

1911   The Triangle Shirtwaist Factory fire in New York City focuses national attention on dangerous working conditions for women. One hundred and forty-six women die in the first fifteen minutes of the fire. The event generates support for the International Ladies' Garment Workers' Union, which signs its first contract in 1913. The contract provides women with some advantages but also formalizes the division of labor that exists in the industry by stating that the more lucrative, skilled jobs are for men; the less skilled, lower-paying jobs are for women.

The federal government establishes mothers' pensions, a predecessor to modern welfare, but the pensions are given to only a small percentage of eligible women.

1914   Amalgamated Clothing Workers of America becomes one of the few unions, prior to 1930, to accept women

1914
cont.

members. The union provides members with health care, housing, adult education, scholarships, and day-care centers but also initially sanctions lower wages for women workers, even though half its members are women.

1917

The Council of Defense sets up a Committee on Women in Industry to advise them on how to protect the welfare of women workers during the war. In July, the first draft of American men to fight in World War I creates a labor shortage. By fall, the U.S. Employment Service launches a campaign to replace men with women in "every position that a woman is capable of filling." The committee produces recommendations, including the statement that its members "view with alarm the increase of employment of married women with young children, and believe that efforts should be made to stem this movement as far as practicable, especially as regards night work."

1918

Ford Motor Company institutes the "Five Dollar Day," a "family wage" twice the going rate for unskilled workers in the area. Eligible workers must be "married men living with and taking good care of their families," or single men over twenty-two years of age, or men and women under the age of twenty-two who are "the sole support of some next of kin or blood relative." Married women are not initially included in the plan at all. Other large corporations also institute some form of family welfare program, with the goal of accommodating and controlling workers.

Woman in Industry Service (WIS) is set up by the War Labor Administration to deal with problems associated with a rapid introduction of women into industry. WIS quickly formulates standards for employment of women in war industries, including a 48 hour workweek, equal pay, lunch breaks, and sanitary and safety rules. The defense departments include these standards in war contracts, though many contractors do not observe them. WIS evolves into the Women's Bureau in 1920.

1919   The First International Congress of Working Women
            meets in Washington, D.C. It later becomes the Inter-
            national Federation of Working Women. Its main pri-
            ority is to promote trade union organizing among
            women.

1920s   Day nurseries continue to serve the temporary needs
            of poor families, and nursery schools become popular
            among psychologists, educators, and wealthier fami-
            lies.

1920   Twenty-four percent of all women are in the labor
            force; 9 percent of married women are in the labor
            force.

            Congress establishes the Women's Bureau, a branch of
            the Department of Labor with a staff of twenty under
            the directorship of Mary Anderson. The goals of the
            bureau are to collect information about women in
            industry and improve working conditions for women.
            Although the bureau seeks better opportunities for
            working women, the first few decades it favors pre-
            serving the role of women as homemakers, and it does
            not encourage young mothers to work outside the
            home unless necessary.

1923   The Classification Act of 1923 is passed, introducing
            the concept of "equal pay for equal work." The new
            law establishes that government salaries should be
            determined by job duties, not gender of employee.

            In *Adkins v. Children's Hospital,* the Supreme Court
            overturns a Washington, D.C., minimum-wage law
            for women. The Court finds that the minimum wage
            law is unconstitutional because it interferes with a
            woman's right to bargain with her employer on the
            subject of wages. Earlier court decisions had held that
            a woman's unique need for protection took prece-
            dence over having the freedom to bargain.

1924   The Vassar School of Euthenics is founded in response
            to a growing demand by women's schools to prepare

1924
cont.

women for domestic life. *Euthenics* is defined as an attempt to improve the physical quality of people through improvements in living conditions. It attempts to elevate homemaking and child rearing to a science.

The Women's Bureau issues numerous reports on women and work, including a report in 1924 titled *Married Women in Industry*.

1925

Rose Knox, president of Knox Company, producers of gelatin for food and industrial purposes, begins to run her successful business "in a woman's way." She institutes one of the first five-day workweeks and keeps her plants clean and comfortable, winning loyalty and dedication from her workers.

The Institute to Coordinate Women's Interests is founded. It is one of the first groups that attempts to assist women in balancing work and family. It addresses the concerns of educated women and attempts to arrange domestic chores around working women's needs. Some of the programs include communal nurseries, laundries, and kitchens as well as joint shopping trips.

1926

The National Association for the Education of Young Children is founded. Child development becomes a field of research.

1930s

Reformers advocate for regulations to be passed so that the approximately 800 day nurseries in the United States can be licensed and adhere to minimal standards of hygiene, health, and nutrition. Some regulations are passed, but there is little enforcement or compliance.

The Works Progress Administration (WPA) establishes government-funded day nurseries as an emergency measure to provide jobs for unemployed teachers, custodians, and cooks. The emphasis is on basic health and nutrition.

1930   Twenty-five percent of all women are in the labor force; 12 percent of married women are in the labor force.

A report from the White House Conference on Children states, "No one should get the idea that Uncle Sam is going to rock the baby to sleep," in response to the suggestion that the federal government become involved in supporting child care.

1931   U.S. colleges sponsor nursery schools that can be used for research and teacher training. By 1932, 500 nursery schools serve thousands of middle- and upper-income families.

1932   Section 213 of the Federal Economy Act requires that one spouse resign if both husband and wife are working for the federal government. A Women's Bureau study later shows that more than 75 percent of those resigning were women. It is one of many public and private pressures on women to give up "pin money" so that men can support families during the Depression.

1934   The Women's Bureau publishes *Women at Work: A Century of Industrial Change* by Eleanor Nelson. The report presents an overview of the history of working women in the United States, covering the move from home to factory, the problem of low wages, labor legislation, war work, employment opportunities, and the contributions of black and immigrant women. In 1936 the bureau publishes *The Employed Woman Homemaker in the U.S.: Her Responsibility for Family Support*, and in 1938 it publishes *The Difference in Earnings of Women and Men*.

1935   The modern welfare system begins with the establishment of Aid to Dependent Children, a program designed to support widows and their children.

1938   The Fair Labor Standards Act sets minimum wages and maximum hours standards to protect workers in the most poorly paid jobs.

1939   The U.S. Tax Court rules that a working mother can-
            not deduct from her gross income the expense of hir-
            ing a nursemaid to care for her child. The court finds
            child care to be an inherently personal duty.

1940   Twenty-seven percent of all women are in the labor
            force; 16 percent of married women are in the labor
            force.

            The Lanham Act is passed to provide funds for build-
            ing defense-related industries. Federal funds for child
            care facilities are included under the act to support
            working mothers who are joining the war effort.
            Though only a small percentage of the children of
            working mothers attend these centers, it sets a prece-
            dent for federal involvement in child care funding. At
            the height of the program, 13 percent of children need-
            ing care receive federal assistance. The Children's
            Bureau criticizes the child care centers, calling them
            "baby parking stations."

1941   The United States enters World War II. A Fair Employ-
            ment Practices Commission is established to help alle-
            viate discrimination against black people in war pro-
            duction. Black women especially want to escape from
            domestic and agricultural jobs into better-paying fac-
            tory work.

1942   The National War Labor Board rules that Brown and
            Sharp Manufacturing cannot pay women only four-
            fifths of what they pay men for the same work. The
            board supports giving women equal pay for the same
            quantity and quality of work in similar jobs.

            The War Manpower Commission urges employers not
            to recruit women with children under the age of four-
            teen. But this same year, Congress appropriates $6
            million to allow 1,150 out of 1,700 WPA nurseries to
            remain open.

            The draft begins to decimate the ranks of male work-
            ers, and the government issues a nondiscrimination

directive, reversing Depression-era restrictions on employment of women, especially married women. For the first time, employers actively seek out women workers for nontraditional jobs, and some offer day care, meals, and transportation to make it easier for women with families to work.

1943   Kaiser Shipbuilding Company uses $750,000 in federal funds to set up two 24-hour child care centers for employees' children ages 18 months to six years. The centers provide high-quality care and a host of services to working mothers.

The Children's Bureau publishes *Maternity-Leave and Maternity-Care Practices in Industry,* the results of a survey on maternity leave policies in the workplace.

1944   From 1940 to 1944, more than 6 million women join the civilian labor force, though fully 75 percent of all women working for wages during the war had worked before the war.

As the war comes to an end, President Franklin D. Roosevelt states: "[We] do not believe further federal funds should be provided for actual operation of child care programs." He stresses that child care is a war need only.

Talcott Parsons publishes *The Social Structure of the Family: Its Function and Destiny.* In this and other works Parsons, an influential sociologist, develops the theory of functionalism—that men are in charge of doing and women are in charge of feeling. Parsons and other researchers support the idea that men should work outside the home and that a woman's natural role is to serve as wife, mother, and homemaker. Though researchers today have refuted this theory, Parsons and others greatly influenced the thinking of many people in the 1950s and later.

1946   Hundreds of child care centers close after the withdrawal of Lanham Act funds, despite President Harry

1946 cont.	S. Truman's authorization of $7 million to extend child care funding through 3 March 1946. In New York City, activist Elinor Guggenheimer leads the battle to save 91 centers that had been supported by the government during the war. Two years later, Guggenheimer founds the New York City Day Care Council to help support day care and unionize staff.
1949	The U.S. Tax Court upholds its decision that working parents cannot deduct the cost of child care from gross income.
1950s	In the early 1950s, hospitals in the United States face a critical shortage of nurses. Surveys find that enough nurses are being trained, but that many women leave nursing when they become mothers. Nursing administrators at many hospitals set up successful on-site day care centers. This sets the stage for employer-sponsored child care in other corporate settings.
	Middle- and upper-income families send their children to nursery schools and view it as an enriching experience. Child care for younger children is still viewed negatively. According to a 1948 Children's Bureau survey, only 4 percent of working mothers use child care centers; 94 percent rely on relatives and friends.
1950	Twenty-three percent of all women are in the labor force; 28 percent of women with children ages six to 17 and 12 percent of women with children under age six are in the labor force.
1952	The National Committee for Equal Pay is established from a coalition of women and labor organizations. The Women's Bureau publishes the conference report from this group, along with its own papers on *Women Workers and Their Dependents* and *Maternity Protection of Employed Women*. In 1953 the bureau publishes additional reports, including *Employed Mothers and Child Care*.

1954   A growing child care movement protests the closing of child care centers. Activists pressure the Internal Revenue Service, and the tax code is changed to allow low-income families to take tax deductions for child care expenses. Married women with working husbands can take a deduction only if they file joint returns and if the couple's total adjusted gross income does not exceed $5,100.

1955   The U.S. Department of Labor sponsors the White House Conference on the Effective Use of Womanpower to explore expanding women's opportunities in the labor market, including greater participation in nontraditional fields.

1960   Thirty-one percent of all women are in the labor force; 39 percent of women with children ages six to 17 and 19 percent of women with children under age six are in the labor force. One-third of all wage-earning women hold clerical jobs. Nearly 80 percent of wage-earning women hold jobs stereotyped as "female," and the gender-gap in earnings widens—median annual earnings of women fall to 60 percent of the rate for men.

The U.S. Agricultural Research Service issues a report titled *Food Consumption and Dietary Levels as Related to Employment of Homemaker*. The report compares food consumption patterns in families with mothers who work in the labor market and families with mothers who do not work in the labor market. The study finds that the nutritional value of food served is the same for both families, but the employed wife spends more money on meat and beverages, and families with a mother in the labor market eat out more often.

1961   At the urging of Eleanor Roosevelt, President John F. Kennedy establishes the President's Commission on the Status of Women to investigate the participation of women in key areas of national life, including employment.

1962   Child care assistance becomes available to mothers on welfare engaged in job training or work.

1963   Congress passes the Equal Pay Act, requiring most companies to pay equal wages regardless of sex to all those performing equal tasks. The act cites equal opportunity for women in employment as a national goal.

Betty Friedan publishes *The Feminine Mystique*. The book helps spark the second wave of the women's movement. Based on surveys of her classmates at Smith College, Friedan found many women who were unhappy in their roles as wives and homemakers. Friedan later helps establish the National Organization for Women, which advocates for more child care centers, legalized abortion, and an end to sex-segregated employment advertising, in addition to other issues.

The U.S. Office of Education publishes *Management Problems of Homemakers Employed Outside the Home: Resources for Teaching*, a curriculum guide for teaching high school and adult women how to deal with household responsibilities while working outside the home.

1964   Congress passes the Civil Rights Act of 1964. The act includes Title VII, which prohibits firms with 15 or more employees from discriminating on the basis of sex, among other characteristics. It also establishes the Equal Employment Opportunity Commission (EEOC) to coordinate efforts to implement the law and to conciliate disputes. Shortly thereafter, the EEOC is flooded with sex discrimination complaints.

1965   Head Start begins as an antipoverty program helping over 500,000 children ages three to five years old, with a budget of almost $100 million.

1968   Executive Order 11246, as amended by 11375, prohibits discrimination in employment on the basis of sex, among other characteristics, by all employers with federal contracts valued over $10,000.

Congress passes the Child Care Food Program to improve the nutritional status of children in child care in low-income areas.

The Federal Interagency Day Care Requirements establish regulations on staff-child ratios, maximum group sizes, and caregiver qualifications for sites caring for children ages three to 14 years old.

1969   The Supreme Court upholds the decision in *Pittsburgh Press v. Human Relations Commission* that ends the practice of running sex-segregated want ads in newspapers.

1970   Forty-one percent of all women are in the labor force; 49 percent of women with children ages six to 17, and 30 percent of women with children under age six are in the labor force.

Caroline Bird publishes *Born Female.* In the book, she documents the unequal status and lower pay of women in the workplace during the 1960s. She also demonstrates that young women need higher grades than men to be accepted by colleges and are relegated to low-paying, sex-segregated industries after graduation. She later publishes a number of other books, including *The Two-Paycheck Marriage* in 1979.

At the White House Conference on Children, thousands of attendees endorse the Comprehensive Child Development Act, which views child care as a right for all children regardless of income, with priority given to those in greatest need. Despite his initial support and widespread bipartisan approval, President Richard M. Nixon vetoes the act the following year, saying it would promote "communal approaches to child rearing over the family-centered approach."

1971   The Women's Legal Defense Fund (WLDF) is founded to use public education and advocacy to help women and men meet the dual demands of work and family. Later WLDF changes its name to the National Part-

1971
cont.

nership for Women and Families. The organization takes a lead role in the passage of the Pregnancy Discrimination Act of 1978 and writes the first draft of the Family and Medical Leave Act (FMLA) in 1984.

The Supreme Court overrules the lower courts' finding in *Phillips v. Martin-Marietta Corporation*. Phillips was denied a job at Martin-Marietta because she had young children. The Supreme Court rules that the company cannot have different hiring policies for men and women. However, the Court leaves open the possibility that gender might be considered a bona fide occupational qualification if parenting can be shown to have a lesser impact on a man's job performance than on a woman's job performance.

1972

The National Council of Jewish Women publishes *Windows on Day Care*, the first definitive nationwide study of day care facilities and services. The report calls attention to the poor health and safety conditions at most day care centers. In 1999 the organization publishes a follow-up report stating that there is a continuing shortage of safe, high-quality, affordable day care centers.

1973

The Children's Defense Fund is founded. Its mission is to provide a voice for children in the United States, especially poor and minority children and those with disabilities.

1974

Title XX of the Social Services Act provides money to be used for child care for low-income women who work.

The Alliance for Displaced Homemakers (later renamed the National Displaced Homemakers' Network in 1978) is established and encourages men and women to view homemaking and child rearing as occupations. The alliance also tries to help women who are not supported by their husbands find employment.

1975   Musician John Lennon announces his withdrawal from the music business and from public life to become a househusband. For five years, Lennon devotes himself to raising Sean, his son with wife Yoko Ono, while she focuses on their business affairs. In an interview, Lennon speaks fondly of the sheer ordinariness of daily life with his son.

The Stepford Wives, a movie about housewives who are replaced by complacent robots who are enthusiastic about housework, is released. The film is labeled misogynist by some, though others see it as supportive of the women's liberation movement. It becomes a cult classic, and the term *Stepford wife* is used as a derogatory name for suburban female homemakers.

Stride Rite opens the first modern, on-site, corporate-sponsored child care center and becomes well known as a company that is supportive of working mothers. By 1978, 105 companies sponsor child care centers.

The U.S. Social Security Administration publishes *The Economic Value of a Housewife* by Wendyce H. Broday. The report describes approaches to determining the economic value of work performed by housewives and estimates that the average value of a housewife in 1972 would be $4,705. The average annual earnings for all workers during this time are $6,697.

About 14.6 percent of all preschoolers are cared for in centers; 43.8 percent are cared for in the home of a relative or a nonrelated provider.

1976   A 20 percent Dependent Care Tax Credit replaces the child care deduction on federal taxes. Child care is seen as an employment-related expense. All taxpayers with children benefit, with larger credit for lower-income earners.

1977   Rosabeth Moss Kanter publishes one of the first scholarly books on work-family, titled *Work and Family in*

1977
cont.

the United States: A Critical Review and Agenda for Research and Policy. Her thesis is that there is a prevailing myth that work and family are separate worlds with their own functions, rules, and territories. For the most part, men are studied in the workplace, and women and family life are studied in the home. Soon after Kanter's work is published, sociologists begin to study the interconnections between these two key areas of life, and the field of work-family begins.

The Family Caregiver Alliance is founded as one of the first community-based nonprofit organizations in the country to address the needs of families and friends providing long-term care for the elderly and disabled at home.

1978

The Center for the Childcare Workforce is founded to improve child care jobs through better pay, improved working conditions, and opportunities for professional development for child care staff.

The National Day Care Study finds that 5 million preschoolers and 6 million school-age children are in need of care.

The Pregnancy Discrimination Act passes, categorizing discrimination based on pregnancy as a type of sex discrimination and requiring employers to treat pregnancy as a temporary disability. Prior to the act, pregnant women were sometimes fired, demoted, or lost seniority.

Psychologist Nancy Chodorow writes *The Reproduction of Mothering: Psychoanalysis and the Sociology of Gender.* In it she argues that women should not be the exclusive caretakers of children but that men and women should share parental responsibilities in order to raise psychologically healthy boys and girls.

1979

The White House Conference on Families is held. It includes more than 500 hearings and forums at the state and community level. Scholars from diverse disciplines come together to discuss family issues as part of the conference, and 2,000 delegates are selected from across the country to develop policy recommendations, many of which relate to work-family concerns. Soon after the conference, President Jimmy Carter establishes the Office for Families.

Kramer vs. Kramer wins an Academy Award for best picture. Primarily about divorce, the movie shows a father who is employed full-time suddenly faced with juggling work and single parenthood when his stay-at-home wife leaves him and his young son.

1980   Fifty-two percent of all women are in the labor force; 68 percent of women with children ages six to 17, and 50 percent of women with children under age six are in the labor force. Labor force participation rates for white women now equal the participation rates of black women.

1981   The Fatherhood Project is founded as a national research and education program concerned with developing practical ways to support the involvement of fathers in child rearing.

Working Mother magazine begins publication in New York.

American Federation of State, County, and Municipal Employees (AFSCME) v. State of Washington is settled out of court. The original decision, recommending that back pay be granted to women who were paid less for jobs of comparable worth, prompts government administrators across the country to take the issue of pay equity more seriously.

1983   The Child Care Action Campaign is founded by Elinor Guggenheimer and other child care activists, with the goal of making the public aware of the child care crisis in the United States. Two years later, the group leads a successful campaign lobbying insurers to provide liability at child care centers after numerous poli-

1983
cont.

cies were canceled in response to several sex abuse cases in centers.

The Bush Center on Child Development and Social Policy at Yale University concludes after a two-year study that "the infant care leave problem in the United States is of a magnitude and urgency such as to require immediate national attention." The committee recommends that the United States adopt a national infant care leave policy that allows parents to take up to six months off with 75 percent of their salary paid for the first three months. Ten years pass before a weaker law, the Family and Medical Leave Act, is approved.

Mr. Mom, a movie about a man who loses his job and becomes a househusband because his wife has a potentially profitable business opportunity, is released in theaters. A formula comedy, the film and even its title poke fun at and draw attention to the implausibility of a man running a household and raising children.

1984

A hearing on the problems of working women is held before the 98th Congress. The hearing draws attention to issues such as child care, flextime, leave for pregnant workers after childbirth, training for better jobs, and provision of day care for children of mothers in poverty.

The National Association for the Education of Young Children begins a voluntary accreditation program to promote high-quality care.

The Women's Bureau changes its focus from women in the workplace to issues of balancing work and family, including eldercare and alternative work arrangements.

In *Guerra v. California Federal Savings and Loan Association,* the Supreme Court rules that a woman has a right to job security following maternity leave. Writing for the 6–3 majority, Justice Thurgood Marshall says that the legislation "promotes equal employment opportunity" because "it allows women, as well as men, to have families without losing their jobs."

The Family Support Act guarantees child care for parents meeting mandatory work and training requirements of welfare and provides one year of transitional child care after a parent leaves welfare for work.

1989   Arlie Hochschild publishes *The Second Shift: Working Parents and the Revolution at Home.* The book describes how working mothers have two full-time jobs: paid employment and what Hochschild calls the "second shift," homemaking and child care duties. For the growing number of single mothers, the dual responsibilities are particularly challenging.

The term *mommy track* enters the popular lexicon, with the publication of an article in the *Harvard Business Review* by Felice Schwartz. Schwartz proposes that some women should be able to choose a slower track during the years when they have children at home to keep valuable women in the labor force from dropping out completely while raising children. The media distorts Schwartz's proposal and suggests that women with children are better suited to part-time and less demanding work labeled the "mommy track."

The Families and Work Institute is founded in 1989 by Dana Friedman and Ellen Galinsky to address the changing nature of work and family life by conducting research to inform policymaking.

1990   Fifty-seven percent of all women are in the labor force; 74 percent of women with children ages six to 17 and 57 percent of women with children under age six are in the labor force.

The 1990 National Child Care Study is released. It shows widespread shortages of infant and toddler care.

1990
cont.

More than 3.5 million school-age children between the ages of five and 15 regularly spend after-school time unsupervised by adults or older teenagers.

About 12 percent of employers offer eldercare assistance of some type to their employees.

1992

President Bill Clinton nominates Zoe Baird for the post of attorney general. Baird later asks the president to withdraw her nomination when it is found that she had hired an immigrant who had entered the country illegally to care for her children because she could not find a qualified nanny in the United States. When asked by the Judiciary Committee how she, as a lawyer, could have ignored employment laws, she responded, "I guess I was thinking more as a mother than a lawyer." Later Kimba Wood's nomination for the same post is withdrawn for a similar reason. Strong reactions from the public ensued, including some questioning as to why a mother with young children would consider working in a post that demanded such long hours and reactions from others questioning whether a male candidate would ever be questioned about his nanny-hiring practices.

1993

President Clinton signs into law the Family and Medical Leave Act. The new law provides for unpaid leave for the birth, adoption, or foster placement of a child; an employee's own serious health condition; or the serious health condition of an immediate family member. Though a major accomplishment, this law covers only 11 percent of U.S. employers (those with 50 or more employees), leaving 41 percent of all workers ineligible. In addition, the law does not provide leave to members of less traditional family arrangements such as gay and lesbian couples or people in common-law marriages.

The U.S. Census Bureau reports that 1.9 million men are stay-at-home fathers.

1994

The Carnegie Corporation releases *Starting Points:*

Meeting the Needs of Our Youngest Children, a report showing the critical importance of good care in the first three years of life. The report documents the "quiet crisis" affecting children in the United States, including increasing rates of poverty and changing family employment patterns, resulting in inadequate child care arrangements being made for young children. The report recommends guaranteeing quality child care choices and other supports for families. This same year the Families and Work Institute releases a report showing that only 9 percent of family child care homes provide high-quality care.

1995   An estimated 22.4 million households, almost one in four, are providing home care for family members or friends over the age of 50.

1996   Vice President Al Gore hosts the sixth annual Family Reunion Conference, which focuses on integrating family and work. He and his wife Tipper moderate the conference, and President Clinton is a featured speaker.

The Alliance of Work/Life Professionals is founded from the merger of the national Work Family Alliance and the Association of Work/Life Professionals. The membership organization is for professionals who work in the work-life or work-family field.

1998   Louise Woodward, an au pair, is found guilty of manslaughter in the death of Matthew Eappen, a toddler under her care. Some members of the public criticize the mother, Deborah Eappen, for working outside the home because she has two young children and her husband makes enough money to support the family. Fears about the safety of care from nannies and au pairs are also widely discussed.

Sixty percent of all women are in the labor force; 80 percent of women with children ages six to 17 and 67 percent of women with children under age six are in the labor force.

1999   The fourth annual convention for "at-home dads" is held in Illinois. More than 80 men from 20 states attend. Another group, Dad-to-Dad, formed two years earlier for stay-at-home dads, reports that it has 30 chapters nationwide. The Bureau of Labor Statistics reports that from 1991 to 1996, the percentage of unemployed men who chose not to look for work because of "home responsibilities" rose to 8.4 percent from 4.6 percent.

Ellen Galinsky's book *Ask the Children: What America's Children Really Think about Working Parents* is published. The book gets a great deal of publicity in the media, and Galinsky is featured on the cover of *Newsweek*.

Two students at Columbine High School in Littleton, Colorado, murder 12 students and one teacher and wound 23 other students. The public response to the shootings raises questions about improving the supervision of teenagers when parents are at work.

Georgia is the only state to offer free universal care for all four-year-olds, but 41 other states offer some kind of free prekindergarten program. Child care costs in other states range from $4,000 to $14,000 a year per child.

3

Biographical Sketches

This chapter provides biographical information on some of the scholars and activists currently involved with work-family issues. In compiling this list, an attempt was made to include people working in a wide range of disciplines who are approaching work-family issues from a variety of perspectives.

Lotte Bailyn (1930–)

Lotte Bailyn received her B.A. from Swarthmore College and her doctorate from Harvard University. She is currently a professor of management at Massachusetts Institute of Technology's Sloan School. Bailyn investigates the relationship between managerial practice and employees' lives. Her areas of expertise include the changing work environment and workforce, telecommuting, gender and organizational change, and work-family issues. In *Breaking the Mold: Women, Men, and Time in the New Corporate World*, she argues that the traditional system of favoring employees who dedicate themselves to work above all else is no longer a tenable model when so many women and a growing number of men are finding they are unable to meet the demands of both work and family. Bailyn challenges the idea that managers need to have tight control over work practices and employee time. Instead, managers need to hold employees accountable for results. Work needs to be organized around tasks and not time, and the perceived relationship between time and both productivity and work commitment needs to be questioned. In a collaborative research project conducted for the Ford Foundation in 1996, *Relinking Life and Work: Toward a Better Future*, Rhona Rapaport and Bailyn contended that work and personal life can be complementary, even synergistic, rather than adversarial. Results from this and other studies indicate that paying attention to employees' personal lives increases corporate productivity.

Rosalind C. Barnett (1937–)

Rosalind Barnett received her B.A. from Queens College and her doctorate from Harvard University. She is a clinical psychologist currently working as a senior scientist in the Women's Studies Program at Brandeis University and a senior scholar in residence at the Murray Research Center at Radcliffe College. She has published many books and articles on work-family issues, including *She Works/He Works: How Two-Income Families Are Happier, Healthier, and Better Off,* which she coauthored with the journalist Caryl Rivers. In this book, Barnett and Rivers studied 300 dual-career couples. Their results challenge the assumption that families benefit when one parent stays home and confirm earlier studies that indicate that mothers who work outside the home tend to benefit both psychologically and physically. Barnett is working on three new projects that focus on work and family. The first explores part-time work in medicine as a strategy for combining work and family; the second investigates mental health correlates for adult children who reside in the parental home; and the third explores the psychological effects of long-term non-tenure-track faculty positions. Barnett has been the recipient of the American Personnel and Guidance Association's Annual Award for Outstanding Research and the Radcliffe College Graduate Society's Distinguished Achievement Medal. She is currently working with Caryl Rivers on a book about the future of gender to be published by Harvard University Press.

Ellen Bravo (1944–)

Ellen Bravo received her B.A. from Cornell University and her M.A. from Cambridge University. She has worked as an instructor in women's studies at several colleges. In 1982, Bravo founded the Milwaukee chapter of 9to5, the National Association of Working Women. In 1993, she became codirector of the national organization of 9to5. This organization works to ensure equal pay, healthy and harassment-free workplaces, and more family-friendly benefits and policies. Also in 1993, Bravo was appointed to the Federal Commission on Leave and was involved in the passage of the Family and Medical Leave Act. Bravo is the author of several books, including *The 9to5 Guide to Combating Sexual Harassment*, cowritten with 9to5 cofounder Ellen Cassedy, and *The Job/Family Challenge: A 9to5 Guide*, published in 1995. In this latter book Bravo points out that only 8 percent of families in the United States have stay-at-home mothers and that the workforce is changing, but the workplace has not kept pace. Bravo was selected as a participant at the 1995 United Nations Fourth World Conference on Women in Beijing. As a working mother and an advocate for working mothers, Bravo has emphasized throughout her career that most women need to work for financial reasons and that balancing the demands of work and family life can be stressful.

Robert Drago (1954–)

Robert Drago received his doctorate in economics from the University of Massachusetts at Amherst in 1983. He is professor of labor studies and industrial relations at Pennsylvania State University and has been a senior Fulbright research scholar. He is the principal investigator for the Faculty and Families Project and the Time, Work, and Family Life Project, both funded by the Sloan Foundation. He serves as moderator of the Work/Family newsgroup, an electronic discussion list that provides information to work-family researchers all over the world. In addition, Drago is a faculty associate at the Population Research Institute and a member of the Children, Youth, and Families Consortium, both at Pennsylvania State University. Recent books include *Unlevel Playing Fields: Understanding Wage Inequality and Discrimination*, an undergraduate textbook he cowrote with Randy Albelda and Steven Shulman. Drago reported on a study of teachers and working time in the *Monthly Labor Review* in 2000. He also serves as a research associate at the National Institute of Labor Studies at Flinders University in Australia. His recent courses have covered the economics of discrimination, as well as work and the family.

Betty Friedan (1921–)

Betty Friedan received her B.A. from Smith College in 1942. She was the founding president of the National Organization for Women and has worked as a feminist organizer, writer, and lecturer worldwide. She helped organize the Women's Strike for Equality in 1970, the International Feminist Congress in 1973, and the Economic Think Tank for Women in 1974. She has served as a consultant for the President's Commission on the Status of Women and as a delegate to the White House Conference on the Family. Her numerous awards and honors include an honorary doctorate from Columbia University in 1994. Her journey to political activism began when she was fired from her newspaper job after requesting her second maternity leave. When her first book, *The Feminine Mystique*, was published in 1963, it helped launch the modern women's movement by questioning the myth that women were contented homemakers who wanted nothing more than to take care of their families and defer their own ambitions and interests. After the success of her book, she became a major leader in the women's movement. In a later book, *The Second Stage*, Friedan explained how the backlash from the first wave of feminism caused a second "feminine mystique" to emerge in the form of a woman who could effortlessly combine family, career, and rewarding personal life. Friedan encouraged the women's movement to make the family its central focus, though many in the movement disagreed with her ideas. In a recent book, *Beyond Gender: The New Politics of Work and Family*, Friedan reports on discussions held by participants of her New Paradigm Seminar, which she organized while a guest scholar at the Woodrow Wilson Institute in 1994. In this book, she argues that researchers and activists should focus energy on women's earnings and economic equality, and she and other participants advocate for a reduced workweek, flexible scheduling of work, and benefits for part-time workers.

Ellen Galinsky (1942–)

Ellen Galinsky received her B.A. from Vassar College and her M.S. in education from Bank Street College of Education in New York. She currently serves as president and cofounder of the Families and Work Institute, which conducts research to inform policy-making on work-family issues. The institute has been involved in studies on work and family, such as the 1997 *National Study of the Changing Workforce* and the 1998 *Business Work-Life Study*, the latter of which analyzes trends and business initiatives that support the family and personal lives of employees. Galinsky was a presenter at the 1998 White House Conference on Child Care and in

1999 was featured on the cover of *Newsweek* magazine, which published an excerpt from her groundbreaking new book, *Ask the Children: What America's Children Really Think about Working Parents*. This book explores work and family issues through interviews with more than 1,000 children, who discuss their feelings about their parents' work and its impact on their family. Galinsky found that having a mother working outside the home was not predictive of how children rated parenting skills. What she did find was that even though the amount of time children and parents spend together is important, most children do not want *more* time with their parents. What children want is to have the time they spend with their parents be less rushed and more devoted to shared activities. Galinsky also serves as the program director of the annual work-life conference co-convened by the Conference Board and the Families and Work Institute. For twenty-five years, she served on the faculty at the Bank Street College, where she helped establish the field of work and family life.

Kathleen Gerson (1947–)

Kathleen Gerson received her B.A. from Stanford University and her doctorate from the University of California at Berkeley. She is a founding member of the Women's Studies Program and the director of undergraduate studies in sociology at New York University. Her book, *Hard Choices: How Women Decide about Work, Career, and Motherhood*, investigated how women make choices between work and family commitments. A more recent book, *No Man's Land: Men's Changing Commitments to Family and Work*, explores how and why men's lives are changing in the wake of the gender revolution at home and at work. Gerson has also published many scholarly articles on gender, the family, links between work and family, and the processes of social change. She is a member of the Council of Research Advisers for the Center for Families at Purdue University; the Ford Foundation Roundtable on the Integration of Work, Family, and Community; and the Council on Contemporary Families. In 1998 she was chosen by the Sociologists for Women in Society to be the Feminist Lecturer on Women and Social Change. Her current research is on how "children of the gender revolution" are responding to living in diverse family situations and how men and women are developing new moral strategies for meeting their needs for autonomy and providing care for others.

Arlie Hochschild (1940–)

Arlie Hochschild received her B.A. from Swarthmore College and her doctorate in politics from the University of California at Berkeley. She is currently a professor of sociology at the University of California at Berkeley and also serves as a member of the board of editors of the *American Prospect* and *Gender and Society*. She has written a number of books and articles, including *The Second Shift: Working Parents and the Revolution at Home*, which analyzed the lives of dual-career couples. Her studies revealed that after putting in a full day at work, women come home to a "second shift" that adds up to an entire month of 24-hour work days each year. Another book, *The Time Bind: When Work Becomes Home and Home Becomes Work*, found that men and women failed to take advantage of benefits that would alleviate strain between work and home. Hochschild discovered that workers in the company she studied were extending their time at work by choice, often at the expense of spending time with their spouses and children. She found that work could sometimes be a pleasurable respite from the complicated demands of home life. Hochschild's books appeal to both scholars and laypeople and have generated a great deal of controversy and discussion. Recently, she was a Fulbright scholar at the Center for Development Studies in Trivandrum, Kerala, India. Her current research involves exploring how different social groups define and experience care and the impact of privatization on the human interactions involved in care.

Rosabeth Moss Kanter (1943–)

Rosabeth Moss Kanter has worked at Yale University and the Massachusetts Institute of Technology and currently is a member of the faculty at the Harvard Business School. A renowned management theorist and adviser to many Fortune 500 companies, Kanter served as editor of the *Harvard Business Review* from 1989 to 1992. Two of Kanter's best-known books, *The Change Masters* and *Men and Women of the Corporation*, focus on how innovation in business can be achieved by putting the needs of people within the corporation first. Kanter has long advocated flattening hierarchical structures and fostering communication between top managers and line staff within an organization. Though Kanter's career has not specifically focused on work-family, much of her work discusses the benefits that an organization receives from listening to the individual needs, including family needs, of workers. In 1977, Kanter published *Work and Family in the United States: A Critical Review and Research and Policy Agenda.* Now considered a classic in the field, this book first called attention to what Kanter has referred to as the "myth of separate worlds." Kanter was one of the first to argue that the assumed separation between work and family was a "myth" and that research must explore the linkages between these two roles. Kanter's most recent book, *Rosabeth Moss Kanter on the Frontiers of Management,* presents a series of articles that reflect many of her management theories. These articles provide support for her thesis that people are the most important asset of business and that providing the conditions that allow people to do their best work leads to the innovation and creativity needed to compete successfully in a constantly changing world.

James A. Levine (1946–)

James Levine is currently the director of the Fatherhood Project at the Families and Work Institute in New York City. Levine founded the project in 1981 to examine the future of fatherhood and support men's involvement in child rearing. Prior to his work at the Fatherhood Project, Levine taught preschool for three years and then founded and directed a comprehensive child care system in the second-largest public housing project in Massachusetts. Levine was also responsible for setting up and directing the National Institute on Out-of-School Time, which continues today as the country's leading source of technical assistance on after-school care. At the Families and Work Institute, Levine and his colleagues provide development and training assistance to community-based organizations such as Head Start. One of Levine's most recent books is *Working Fathers: New Strategies for Balancing Work and Family,* written with Todd Pittinsky of the Harvard Business School. Levine also serves as contributing editor for *Child* magazine and conducts seminars for Fortune 500 companies on "Daddy stress," aimed at a growing population of men who are trying to balance work and family responsibilities. He has appeared frequently on national television and has served as a consultant to organizations such as Apple Computer, Children's Television Workshop, and IBM. Levine served as a consultant to Vice President Al Gore in drafting the new federal initiative on fatherhood, created by executive order in 1995. In 1997, *Working Mother* magazine recognized him as one of the top twenty-five men in the United States who have made a difference in the lives of working mothers.

Judith L. Lichtman (1940–)

Judith Lichtman received her B.S. and law degrees from the University of Wisconsin. She chose to study law because being a lawyer meant "having a license to be an activist." She has been a vocal member of the women's and civil rights movements for more than 25 years and has worked at the Urban Coalition, at the U.S. Commission on Civil Rights, and as a legal adviser to the Commonwealth of Puerto Rico. In 1974 she became the first executive director of the Women's Legal Defense Fund, which later became the National Partnership for Women and Families. She currently serves as president of this organization. The national partnership is a nonprofit organization that uses public education and advocacy to promote fairness in the workplace, policies that help men and women meet the dual demands of work and family, and quality health care for all. It has been at the forefront of every major piece of legislation related to women and families for the past 25 years, including the Pregnancy Discrimination Act, the Family and Medical Leave Act, and the Health Insurance Portability and Accountability Act. In addition, with a coalition of health care and consumer organizations, it helped support the passage of the Patients' Bill of Rights Act. Former president Bill Clinton called Lichtman "a remarkable national treasure."

Phyllis Moen (1942–)

Phyllis Moen received her doctorate in sociology from the University of Minnesota. She is currently a sociology professor and director of the Employment and Family Careers Institute at Cornell University. Moen also serves as the director of the Bronfenbrenner Life Course Center, a multidisciplinary center at Cornell University that focuses on the study of life-course paths and transitions. In addition to teaching courses related to family studies and gender and the workforce, she conducts research on life-course transitions related to work and family. She is involved in research examining baby boomers' transitions into retirement. In addition, she is studying the links between social and economic changes in China and the lives of Chinese citizens at various stages in the life course. Much of her work focuses on gender as an important social marker shaping the life course. One of her most widely read books is *Women's Two Roles: A Contemporary Dilemma*, published in 1992. This work was inspired by Alva Myrdal and Viola Klein's classic study, *Women's Two Roles: Home and Work*, which suggested that women leave the labor force to raise their young children and resume work when their children enter school. Moen sees women today as having more options. Her most recent book, cowritten with Dempster-McClain and Walker, is titled *A Nation Divided: Diversity, Inequality, and Community in American Society*. She is currently serving as a fellow at the Radcliffe Institute for Advanced Study at Harvard University.

Karen Nussbaum (1950–)

Karen Nussbaum received her B.S. from Goddard College in 1975. She became an activist while serving as a secretary at Harvard University in 1973. She was alone in the office one day when "a male student came in, looked me right in the eye, and asked, 'Isn't anybody here?'" Soon afterward Nussbaum cofounded 9to5, the National Association of Working Women, with the goal of organizing "pink-collar" workers to improve their wages and working conditions. She led 9to5 for twenty years. In 1981, she also became president of District 925 of the Service Employees International Union. She served on its executive board and headed up the union's 170,000-member Office Workers Division. Later, she was appointed director of the Women's Bureau in the Department of Labor, the highest seat in the federal government devoted to women's issues. President Bill Clinton declared her uniquely qualified to serve as chief advocate for the nation's 60 million working women. In 1994, while serving as director of the Women's Bureau, Nussbaum surveyed more than a quarter of a million American women in the workforce about what was right and wrong with their jobs, collecting their responses in a document titled *Working Women Count!* This report solidified women's concerns into three areas: pay and benefits; work and family, especially child care and family leave; and valuing women's work through training, advancement, and respect on the job. These issues provided the framework for developing programs at the bureau. Currently, Nussbaum is working as the first director of the newly created Working Women's Department of the American Federation of Labor–Congress of Industrial Organizations (AFL-CIO). The department is charged by AFL-CIO president John Sweeney with developing a program that will inject the concerns of working women into every aspect of the AFL-CIO's work. Nussbaum is coauthor with Sweeney of *Solutions for the New Workforce: Policies for a New Social Contract* and coauthored with Ellen Cassedy *9 to 5: A Working Woman's Guide to Office Survival.*

Juliet Schor (1955–)

Juliet Schor received her B.A. from Wesleyan University and her doctorate from the University of Massachusetts. An economist who has taught at Harvard University and the University of Tilburg, she was also a 1999 Guggenheim fellow. Her areas of expertise include voluntary simplicity and working hours. She has written several books, including *The Overworked American: The Unexpected Decline of Leisure.* In this book, Schor argues that U.S. employees are spending increasing amounts of time working at the expense of being involved in other activities such as volunteer service, rest, and self-improvement. She also documents the effect that working long hours has on families. Schor advocates for white-collar workers to spend a set number of hours at work with compensation for any overtime. Schor also cites studies that show that shortening the workweek often results in no drop-off in productivity and in some cases results in a rise. Schor's most recent book, *The Overspent American: Why We Want What We Don't Need,* uses a variety of research strategies to analyze the American passion for spending money. She is currently working on a new project investigating the commercialization of childhood.

Sue Shellenbarger

Sue Shellenbarger received her master's degree in journalism from Northwestern University. She has worked as a *Wall Street Journal* reporter, editor, bureau chief, and columnist for more than 16 years. While working as a bureau chief, Shellenbarger began to feel overwhelmed by her career and family responsibilities. Looking around, she saw many other people facing similar struggles. In 1991 she left her position as bureau chief and began writing a weekly column for the *Wall Street Journal* called "Work and Family." The column became very popular, and soon other newspapers, such as the *New York Times* and *Chicago Tribune,* assigned reporters to cover similar terrain. The goal of her column is to help readers better manage their work and family lives. The column focuses on innovative solutions to work-family conflict, new trends and developments that affect work-life activities, and personal profiles of all types of workers who are trying to juggle competing demands. Her recent book, *Work and Family,* is a collection of past columns covering all types of work and family challenges. Shellenbarger is also a former contributing editor to *Parenting* magazine. She received the "Exceptional Merit Media Award" in 1994 from the National Women's Political Caucus and Radcliffe College for outstanding coverage of issues of special concern to women.

Faith Wohl (1936–)

Faith Wohl received her B.A. in economics from Adelphi University. She worked for DuPont as one of their first women in senior management. While there, she held a number of positions, including director of corporate communications and director of human resources. Her last position at DuPont involved working on initiatives to help employees balance their family lives and careers and to improve the workplace for women and minority employees. Following her corporate work, Wohl served as director of the Office of Workplace Initiatives at the U.S. General Services Administration, where she supervised the operation of over 100 child care centers located in federal buildings across the nation. While an employee of the federal government, Wohl spent a year working with then Vice President Al Gore on the National Performance Review, during which time she helped accelerate the use of family-friendly workplace policies by federal agencies and departments. In 1997 Wohl helped create the Child Care Action Campaign (CCAC). She currently serves as president of CCAC, a national nonprofit organization dedicated to advancing the well-being of children and families through advocacy for affordable, quality child care. Wohl has been the recipient of many awards and honors relating to work-family issues, including the national Lewis Hine Award from the National Child Labor Committee for her work in developing quality child care programs. She has also received an award from the Delaware Chamber of Commerce for her role in creating

Child-Care Connection, a statewide resource and referral agency, and was named one of the 10 "Most Admired Women Managers" in the United States by *Working Woman* magazine. In addition, she was selected as one of "10 People of the Year" by *New Woman* magazine.

4

Statistics on Work-Family

This chapter provides statistics on key work-family issues in the United States and in other countries throughout the world. Statistics on the growth in women's participation in the paid workforce, the enduring wage inequity between women and men, the changes in family structures and roles, the outsourcing of child care duties, and the growth of corporate family-ly-friendly benefits are provided for the United States and other countries.

Statistics on Work-Family in the United States

Women and Employment in the United States

Women's increasing involvement in paid employment over the twentieth century is the single most important change influencing the relationship between work and family in the United States. Though women have always worked, on the farm, in the house, and in the labor force, what has changed is the percentage of women who are now formally participating in the labor force. In 1999, about three-fifths of women ages 16 and over were employed outside the home, a rate three times as high as the participation rate in 1900. The participation of women ages 25 to 44 in the labor force (i.e., those most likely to have children) has increased even more substantially, from less than 20 percent in 1900 to more than 75 percent today. Figure 4.1 traces the increase in labor force participation by women from 1900 to the present.

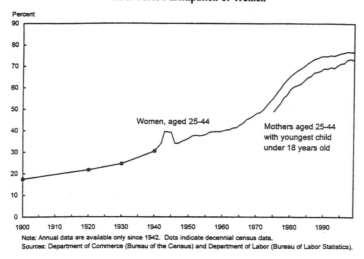

FIGURE 4.1
Labor Force Participation of Women

Percent

Women, aged 25–44

Mothers aged 25–44
with youngest child
under 18 years old

Note: Annual data are available only since 1942. Dots indicate decennial census data.
Sources: Department of Commerce (Bureau of the Census) and Department of Labor (Bureau of Labor Statistics).

Married and single mothers with very young children frequently work at least part-time. Fifty-nine percent of women with babies younger than 12 months were employed in 1998, compared to 31 percent in 1976 (U.S. Bureau of the Census 2000). In the last few years there has been a large jump in the number of single parents who are employed. In 1993, 44 percent of single parents were employed, and in 1999, 65 percent were employed (U.S. Bureau of the Census 2000). The strong economy is partly responsible for this trend because the quality of low-wage jobs has improved. More important, perhaps, is that welfare recipients are now required to work under federal and state welfare laws, and states have increased spending on child care, which has resulted in many single mothers finding they are financially better off if they enter the paid workforce.

Historically, the most significant, steady increase in women's participation in the workforce started toward the end of World War II and continues to the present day. But the trend for women to work outside the home first began toward the end of the nineteenth century, as the United States shifted from an agricultural to an industrial economy. This shift created a need for both male and female factory workers. Younger unmarried women were frequently hired to work in factories and mills. Later, with the rise of the service sector of the economy in the early twentieth century, the need for clerical help increased, and women, especially young single women, were encouraged to enter the labor market. As the demand for workers increased between 1890 and 1920, married women also entered the workforce. Though the rise in employment slowed between 1920 and 1940, married women's participation in the workforce continued to gradually increase. Then, in the 1950s and 1960s, it became more common for women to stay home with their children and enter the labor force later, when their children were close to adulthood.

Today, many women complete their education and establish themselves in the labor force before having children. Most women also remain connected to the labor force, though usually part-time, while raising children. In 1999, almost half the U.S. labor force was female, up from 20 percent in 1900 (Spain and Bianchi 1996). The increase in labor force participation rates for black women climbed more slowly during the latter half of the twentieth century, for the most part because a greater percentage of black women were already participating in the labor market.

The recent rise in women's participation in the workforce can be explained by a number of factors. The women's movement, women's rising levels of education, the postponement of marriage, and the higher divorce rate all contributed to the rise in women working outside the home. The greater public acceptance of women working outside the home, fueled partly by higher consumption standards and partly by women's realization that they might be faced with providing financially for themselves and their children, also contributed to women's higher rate of participation in the workforce. For low-income women especially, the stagnation of men's wages in the 1970s created a need for two wage earners in the family.

Wage Inequality in the United States

Though women's participation in the workforce climbed steadily, the wage gap remained relatively constant between 1955 and 1980, with women earning about 60 percent of what men were earning. By 1980 the wage gap began to narrow as college enrollment rates for men and women became almost equal and as many women began entering nontraditional, better-paying fields such as law and medicine. Minority women and Latino men continued to lag behind white women in wages. The gap in wages also narrowed as older women with less education, fewer skills, and less continuous attachment to the labor force began to retire at the same time that better-educated women entered the labor force. For educated women entering the labor force, pay rates began to increase, but for women without a college education, wages did not increase significantly. Table 4.1 illustrates the changes in the wage gap over time.

TABLE 4.1
Changes in the Wage Gap: Median Annual Earnings of Black Men and Women, Hispanic Men and Women, and White Women as a Percentage of White Men's Median Annual Earnings (in percent)

Year	White Men	Black Men	Hispanic Men	White Women	Black Women	Hispanic Women
1970	100	69.00	N/A	58.70	48.20	N/A
1975	100	74.30	72.10	57.50	55.40	49.30
1980	100	70.70	70.80	58.90	55.70	50.50
1985	100	69.70	68.00	63.00	57.10	52.10
1990	100	73.10	66.30	69.40	62.50	54.30
1992	100	72.60	63.35	70.00	64.00	55.40
1994	100	75.10	64.30	71.60	63.00	55.60
1995	100	75.90	63.30	71.20	64.20	53.40
1996	100	80.00	63.90	73.30	65.10	56.60
1997	100	75.10	61.40	71.90	62.60	53.90
1998	100	74.90	61.60	72.60	62.60	53.10
1999	100	80.61	61.63	71.58	65.05	52.11

Source: U.S. Bureau of the Census, *Current Population Reports,* Series P-60, Washington, DC: U.S. Government Printing Office.

The wage gap also decreased for all women because there was a decrease in higher-paying manufacturing jobs for blue-collar men and an increase in slightly better-paying service sector jobs predominantly filled by women, though women often had to work longer hours or take on more than one job to approach the wages paid to men working in blue-collar jobs. The narrowing of the gap for these workers had less to do with a significant increase in women's wages and more to do with men's wages stagnating and then declining. For all levels of workers, the ratio of women's earnings to men's increased to between 70 percent and 72 percent by the early 1980s, up from 60 percent. Despite some progress in the 1980s, women's earnings relative to men's in the 1990s have once again leveled off, with figures from 1997 indicating 74 percent. In 1999 women's median annual earnings averaged $26,324, whereas men's median annual earnings averaged $36,476.

Many explanations have been put forward regarding the continuing disparity between the wages of women and men. Women tend to leave the labor market more frequently because of family responsibilities; they have lower-skill levels and educational levels; and discrimination continues to occur in hiring, pay, and promotion. In addition, gender differences in occupational participation are decreasing but remain quite pronounced; in 1990 women held 77 percent of clerical administrative support positions and only 10 percent of skilled craft or transportation jobs. Occupations that are largely dominated by female employees usually pay less than occupations that are dominated by male employees.

The Changing Family in the United States

The American family no longer resembles the 1950s notion of the "traditional family"—a breadwinning father and stay-at-home mother. At the beginning of the twenty-first century, only 27 percent of all families have mothers who stay at home to take care of children and household duties; in 1952 the number of stay-at-home mothers was 67 percent (Figure 4.2).

FIGURE 4.2
Composition of Families by Family Structure

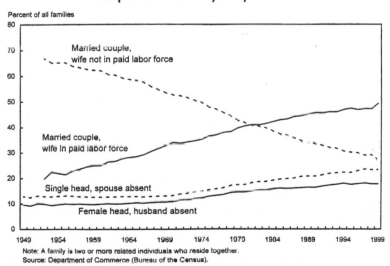

Percent of all families

Married couple, wife not in paid labor force

Married couple, wife in paid labor force

Single head, spouse absent

Female head, husband absent

Note: A family is two or more related individuals who reside together.
Source: Department of Commerce (Bureau of the Census).

The family in the United States underwent a set of dramatic transformations during the twentieth century. In 1900 about 80 percent of children lived in two-parent families with a mother who was not engaged in the paid workforce. Only one-fifth of all women worked for pay, and those that did tended to be single and poor. In the early 1900s women married earlier, had more children, and died younger than women today. Average life expectancy for men and women was less than 50 years, whereas today it is 73 and 79 years for men and women, respectively. As people live longer, they spend a smaller percentage of their life married, and the proportion of elderly people has increased. These factors require many families to provide care for aging and disabled relatives who have been widowed or divorced. A 1997 survey estimated that 22 percent of all households in the United States provide care for an elderly person (Spain and Bianchi 1996).

In addition to women joining the labor force in increasing numbers, one of the most striking transformations in family life is the emergence of the single-parent family as an increasingly common family form. Though the proportion of men and women who have married has remained static since 1900, the divorce rate has risen. In addition, a much larger proportion of children are born to unmarried mothers, and the percentage of children living in single-parent households has increased from 9 percent in 1900 to 28 percent in 1998. For unmarried women ages 15 to 44, the number of births per 1,000 increased dramatically, from 7.1 in 1940 to 46.9 in 1994. Since 1994 this rate has stabilized and even declined slightly (*Economic Report of the President* 2000). Although most children living in single-parent families live with their mothers, the share of single-parent families headed by fathers has more than doubled since 1975, reaching 19 percent in 1999 (*Economic Report of the President* 2000). Another significant trend is the number of women who do not ever give birth. Childlessness is on the rise. For women ages 40 to 44, 19 percent were childless, compared with only 10 percent in 1976 (U.S. Bureau of the Census 2000).

The number of people living in a household containing a mother, father, and children has declined substantially. In 1970, 40 percent of families fit this description, but in 1998 only 25 percent of families fit this description. The number of Americans living in unmarried-partner households is growing rapidly. From 1994 to 1998, the number of married-couple households increased by 2 percent, and the number of unmarried-partner households increased by 16 percent. In 1998 about 1.7 million households, or

1.6 percent, were made up of same-sex partnerships (*Economic Report of the President* 2000).

Since 1950 there has been a growing inequality in men's and women's poverty rates. Women today are 50 percent more likely than men to live in poverty. This phenomenon has been called the "feminization of poverty" and is a trend worldwide. Higher wage growth for men because of their higher degree of attachment to the labor force is partly responsible for the fact that fewer men are living below the poverty line. In addition, changes in family structure have had a greater financial impact on women than on men because women are more likely to remain the primary caretakers of their children. Women also have higher life expectancies than men and live a longer part of their life relying on frequently insufficient social security benefits.

The Role of Men in Family Care and Housekeeping in the United States

As women have become more involved in the paid workforce, men's participation in child care and household chores has increased gradually. Women, however, even those that work full-time, are still responsible for a much greater proportion of housekeeping and child care duties. Married men with children have increased their household work from about five hours a week to about 10 hours a week, as compared to married mothers, whose household labor has declined to about 20 hours a week. By 1985 married women with children performed about two-thirds of all housework, compared with taking care of about three-quarters of all housework duties in 1965 (Robinson 1988).

Household duties differ by gender as well, with husbands taking care of about 40 percent of the duties associated with child care, yard work, and home maintenance. Married men take care of less than 25 percent of the cooking, cleaning, and laundry and share in just over 25 percent of the grocery shopping (Goldscheider and Waite 1991). In families in which the wife works outside the home, however, husbands take on a higher percentage of household responsibilities. Research has shown that the greater the wife's salary in relationship to the husband's, the more the husband participates in housework. In addition, almost 20 percent of two-parent, dual-income couples work different shifts in order to share equally in child care and save money on child care expenses (U.S. Bureau of the Census 2000).

Statistics on stay-at-home fathers, who are the primary caregivers for their children, are difficult to compile. The Census Bureau reports that in 1993, 1.9 million unemployed men were the primary caregivers of children up to 14 years old—down from a recession high of more than 2 million in 1991. A Bureau of Labor Statistics study released in September 1999 showed that from 1991 to 1996, unemployed men ages 25 to 54 who chose not to look for work because of "home responsibilities" rose to 8.4 percent from 4.6 percent.

Caregiving in the United States
Child Care
In 1997, 75 percent of children under five were in some type of child care (Capizzano, Adams, and Sonenstein 2000). Of this group, about one-third were cared for in their own home by parents working different shifts, nannies, relatives, or babysitters; one-third were cared for in the home of a relative, neighbor, or home day care provider; and one-third were cared for in a center or preschool (Hofferth 1999). As Table 4.2 indicates, since 1980 more children have been enrolled in day care centers, the number of children in family day care has remained fairly constant, and the use of care by relatives and babysitters has declined.

Many children are involved in more than one caregiving arrangement at any given time. Nearly 40 percent of children under age five are in two or more nonparental caregiving arrangements, with low-income children no more likely to be in multiple arrangements than children from higher-income families. Three- and four-year-olds were much more likely to be in three or more caregiving arrangements in any given week (Capizzano, Adams, and Sonenstein 2000).

The shortage of high-quality child care makes finding child care a difficult task for working parents. A 1994 study by the Families and Work Institute found only 9 percent of home care arrangements it surveyed could be rated "good," 56 percent were rated "adequate" or merely "custodial," and 35 percent were rated "poor" or "disadvantageous" (Galinsky et al. 1994). Working parents often have trouble locating quality child care options and after-school programs. A recent study indicated that for parents who have day care and backup arrangements, nearly one-third experience breakdowns in their arrangements over a three-month period (Parasuraman and Greenhaus 1997).

TABLE 4.2
Primary Child Care Arrangements Used for Preschoolers by Families with
Employed Mothers: Selected Years, 1977 to 1994

Type of Arrangement	1994	1993	1991	1990	1988	1987	1986	1985	1977
Number of children	10,288	9,937	9,854	9,629	9,483	9,124	8,849	8,168	4,370
Percent	100.0	100.0	100.0	100.0	100.0	100.0	100.0	100.0	100.0
Care in child's home	33.0	30.7	35.7	29.7	28.2	29.9	28.7	31.0	33.9
By father	18.5	15.9	20.0	16.5	15.1	15.3	14.5	15.7	14.4
By grandparent	5.9	6.5	7.2	5.2	5.7	5.1	5.2	5.7	(NA)
By other relative	3.5	3.3	3.2	2.9	2.2	3.3	3.4	3.7	12.6
By nonrelative	5.1	5.0	5.4	5.0	5.3	6.2	5.5	5.9	7.0
Care in another home	31.3	32.1	31.0	35.1	36.8	35.6	40.7	37.0	40.7
By grandparent	10.4	10.0	8.6	9.1	8.2	8.7	10.2	10.2	(NA)
By other relative	5.5	5.5	4.5	5.9	5.0	4.6	6.5	4.5	18.3
By nonrelative	15.4	16.6	17.9	20.1	23.6	22.3	24.0	22.3	22.4
Organized facilities	29.4	30.1	23.0	27.5	25.8	24.4	22.4	23.1	13.0
Day/group care center	21.6	18.3	15.8	20.6	16.6	16.1	14.9	14.0	(NA)
Nursery/ preschool	7.8	11.6	7.3	6.9	9.2	8.3	7.5	9.1	(NA)
School-based activity	0.2	0.2	0.5	0.1	0.2	(NA)	(NA)	(NA)	(NA)
Child cares for self	0	0	0	0.1	0.1	0.3	0	0	0.4
Mother cares for child at work[a]	5.5	6.2	8.7	6.4	7.6	8.9	7.4	8.1	11.4
Other arrangements[b]	0.9	0.9	1.1	1.1	1.3	1.0	0.8	0.8	0.6

Notes:　a. Includes mothers working for pay at home or away from home.
　　　　 b. Includes children in kindergarten/grade school.

Source: U.S. Bureau of the Census, Historical Time Series Tables. Internet Release Date: 14 January 1998. http://www.census.gov/population/socdemo/child/p70-62/tableA.txt.

After-School Care for Older Children

School-age children are less likely to be in formal after-school programs than their preschool counterparts. In 1991, of the 36 million children between the ages of five and 14, about 24 million were in families with employed parents but only 2 million were enrolled in formal after-school programs. About one-third of children of working parents are "latchkey" children who come home to empty houses while their parent or parents are still at work (Seppanen, DeVries, and Seligson 1993). Hofferth reported that in 1990, 3.5 million school-age children regularly spent after-school time unsupervised by adults or older teenagers (Hofferth 1991).

Eldercare

An increasing proportion of the population is elderly, and this trend will continue. In 1990 one in eight people were over 65; the projected ratio for 2030 is one in five. The most rapidly growing sector of the population, those ages 85 and older, are also the most likely to need care (Vierck 1990). For the first time in history, families will soon spend more time caring for elderly parents than for children (Harrington 1999). In 1900, the number of 40-year-olds with at least one surviving parent was 70 percent; today, it is more than 95 percent (Cordtz 1990). In the mid-1990s, an estimated 22.4 million households, or almost one in four, were providing home care for family members or friends over the age of 50 (Harrington 1999). More than 65 percent of disabled elderly people live at home or with relatives, with most of their care coming from family members with minimal governmental support (Harrington 1999). Because women are marrying later and having children later, there is also an increasing likelihood that they will be part of the "sandwich generation"—women who are responsible for the care of both young children and elderly parents at the same time. Of women caring for elderly relatives, nearly 40 percent are still raising children of their own (England 1989).

Work-Family Benefits in the United States

The dramatic changes in work and family life have given rise to a new area within human resources departments—work-family or the more encompassing work-life programs. Corporate work-life programs have grown enormously since they were introduced just a few decades ago. Though there was some minor corporate support for child care during World War II and in the 1960s, serious corporate work-family programs were not instituted until the early 1980s. With growing concerns about productivity and competition, employers became increasingly interested in programs designed to assist employees in balancing work with demands outside the workplace.

A 1991 study by the Families and Work Institute found that the strongest predictor of a particular corporation developing work-family benefits was institutional change—downsizing, mergers, or replacement of the CEO. The programs were often initiated in an effort to support remaining employees in coping with growing work demands and flagging morale at times when other employees were being terminated. As the field of work-family grew, research supporting the benefits of instituting work-family programs became more widely known, and corporations developed more competitive programs to aid in recruitment and retention, and to address productivity issues. The Families and Work Institute's *1997 National Study of the Changing Workforce* surveyed employees and found that those with more supportive family-friendly workplaces were more likely than other workers to have "higher levels of job satisfaction; more commitment to their companies' success; greater loyalty to their companies; a stronger intention to remain with their companies."

In 1998, the Families and Work Institute's *1998 Business Work-Life Study* (BWLS, see Galinsky and Bond 1998) detailed the extent of family-friendly benefits currently being offered by a representative sample of 1,057 for-profit and nonprofit U.S. companies with 100 or more employees. The BWLS found that 88 percent of the companies studied allowed employees to take time off to attend school and child care functions and that 81 percent allowed employees to return to work on a gradual basis following childbirth and adoption. More than two-thirds of employers allowed traditional flextime schedules (e.g., a consistent four-day workweek), and more than half allowed employees to move back and forth between full-time and part-time work and to work at home occasionally. Job sharing, regular work at home, and daily flextime were less common arrangements (Table 4.3).

Under the Family and Medical Leave Act of 1993, almost all the companies surveyed by the BWLS were required to provide 12 weeks of unpaid leave for childbirth, adoption, foster care placement, a serious personal medical condition, or the serious medical condition of an immediate family member. Roughly 2 percent of companies studied by BWLS were not complying with the law. Between 7 and 10 percent of companies provided fewer than 12 weeks of leave (most were in compliance with the law because they had fewer than 50 employees per worksite), and 15 to 33 percent provided 13 weeks or more (Table 4.4).

TABLE 4.3
Flexible Work Arrangements (percentage of companies offering)

Does your company allow employees...	Yes	No, but Considering
To periodically change starting and quitting times?	68	9
To change starting and quitting times on a daily basis?	24	7
To return to work gradually after childbirth or adoption?	81	7
To move from full-time to part-time and back again while remaining in the same position or level?	57	5
To share jobs?	37.5	17
To work at home occasionally?	55	6
To work at home or off-site on a regular basis?	33	14
To take time off for school/child care functions?	88	Not asked

Source: Galinsky, Ellen, and James T. Bond. 1998. *1998 Business Work-Life Study: A Sourcebook.* New York: Families and Work Institute. Reprinted by permission.

TABLE 4.4
Summary of Leave Policies (percentage of companies offering)

Leave Policy	Less than 12 Weeks	12 Weeks	13–26 weeks	>26 weeks	Median and Mean Number of Weeks
Maternity Leave	9	58	25	8	Median: 12 weeks Mean: 17 weeks
Paternity	10	74	13	3	Median: 12 weeks Mean: 14 weeks
Adoption/Foster Care Leave	10	74.5	13	3	Median: 12 weeks Mean: 14
Care of Seriously Ill Child	7	78	11	4	Median: 12 weeks Mean: 14 weeks

Source: Galinsky, Ellen, and James T. Bond. 1998. *1998 Business Work-Life Study: A Sourcebook.* New York: Families and Work Institute. Reprinted by permission.

Care for mildly sick children was provided by 5 percent of the companies studied, though there was no legal requirement to provide this type of leave. Just over half of companies provided some pay for women for maternity leave, with funds usually coming from a temporary disability fund; 13 percent provided some pay for paternity leave; and 12.5 percent provided some pay for adoption/foster care leave. The most common type of child care assistance programs offered were those that cost little or no money. About 35 percent of companies in the BWLS study provided information to help locate child care, and 50 percent had dependent care assistance plans that helped employees pay for child care with pretax dollars. Table 4.5 shows that few companies provided other types of child care assistance, including on-site care.

TABLE 4.5
Child Care Assistance (percentage of companies offering)

Does your company provide…	Yes	No, but Considering
Access to information to help locate child care in the community?	36	12
Child care at or near the worksite?	9	12
Payment for child care with vouchers or other subsidies that have direct costs to the company?	5	5
Dependent care assistance plans that help employees pay for child care with pretax dollars?	50	Not asked
Reimbursement for child care costs when employees work late?	4	Not asked
Reimbursement of child care costs when employees travel for business?	6	Not asked
Child care for school-age children on vacation?	6	2.5
Backup or emergency care for employees when their regular child care arrangements fall apart?	4	4.5
Sick care for the children of employees?	5	3
Financial support of local child care through a fund or corporate contributions beyond United Way?	9	Not asked
Public-private partnership in child care	5	Not asked

Source: Galinsky, Ellen, and James T. Bond. 1998. *1998 Business Work-Life Study: A Sourcebook.* New York: Families and Work Institute. Reprinted by permission.

Only 9 percent of companies offer long-term care insurance for family members, and only 5 percent make direct financial contributions to eldercare programs in the communities where they operate, but 23 percent currently offer eldercare resource and referral services.

Statistics on Work-Family: International Comparisons

Women and Employment: An International Perspective

In developed countries, women's and mother's labor force participation rates have increased significantly since the 1960s. The increase in women's work outside the home has occurred across age groups, except for teenagers in Japan and Europe and elderly women in most countries. One of the most significant increases has been in labor force participation for women in the 25- to 34-year-old age bracket, women who are in the primary childbearing and child-rearing ages (see Tables 4.6, 4.7, and 4.8). With the exception of Italy, women with younger children tend to participate in the labor force less than women with older children. In the United States, about 50 percent of women with children under three participate in the labor force, whereas in Germany and Great Britain, the percentages are significantly lower.

TABLE 4.6
Increase in Labor Force Participation of Women from 1970 to 1988
(percentage of women working)

Country	1970	1988
United States	44.7	72.6
Canada	41.2	74.9
Japan	46.8	54.5
Denmark	N/A	90.0
France	52.2	74.5
Germany	47.6	61.5
Italy	44.1(1977)	60.8
Netherlands	23.9	55.4
Sweden	60.7	89.4
United Kingdom	43.3	66.0

Source: Sorrentino, Constance. 1990. "The Changing Family in International Perspective." *Monthly Labor Review* (March): 41–58.

In developing countries, women's participation rate in the labor force has increased as well, with the largest increase taking place in Latin America (Table 4.9). In 1980, women accounted for only one-quarter of the labor force in Central and South America;

TABLE 4.7
Female Labor Force Participation Rates, by Country, 1980–1997

Country	1980	1990	1995	1997
Australia	52.7	62.9	64.8	64.7
Austria	48.7	55.4	62.3	61.4
Belgium	47.0	52.4	56.1	N/A
Canada	57.8	67.8	67.6	67.8
Czech Republic	N/A	69.1	65.4	64.4
Denmark	N/A	78.5	73.6	75.1
Finland	70.1	72.9	70.3	71.3
France	54.4	57.6	59.3	59.8
Germany	52.8	57.4	61.7	61.8
Greece	33.0	43.6	45.9	N/A
Hungary	N/A	N/A	50.5	49.4
Iceland	N/A	N/A	82.4	N/A
Ireland	36.3	38.9	47.8	50.4
Italy	39.6	45.9	43.3	44.1
Japan	54.8	60.3	62.1	63.7
Korea, South	N/A	51.3	53.2	54.8
Luxembourg	39.9	50.7	58.0	60.9
Mexico	33.7	23.6	40.1	42.8
Netherlands	35.5	53.1	59.0	62.2
New Zealand	44.6	62.9	63.3	64.9
Norway	62.3	71.2	72.4	75.8
Poland	N/A	N/A	61.1	60.0
Portugal	54.3	62.9	62.4	65.1
Spain	32.2	41.2	45.1	47.1
Sweden	74.1	80.1	76.1	74.5
Switzerland	54.1	59.6	67.8	69.4
Turkey	N/A	36.7	34.2	30.2
UK	58.3	65.5	66.0	67.5
United States	59.7	68.9	70.7	71.3

Note: Numbers given are percentages. The female labor force of all ages is divided by the female population 15-64 years old.

Source: U.S. Bureau of the Census. 1999. *Statistical Abstract of the United States.* Washington, DC: Government Printing Office.

by 1997 women made up one-third of the labor force in Central America and nearly two-fifths in South America. In North Africa and western Asia, women's participation increased as well, but in eastern Europe and sub-Saharan Africa, rates have remained roughly the same since 1980. Usually there are cultural and religious explanations for low rates of labor force participation for women in particular countries, such as strict gender segregation or concerns about working and the effect working might have on future marriage prospects for women.

TABLE 4.8
Labor Force Participation Rates for All Women under Age 60 and Women with Children under the Ages of 18 and Three in the United States, Canada, and Sweden in 1988 and Five Other Countries in 1986 (in percent)

Country	All Women	Women with Children under 18	Women with Children under 3	Single Mothers with Children under 18	Single Mothers with Children under 3
United States	68.5	65.5	52.5	65.3	45.1
Canada	66.8	67.0	58.4	63.6	41.3
Denmark	79.2	86.1	83.9	85.9	80.9
Germany	55.8	48.4	39.7	69.7	50.4
France	60.1	65.8	60.1	85.2	69.6
Italy	43.3	43.9	45.0	67.2	68.0
Sweden	80.0	89.4	85.8	N/A	N/A
United Kingdom	64.3	58.7	36.9	51.9	23.4

Source: Sorrentino, Constance. 1990. "The Changing Family in International Perspective." *Monthly Labor Review* (March): 41–58.

TABLE 4.9
Percentage of the Labor Force Who Are Women

	1980	1997
Africa		
Northern Africa	20	26
Sub-Saharan Africa	42	43
Southern Africa	40	40
Rest of sub-Saharan Africa	43	43
Latin America and the Caribbean		
Caribbean	38	43
Central America	27	33
South America	27	38
Asia		
Eastern Asia	40	43
Southeastern Asia	41	43
Southern Asia	31	33
Central Asia	47	46
Western Asia	23	27

Source: United Nations. 2000. *The World's Women: Trends and Statistics.* New York: United Nations. Reprinted by permission.

Wage Inequality: An International Perspective

Measuring the extent of the difference in pay between men and women working in the same or similar occupations is difficult. Data on hourly pay rates for men and women by occupation, which provide one of the most reliable ways to compare pay scales, are not available from many countries. In addition, statistical information on occupations is difficult to compare across countries because countries define occupational categories in different ways. If an occupation such as "office clerk" is broadly defined, larger pay differentials appear to exist; if it is broken down into more narrow categories, then pay differentials are minimized.

Most researchers agree that in most countries, significant pay differentials exist between men and women, even between men and women in the same occupation (Robinson 1998). Women earn lower average wages and average earnings than men in most occupations for which data are available, and the pay gap between men and women remains significant. Though a comparison of overall pay differentials between countries is not possible with the current data available, researchers have found that different countries experience different degrees of pay inequity across occupations. In some countries, such as Nigeria, Ghana, Cyprus, Estonia, Finland, the United Kingdom, and the United States, women are paid less than men across all occupations. In countries with industrialized market economies, the gap is more narrow and consistent across occupations. Countries that had centrally planned economies have a much larger variation, with larger pay differentials found in some occupations and not others. Nigeria, some Latin American countries, Cyprus, China, Tajikistan, and Singapore all have varied gaps across occupations (Robinson 1998).

Determining why these pay differentials exist is also complicated. Though discrimination clearly plays some role, the degree to which other factors come into play is difficult to determine. Men, who are more likely to work full-time and have continuous attachment to the labor force, have more seniority than women and are paid higher rates as a result. In addition, many occupations remain largely segregated by gender, with female-dominated occupations tending to pay lower salaries than male-dominated occupations. In a number of countries, including the

United States, legislation now mandates equal pay for women and men performing similar work in the same workplace.

The Changing Family: An International Perspective

Constance Sorrentino (1990) has identified four major demographic trends occurring to greater or lesser degrees in many developed countries. Declining fertility, aging of the population, rising divorce rates, and an increasing number of children born out of wedlock are all factors that have dramatically altered the composition of the modern family. Declining fertility and the aging of the population have led to a decline in the size of the average household. Many developed countries had household sizes of four or five members per household 80 years ago; today the average household size is only two or three people living together (Table 4.10).

TABLE 4.10
Average Number of Members per Household in 10 Countries, Selected Years, 1960–1988

Country	1960	1970	1977	1985–1988
United States	3.3	3.1	2.9	2.6
Canada	3.9	3.5	2.9	2.8
Japan	4.1	3.4	3.3	3.1
Denmark	2.9	2.7	N/A	2.3
France	3.1	2.9	2.8	2.6
Germany	2.9	2.7	2.5	2.3
Italy	3.6	3.4	3.1	2.8
Netherlands	3.6	3.2	2.9	2.5
Sweden	2.8	2.6	2.4	2.2
United Kingdom	3.1	2.9	2.7	2.6

Source: Sorrentino, Constance. 1990. "The Changing Family in International Perspective." *Monthly Labor Review* (March): 41–58.

The phenomenon known as the feminization of poverty is also occurring worldwide: families headed by single women have the highest rates of poverty as compared to other family types. In comparison to Canada and Europe, the United States has higher rates of marriage and divorce, slightly larger families, and higher rates of single-parent families. In the United States, as compared to Europe, fewer couples live together without marrying, and fewer people live alone.

The Role of Men in Family Care and Housekeeping: An International Perspective

Since 1995 there has been a concerted effort to collect statistics and provide better data on how men and women spend their paid and unpaid time. Historically, unpaid time spent caring for children or performing household duties has not been recorded and is generally not available from official statistics. Time-use surveys and other data collection techniques have begun to improve measures of unpaid time in a number of countries. Time-use surveys are now being used to understand how men and women allocate their time outside of paid employment and to formulate policies relating to child care, education, and leisure activities.

Though time-use surveys have not been in use for enough countries for a long enough period of time to discern trends in how men and women use their time, it appears that the number of hours spent on unpaid work is slowly increasing for men and decreasing for women. For seven countries for which recent data are available, women and men work between 35 and 50 hours a week in paid and unpaid work combined, except in Latvia where they work more than 50 hours a week on average (Table 4.11). Women's total work time exceeded men's by two or more hours in most countries. In most countries, more than half of women's total work time is spent on unpaid work. Women spend 50 to 70 percent as much time as men do on paid work but almost twice as much or more time as men on unpaid work (Table 4.11). Men spend one to seven hours more per week on leisure than women do, but women spend a few hours more than men do attending to basic needs. Three countries—Australia, the Netherlands, and New Zealand—provide statistics demonstrating that small children greatly increase women's unpaid work but not men's (Table 4.12).

Caregiving Activities: An International Perspective

In European Union (EU) countries, most preschool and child care programs are publicly funded to some degree, with the exception of Great Britain and to some extent Portugal (Tietze and Cryer 1999). As of the early 1990s, most European countries were moving toward comprehensive early childhood education coverage for children from age three until the time they start compulsory

TABLE 4.11

Time Spent in Hours per Week in 1995–1999 for Women (W) and Men (M)

	Total Work Hours		Paid		Unpaid		Leisure		Basic Needs	
	W	M	W	M	W	M	W	M	W	M
Australia	51	49	15	30	35	18	35	38	78	77
France	46	42	15	26	31	17	29	34	85	84
Japan	46	42	20	39	26	3	42	44	75	73
Latvia	62	56	22	32	40	24	28	33	75	76
Netherlands	36	37	10	25	26	11	47	48	76	74
New Zealand	49	49	16	29	33	19	32	33	82	80
Korea, South	40	38	23	36	17	2	30	37	79	79

Source: United Nations. 2000. *The World's Women: Trends and Statistics.* New York: United Nations. Reprinted by permission.

TABLE 4.12

Time Spent in Hours per Week in 1995–1999 in Paid and Unpaid Work, with or without Children under Age Five

	Unpaid Work				Paid Work			
	No Children under Five		Children under Five		No Children under Five		Children under Five	
	W	M	W	M	W	M	W	M
Australia	40	22	49	22	14	30	16	43
Netherlands	36	18	47	23	12	29	9	34
New Zealand	34	23	50	23	20	29	11	41

Source: United Nations. 2000. *The World's Women: Trends and Statistics.* New York: United Nations. Reprinted by permission.

schooling. In eight of 15 countries within the EU, child care slots are available for more than 80 percent of the children who are age three or older, doubling and in some cases more than tripling from the number of slots available a few decades earlier (Table 4.13).

For some countries, such as Sweden and Denmark, publicly funded programs are available from ages one through six. For most EU countries, however, the number of publicly funded slots available is much lower for children under three, though many of these countries have more extensive parental leave programs than the programs found in the United States. In many EU countries, the cost of the programs is free for children three or older or

TABLE 4.13
Publicly Funded Care and Education Services for Children before Compulsory Schooling
in a Sample of EU Countries

Percentage of children younger than 3 served	BE	DK	DE	EL	ES	FR	IT	SV	UK
1988	20	48	2	4	5	22	5	N/A	2
1993	30	50	4	3	5	23	6	33	2
Percentage of children ages 3–6 served									
1970	95	20	33	N/A	42	87	58	22	16
1993	>95	79	78	64	84	99	97	79	53

Note: BE=Belgium, DK=Denmark, DE=Western Germany, EL=Greece, ES=Spain, FR=France, IT=Italy, SV=Sweden, and UK=United Kingdom.

Source: This table abstracts data available in Wolfgang Tietze and Debby Cryer. 1999. "Current Trends in European Early Child Care and Education." *Annals of the American Academy of Political and Social Science* 563 (May): 162–174.

is based on a sliding scale according to income. For children under three who need full-time care (more often from lower-income families), the parents frequently pay a larger percentage of the cost, and there is a significant shortage of affordable programs in many countries. The majority of children under three in Scandinavian countries are in family-based care, whereas in Belgium, France, and eastern Germany, the care is more likely to be center-based.

Comparative data on eldercare in other countries has not yet been widely studied, though common themes include maintaining integration of the elderly person within the community and reducing the rising costs of care. Scandinavian governments compensate family members caring for aging relatives, but many countries continue to depend on family members to either leave work or reduce their work hours to look after frail relatives.

Maternity and Parental Leave Policies: An International Perspective

In 1952, the International Labour Organization Maternity Protection Convention was adopted. The convention calls for a standard maternity leave of at least 12 weeks. Currently, 119 countries meet this standard of 12 weeks or more; 20 countries provide 17 weeks or more, and 31 countries provide less than 12 weeks (Table 4.14). Implementation of the maternity leave allowance varies greatly—in some countries, there is a mandatory minimum level required of all employers, and in other countries, such as the United States, it is optional for some employers.

TABLE 4.14
Maternity Leave Benefits, as of 1998

Country or Area	Length of Maternity Leave	Percentage of Wages Paid in Covered Period	Provider of Coverage
Africa			
Algeria	14 weeks	100	Social Security
Angola	90 days	100	Employer
Benin	14 weeks	100	Social Security
Botswana	12 weeks	25	Employer
Burkina Faso	14 weeks	100	S.S. / Employer
Burundi	12 weeks	50	Employer
Cameroon	14 weeks	100	Social Security
Central African Rep.	14 weeks	50	Social Security
Chad	14 weeks	50	Social Security
Comoros	14 weeks	100	Employer
Congo	15 weeks	100	50% Employer / 50% S.S.
Côte d'Ivoire	14 weeks	10.0	Social Security
Dem. Rep. of the Congo	14 weeks	67	Employer
Djibouti	14 weeks	50 (100% for public employees)	Employer / S.S.
Egypt	50 days	100	S.S. / Employer
Equatorial Guinea	12 weeks	75	Social Security
Eritrea	60 days	—	—
Ethiopia	90 days	100	Employer
Gabon	14 weeks	100	Social Security
Gambia	12 weeks	100	Employer
Ghana	12 weeks	50	Employer
Guinea	14 weeks	100	50% Employer / 50% S.S.
Guinea-Bissau	60 days	100	Employer / S.S.
Kenya	2 months	100	Employer
Lesotho	12 weeks	0	—
Libyan Arab Jamahiriya	50 days	50	Employer
Madagascar	14 weeks	100[a]	50% Employer / 50% S.S.
Mali	14 weeks	100	Social Security
Mauritania	14 weeks	100	Social Security
Mauritius	12 weeks	100	Employer
Morocco	12 weeks	100	Social Security
Mozambique	60 days	100	Employer
Namibia	12 weeks	as prescribed	Social Security
Niger	14 weeks	50	Social Security
Nigeria	12 weeks	50	Employer
Rwanda	12 weeks	67	Employer
Sao Tome and Principe	70 days	100 for 60 days	Social Security
Senegal	14 weeks	100	Social Security

(continues)

Country or Area	Length of Maternity Leave	Percentage of Wages Paid in Covered Period	Provider of Coverage
Seychelles	14 weeks	flat rate for 10 weeks	Social Security
Somalia	14 weeks	50	Employer
South Africa	12 weeks	45	Unemployment Insurance
Sudan	8 weeks	100	Employer
Swaziland	12 weeks	0	—
Togo	14 weeks	100	50% Employer / 50% S.S.
Tunisia	30 days	67	Social Security
Uganda	8 weeks	100 for one month	Employer
United Rep. of Tanzania	12 weeks	100	Employer
Zambia	12 weeks	100	Employer
Zimbabwe	90 days	60/75	Employer
Latin America and the Caribbean			
Antigua and Barbuda	13 weeks	60	S.S. + possible employer supplement
Argentina	90 days	100	Social Security
Bahamas	8 weeks	100	40% Employer / 60% S.S.
Barbados	12 weeks	100	Social Security
Belize	12 weeks	80	Social Security
Bolivia	60 days	100% of nat'l min wage + 70% of wages above min wage	Social Security
Brazil	120 days	100	Social Security
Chile	18 weeks	100	Social Security
Colombia	12 weeks	100	Social Security
Costa Rica	4 months	100	50% Employer / 50% S.S.
Cuba	18 weeks	100	Social Security
Dominica	12 weeks	60	S.S. / Employer
Dominican Republic	12 weeks	100	50% Employer / 50% S.S.
Ecuador	12 weeks	100	25% Employer / 75% S.S.
El Salvador	12 weeks	75	Social Security
Grenada	3 months	100 (2 months), 60% for 3rd month	S.S. / Employer
Guatemala	12 weeks	100	33% Employer / 67% S.S.
Guyana	13 weeks	70	Social Security
Haiti	12 weeks	100 for 6 weeks	Employer
Honduras	10 weeks	100 for 84 days	33% Employer / 67% S.S.
Jamaica	12 weeks	100 for 8 weeks	Employer
Mexico	12 weeks	100	Social Security
Nicaragua	12 weeks	60	Social Security
Panama	14 weeks	100	Social Security
Paraguay	12 weeks	50 for 9 weeks	Social Security
Peru	90 days	100	Social Security
Saint Lucia	13 weeks	65	Social Security
Trinidad and Tobago	13 weeks	60-100	S.S./Employer
Uruguay	12 weeks	100	Social Security
Venezuela	18 weeks	100	Social Security

(continues)

Country or Area	Length of Maternity Leave	Percentage of Wages Paid in Covered Period	Provider of Coverage
Asia			
Afghanistan	90 days	100	Employer
Azerbaijan	18 weeks	—	—
Bahrain	45 days	100	Employer
Bangladesh	12 weeks	100	Employer
Cambodia	90 days	50	Employer
China	90 days	100	Employer
Cyprus	16 weeks	75	Social Security
India	12 weeks	100	Employer / S.S.
Indonesia	3 months	100	Employer
Iran (Islamic Republic of)	90 days	66.7 for 16 weeks	Social Security
Iraq	62 days	100	Social Security
Israel	12 weeks	75[a]	Social Security
Jordan	10 weeks	100	Employer
Kuwait	70 days	100	Employer
Lao People's Dem. Rep.	90 days	100	Social Security
Lebanon	40 days	100	Employer
Malaysia	60 days	100	Employer
Mongolia	101 days	—	—
Myanmar	12 weeks	66.7	Social Security
Nepal	52 days	100	Employer
Pakistan	12 weeks	100	Employer
Philippines	60 days	100	Social Security
Qatar	40–60 days	100 for civil servants	Agency concerned
Republic of Korea	60 days	100	Employer
Saudi Arabia	10 weeks	50 or 100	Employer
Singapore	8 weeks	100	Employer
Sri Lanka	12 weeks	100	Employer
Syrian Arab Republic	75 days	100	Employer
Thailand	90 days	100 for 45 days then 50% for 15 days	Employer for 45 days, then S.S.
Turkey	12 weeks	66.7	Social Security
United Arab Emirates	45 days	100	Employer
Viet Nam	4–6 months	100	Social Security
Yemen	60 days	100	Employer
Oceania			
Fiji	84 days	Flat rate	Employer
Papua New Guinea	6 weeks	0	—
Solomon Islands	12 weeks	25	Employer
Developed regions			
Australia	1 year	0	—
Austria	16 weeks	100	Social Security
Belarus	126 days	100	Social Security
Belgium	15 weeks	82% for 30 days, 75% thereafter[a]	Social Security
Bulgaria	120–180 days	100	Social Security

(continues)

TABLE 4.14, continued

Country or Area	Length of Maternity Leave	Percentage of Wages Paid in Covered Period	Provider of Coverage
Canada	17–18 weeks	55 for 15 weeks	Unemployment Insurance
Croatia	6 months+ 4 weeks	—	—
Czech Republic	28 weeks	—	—
Denmark	18 weeks[b]	100[a]	Social Security
Estonia	18 weeks	—	—
Finland	105 days	80	Social Security
France	16–26 weeks	100	Social Security
Germany	14 weeks	100	S.S. to ceiling; employer pays difference
Greece	16 weeks	75	Social Security
Hungary	24 weeks	100	Social Security
Iceland	2 months	Flat rate	Social Security
Ireland	14 weeks	70% or fixed rate[a]	Social Security
Italy	5 months	80	Social Security
Japan	14 weeks	60	Health insurance
Liechtenstein	8 weeks	80	Social Security
Luxembourg	16 weeks	100	Social Security
Malta	13 weeks	100	Social Security
Netherlands	16 weeks	100	Social Security
New Zealand	14 weeks	0	—
Norway	18 weeks	100, and 26 extra paid weeks by either parent	Social Security
Poland	16–18 weeks	100	Social Security
Portugal	98 days	100	Social Security
Romania	112 days	50–94	Social Security
Russian Federation	140 days	100	Social Security
Spain	16 weeks	100	Social Security
Sweden	14 weeks	450 days paid parental leave: 360 days at 75% and 90 days at flat rate	Social Security
Switzerland	8 weeks	100	Employer
Ukraine	126 days	100	Social Security
United Kingdom	14–18 weeks	90 for 6 weeks, flat rate after	Social Security
United States	12 weeks[c]	0	—

[a]Up to a ceiling.

[b]10 more weeks may be taken up by either parent.

[c]The Family and Medical Leave Act (FMLA) of 1993 provided a total of 12 work weeks of unpaid leave during any 12-month period for the birth of a child and the care of the newborn. FMLA applies only to workers in companies with 50 or more workers.

Technical notes: Table 4.14 presents data on maternity leave benefits currently available to women in countries surveyed by the ILO, including the length of time for which benefits are provided, the extent of compensation and the institution responsible for providing the coverage. The data presented was compiled by the ILO, based on information provided by countries as of 1998.

Source: Reprinted by permission from United Nations, Statistics Division, *The World's Women 2000: Trends and Statistics.* New York: United Nations. Table 5.C, based on International Labour Office, press release of 12 February 1998, ILO/98/7 (Geneva). http://www.un.org/Depts/unsd/ww2000/table5c.htm — The World's Women

Many women can take advantage of maternity leave only if it is paid. Most countries provide for full payment or close to full payment for the duration of the leave (see Table 4.14). In many countries, social security systems fund maternity leaves, but some part-time and temporary workers do not qualify for paid leave under these systems. Many countries have laws that safeguard a woman's right to return to her job after her maternity leave, but even in countries where it is illegal, termination due to pregnancy continues to occur.

Parental leave, which allows both men and women to stay home with their children when needed, is becoming increasingly recognized as an important component in providing equal opportunity for men and women in the workplace and in the home. In a review of 138 countries, the International Labour Organization found that 36 countries provide some type of parental leave. In 25 of the countries providing this benefit, the leave is paid. The Nordic countries provide the most generous paid leave to parents, whereas the United States, New Zealand, and Australia provide no pay for parental leave. Parental leave laws are widely used by women in most countries, especially when the leave is paid, but men do not tend to take advantage of parental leave policies (in most countries for which data are available). In Denmark and Germany in 1996, more than 90 percent of those taking leave were women (United Nations 2000). The culture of the workplace and fears about career advancement often inhibit a father's ability or willingness to take advantage of parental leave benefits.

References

Bond, James T., Ellen Galinsky, and Jennifer E. Swanberg. 1998. *1997 National Study of the Changing Workforce.* New York: Families and Work Institute.

Capizzano, Jeffery, Gina Adams, and Freya Sonenstein. 2000. "Child Care Arrangements for Children under Five: Variation Across States." No. B-07 in New Federalism: National Survey of America's Families. Washington, DC: Urban Institute. http://newfederalism.urban.org (cited 5 December 2001).

Cordtz, Dan. 1990. "Hire Me, Hire My Family." *Financial World* 159 (September 18): 76–79.

Economic Report of the President. 2000. Washington, DC: Government Printing Office.

England, Suzanne E. 1989. "Eldercare Leaves and Employer Policies: Feminist Perspectives." Pp. 117–121 in *Proceedings of the First Annual Women's Policy Research Conference*. Washington, DC: Institute for Women's Policy Research.

Galinksy, Ellen, and James T. Bond. 1998. *1998 Business Work Life Study: A Sourcebook*. New York: Families and Work Institute.

Galinsky, Ellen, Carollee Lowes, Susan Kontos, and Marybeth Shinn. 1994. *The Study of Children in Family Child Care and Relative Care*. New York: Families and Work Institute.

Goldscheider, Frances, and Linda J. Waite. 1991. *New Families, No Families? The Transformation of the American Home*. Berkeley: University of California Press.

Harrington, Mona. 1999. *Care and Equality: Inventing a New Family Politics*. New York: Alfred A. Knopf.

Hofferth, Sandra L. 1991. *National Child Care Survey, 1990*. Washington, DC: Urban Institute.

———. 1999. "Child Care, Maternal Employment, and Public Policy." *Annals of the American Academy of Political and Social Science* 563: 20–38.

Parasuraman, Saroj, and Jeffrey H. Greenhaus. 1997. "The Changing World of Work and Family." In *Integrating Work and Family: Challenges and Choices for a Changing World*. Edited by Saroj Parasuraman and Jeffrey H. Greenhaus. Westport, CT: Quorum.

Robinson, Derek. 1998. "Differences in Occupational Earnings by Sex." *International Labour Review* 137, no. 1: 3–31.

Robinson, John P. 1988. "Who's Doing the Housework?" *American Demographics* 10: 24–28.

Seppanen, Patricia S., Diane K. DeVries, and Michelle Seligson. 1993. *National Study of Before- and After-school Programs: Executive Summary*. Washington, DC: U.S. Department of Education.

Sorrentino, Constance. 1990. "The Changing Family in International Perspective." *Monthly Labor Review* (March): 41–58.

Spain, Daphne, and Suzanne M. Bianchi. 1996. *Balancing Act: Motherhood, Marriage, and Employment among American Women*. New York: Russell Sage Foundation.

Tietze, Wolfgang, and Debby Cryer. 1999. "Current Trends in European Early Child Care and Education." *Annals of the American Academy of Political and Social Science* 563: 175–193.

United Nations. *The World's Women: Trends and Statistics*. 2000. New York: United Nations.

U.S. Bureau of the Census. 1999. *Statistical Abstracts of the United States.* Washington, DC: Government Printing Office.

————. 2000. *Statistical Abstracts of the United States.* Washington, DC: Government Printing Office.

Vierck, Elizabeth. 1990. *Fact Book on Aging.* Santa Barbara, CA: ABC-CLIO.

5

Legislation and Case Law

Protective Legislation — Women in the Workforce

Much of the legislation and case law that relates to work-family concerns the treatment of women in the workplace. Prior to 1963, protective legislation dominated the legal landscape. It was a legal approach founded on the assumption that workers and employers were not equal in bargaining power and therefore workers needed legal protection. Though protective legislation originally focused on all workers, the focus shifted to women and in some cases children by the beginning of the twentieth century. This shift in focus was due partly in response to events such as the Triangle Shirtwaist fire in March of 1911, in which 146 young women lost their lives working in extremely hazardous factory conditions.

Proponents viewed one-sex protective legislation as a way to protect women from unsafe and "immoral" work environments, and some protective legislation served to provide women workers with benefits such as maximum hours and mandatory rest periods. In *Muller v. State of Oregon* in 1908, the Supreme Court upheld the constitutionality of an Oregon maximum-hour law asserting that because of their physical structure, women needed to be protected from overly strenuous work and long hours. Much of the protective legislation passed, however, resulted in discrimination against women in the workforce and limited their employment opportunities. For example, in *Radice v. New York* in 1924, the Supreme Court upheld the constitutionality of a

New York law that prohibited women from being employed from 10:00 P.M. to 6:00 A.M. in restaurants. The Court felt the loss of sleep at night would be too difficult for women because of their delicate nature.

From "Special Treatment" to "Equal Treatment"

The fact that women bear children and were viewed as the weaker sex was treated as a legal justification not only for limiting women's work hours and amount of pay but for firing women who became pregnant or excluding women from working in certain occupations. The Equal Pay Act of 1963 and the Civil Rights Act of 1964 prohibited discrimination in employment on the basis of sex and other characteristics. Both laws represented a dramatic shift away from one-sex protective legislation and special treatment of women toward "equal treatment" for men and women in the workplace. These laws have led courts and the legislature to support and enact gender-neutral laws that hold men and women to the same standard. For example, in dealing with the issue of pregnancy discrimination and family leave, the courts followed this gender-neutral stance. Pregnancy is treated as a disability, and pregnant workers are subjected to the same standards as other disabled workers. Similarly, under the Family and Medical Leave Act of 1993 (FMLA), all eligible employees with family responsibilities are allowed leave.

The FMLA represents one of the most important pieces of recent legislation for families struggling to balance work and home responsibilities. Unfortunately, only 59 percent of the United States workforce are eligible under the FMLA, and many workers who are eligible are unable to afford taking unpaid time off from work. In addition, some workers face a hostile work environment that discourages them from taking advantage of the FMLA. In a 1999 case, *Knussman v. State of Maryland,* a helicopter paramedic sued the state police after he was denied 12 weeks leave following the birth of his daughter. He was given ten days off but sought more time because his wife experienced childbirth complications. In the first sex discrimination case under the FMLA, a jury awarded the paramedic $375,000 in damages for mental anguish. As of this writing, the case is under appeal.

Because the FMLA did not provide paid leave, in 2000 the Department of Labor issued a regulation allowing U.S. states to use unemployment insurance funds to provide partial income replacement for new adoptive or biological parental leave. State legislators and activists are currently investigating innovative ways to make family leave more affordable by using unemployment compensation. Many states are holding hearings and funding studies, and more than a dozen states have introduced bills to propose paid family leave benefits. States are also exploring ways to support workers who need to take brief periods of time off to attend a school play, to take an elderly relative to a medical appointment, or to meet other pressing family responsibilities during work hours. The Small Necessities Leave Act, passed in Massachusetts in 1998, allows workers to take up to 24 hours off from work during each year to meet family responsibilities.

Child Care and the Law

Until the 1960s, when married women became increasingly involved in the labor force, the issue of child care was rarely addressed by the legal system. Prior to 1960, most child care services were offered through philanthropic organizations and were rarely supported by business or government funds. Under the New Deal the federal government sponsored some child care through the Works Progress Administration's Emergency Nursery Schools program, and during World War II the government provided limited funds for child care centers under the Lanham Act, but in general government involvement with child care has been minimal. In 1968 and 1969, Congress held hearings on bills to expand and improve child care programs. These hearings led to the proposed Comprehensive Child Development Act of 1971. The act passed both houses of Congress but was vetoed by President Richard M. Nixon. Though literally thousands of bills have been introduced to improve day care programs and standards, few have passed because the issue remains controversial, with some constituents advocating child care support for working families but others encouraging women to stay home and look after their children.

During the latter half of the twentieth century, child care policies and programs developed along two tiers. Middle- and upper-income married working women either purchased quality care from the private sector or were provided with high-quality employer-sponsored child care programs. Mothers receiving welfare were increasingly being required to enter the workforce but faced few options with regard to high-quality or affordable child care. In 1974, Congress passed Title XX of the Social Services Act and in 1975, the Aid to Day Care Centers Act. Both pieces of legislation attempted to improve child care options for low-income women. Despite the passage of these laws, there continues to be a shortage of affordable quality child care for many working families. At the same time, recent welfare legislation, including the Family Support Act of 1988 and the Personal Responsibility and Work Opportunity Reconciliation Act of 1996, have put increased pressure on welfare mothers to join the workforce.

Recent Lower Court Cases and Work-Family

Recent lower court rulings involving work-family issues provide examples of current attitudes about working parents and shed some light on the way the legal system is addressing work-family-related issues. The examples below are of cases that created conflicting and sometimes polarized public responses toward working mothers, single parents, day care, and the role of fathers as caretakers.

Commonwealth v. Woodward, 1998

In a Massachusetts case, *Commonwealth v. Woodward,* an au pair was convicted of manslaughter for the death of Matthew Eappen, a toddler in her care. Similar to a handful of high-profile day care sexual abuse scandals throughout the 1970s and 1980s, the case received national attention and raised fears and anxieties about the safety of child care and about mothers working outside the home. The judge reduced the initial charge of murder to manslaughter, ruling that Louise Woodward had unintentionally caused the baby's death by rough handling. The public response was somewhat sympathetic to Woodward, who was viewed as an overwhelmed eighteen-year-old caring for two young charges, but less sympathetic to the mother, Deborah Eappen, who had just lost her son. Some members of the press and public criticized Deborah Eappen for working and leaving her young children in the care of a teenager when her husband made enough money to support the family. At the same time, working mothers and their supporters came to her defense, pointing out that little was being said in the press about Deborah Eappen's husband and that Deborah Eappen was working only part-time.

Upton v. JWP Businessland, 1997

Another 1997 Massachusetts case, *Upton v. JWP Businessland*, involved a single mother of a young son who sued her former employer for wrongful dismissal. She was fired because her employer frequently requested that she work overtime, often until 9:00 or 10:00 P.M., and she refused. Upton stated that because of family responsibilities, she was unable to stay late, especially when given short notice. Upton argued that the dismissal was a violation of Massachusetts law that supports the care and protection of children, but the court ruled that her domestic situation was irrelevant because an employee at-will can be fired for any reason or no reason.

Maggiore v. Ocon, 1997

In the *Maggiore v. Ocon* California custody case, a teenage mother who had graduated from high school with honors and won a scholarship to a prestigious college took her two-year-old daughter with her to college. She enrolled her daughter in a university day care center, while she attended classes. When faced with child support expenses, the child's father appealed for and won custody. The court ruled in favor of the father because the father's mother would be staying home with the child full-time. The judge stated that though the mother and child had a good bond and the day care was of high quality, leaving the child with the mother meant that the child would be raised and supervised for the most part by strangers. Many people condemned the judge's decision, and the case was reversed on the appeals court finding that custody could not be awarded solely on the day care issue.

Merrill Lynch Class Action Lawsuit, Settled out of Court, 1998

In a 1998 case that was settled out of court in favor of the claimants, 900 current and former Merrill Lynch employees filed claims of workplace discrimination. In the suit, the women employees recalled their supervisors saying that women "couldn't combine work and family" and that women were paid less than men were "because their husbands could support them." Most of the complaints in the case involved economic discrimination whereby tips, clients, and business were funneled to male brokers. Women at Merrill Lynch were often paid a lower salary than men, even when the women and men possessed similar qualifications.

Prickett v. Circuit Science, 1994

A recent case represents what some legal scholars view as an emerging trend—the recognition by the courts that workers have family obligations that conflict with the demands of their jobs and limit their availability in the labor market. In *Prickett v. Circuit Science*, the employer changed an employee's schedule from a day shift to an evening shift. The employee, a single father, was suspended and later fired when, over the course of several days, he was unable to obtain child care and work the required change in shift. The Minnesota Supreme Court held that Prickett was entitled to unemployment compensation because, given the reality today of dual-income and single-parent families, his attempt to attend to family needs did not constitute misconduct justifying denial of unemployment compensation benefits. This ruling appears to reflect a trend, though a somewhat uneven one, of decisions that recognize that employees deserve some workplace accommodations for family responsibilities in terms of unemployment compensation.

Key Federal Legislation

Below is a chronological summary of key legislation followed by a chronological summary of important case law relating to work-family issues, especially women's involvement in the paid workforce.

Women's Bureau Act, 1920 (PL 66-259)

This act created the Women's Bureau, a new agency charged with conducting research about working women.

The Federal Economy Act of 1932 (47 Stat. 406)

Section 213 of the Federal Economy Act, the "married persons clause," required that one spouse resign if both husband and wife were working for the federal government, to limit the number of jobholders in each family to one. A Women's Bureau study later found that more than 75 percent of those resigning were women. It was one of a number of public and private pressures on women to give up "pin money" so that men could support their families during the Depression. Though this legislation was eventually repealed, by 1939 twenty-six states had proposed "married person's clauses," more than 1,500 women had been discharged, and additional women resigned to protect their husband's jobs. As recently as 1962 more than 40 states had laws that set maximum daily or weekly hours for women to work outside the home. It was not until the passage of Title VII of the Civil Rights Act of 1964 that these limitations on women's employment were declared illegal.

The Fair Labor Standards Act of 1938 (52 Stat. 1060–1069; 29 USC 201)

The Fair Labor Standards Act, popularly known as the "Wages and Hours Law," mandated a minimum wage, initially 25 cents, and a 40-hour workweek for women and men, excluding farm and domestic workers. The law also required employers to pay eligible workers "time and a half," or one and one-half times the customary pay, for hours worked that exceeded the maximum allowance. One of the original goals of the law was to discourage employers from requiring employees to work long hours that might interfere with their personal and family lives. The extra compensation for overtime work applies to hourly workers but not salaried workers.

The Lanham Act, 1940 (PL 76-849)

The Lanham Act provided funds for building defense-related industries. Federal funds for child care facilities were included under the act to support working mothers who were joining the war effort. Though only a small percentage of the children of working mothers attended these centers, it set a precedent, along with the emergency aid provided by the Works Progress Administration in the 1930s, for federal involvement in child care funding. At the height of program, 13 percent of children needing care received federal assistance. At the end of the war, most of these centers were rapidly phased out.

Equal Pay Act, 1963 (PL 88-38)

The Equal Pay Act of 1963, an amendment to the Fair Labor Standards Act, prohibited unequal pay for equal or "substantially equal" work performed by men and women. It was the first federal law aimed at preventing sex discrimination by making it illegal to pay unequal wages to men and women who worked in the same place and whose work required the same set of skills and responsibilities.

Title VII of the Civil Rights Act of 1964 (PL 88-352; 42 USC 2000e)

Title VII was a major legislative achievement that mandated equal employment opportunity for women. Passed by Congress in 1964 as part of the Civil Rights Act, Title VII prohibits firms with 15 or more employees from wage discrimination on the basis of gender, among other characteristics. Title VII established the Equal Employment Opportunity Commission (EEOC) to coordinate efforts to implement the law and to conciliate disputes. Soon after being established, the EEOC was inundated with sex discrimination complaints.

Economic Opportunity Amendments of 1966 (PL 89-794)

The Economic Opportunity Amendments of 1966 authorized Head Start, a preschool day care program for children from low-income families, and required that 23 percent of Job Corps positions go to women workers.

Equal Employment Opportunity Act of 1972 (PL 92-261)

The Equal Employment Opportunity Act of 1972 was passed to provide the EEOC the power to enforce the provision against job discrimination on the basis of race, color, religion, national origin, or gender under Title VII of the Civil Rights Act of 1964. The National Organization for Women and other groups actively pressed for the passage of this legislation so that the EEOC, which had been reluctant to enforce Title VII, would have the ability to sue employers for compliance. Previously, the EEOC had been limited to requesting only voluntary compliance. In addition, this law expanded the territory of the Civil Rights Act to include small businesses, government employees, and educational institutions.

The Tax Reform Act of 1976, Dependent Care Tax Credit (IRC 21)

The Dependent Care Tax Credit, in essence, provided for a 20 percent tax credit that replaced the child care deduction on federal taxes. The view of child care shifted from that of a personal expense to that of an employment-related expense with the passage of this law. All taxpayers with children benefit from the law, with a larger credit provided for lower-income earners. The child care tax credit was expanded from 1977 to 1988 by a factor of more than 7.5, and the Internal Revenue Code was modified to allow taxpayers to shelter pretax dollars for child care and other dependent care services in a "flexible spending plan." Families choose between flexible spending and the tax credit. These policies are intended to facilitate parent choice for child care and minimize the direct involvement by government in specific types of child care.

The Pregnancy Discrimination Act of 1978 (PL 95-555; 42 USC 2000e[k])

The Pregnancy Discrimination Act of 1978, an amendment to Title VII of the Civil Rights Act of 1964, prohibited workplace discrimination for pregnancy, childbirth, or related medical conditions. The act stated that pregnancy should be treated the same as other disabilities. Congress passed the act to correct a perceived gap in the way the courts were interpreting Title VII.

The Family Support Act of 1988 (102 Stat. 2343)

The Family Support Act (FSA) was one of the most significant changes in the welfare system in the United States since the 1930s. At a time when more than half of all married women with children under six were in the workforce, public support declined for mothers on welfare remaining in the home. The notion of welfare-to-work programs was incorporated into the passage of the FSA. The goal of the FSA was to help families on public assistance become self-sufficient, unlike the traditional welfare goal embodied in the Aid to Families with Dependent Children (AFDC) program established by the Social Security Act of 1935, which provided financial support for single-parent families. The FSA emphasized that the relationship between the welfare system and families was one of "mutual obligations." Recipients were expected to work toward economic independence, either through employment or participation in educational or training activities. Under the FSA, states were required to implement a Job Opportunities and Basic Skills Training Program (JOBS). These programs were designed to assist recipients in supporting their children while working, and recipients were guaranteed child care.

The Omnibus Budget Reconciliation Act, Title V: Child Care, 1990 (PL 101-508)

The child care provision of the Budget Reconciliation Act provided grants to states for funding child care assistance and tax benefits to families.

Family and Medical Leave Act of 1993 (107 Stat. 6)

The passage of the Family and Medical Leave Act of 1993 (FMLA), after more than a decade of delay that included two vetoes by President George Bush, was finally signed into law by President Bill Clinton in 1993. The FMLA provided for unpaid leave of up to 12 weeks for the birth, adoption, or foster placement of a child; an employee's own serious health condition; or the serious health condition of an immediate family member. The FMLA covered employees who have been working for a particular employer for more than one year, required employers to continue to provide health insurance during a worker's leave, and guaranteed workers the same or equivalent job upon their return.

Some have criticized the FMLA as being largely symbolic because it covers only 11 percent of U.S. employers (those with 50 or more employees), leaving 41 percent of all workers ineligible. The FMLA does not provide leave to members of less traditional family arrangements such as gay and lesbian couples or people in common-law marriages, and because the leave is unpaid many workers cannot afford to take the time off.

The following is a fact sheet (no. 028) issued by the Department of Labor that outlines the key provisions of the FMLA.

The U.S. Department of Labor's Employment Standards Administration, Wage and Hour Division, administers and enforces the Family and Medical Leave Act (FMLA) for all private, state and local government employees, and some federal employees. Most Federal and certain congressional employees are also covered by the law and are subject to the jurisdiction of the U.S. Office of Personnel Management or the Congress.

FMLA became effective on August 5, 1993, for most employers. If a collective bargaining agreement (CBA) was in effect on that date, FMLA became effective on the expiration date of the CBA or February 5, 1994, whichever was earlier. FMLA entitles eligible employees to take up to 12 weeks of unpaid, job-protected leave in a 12-month period for specified family and medical reasons. The employer may elect to use the calendar year, a fixed 12-month leave or fiscal year, or a 12-month period prior to or after the commencement of leave as the 12-month period.

The law contains provisions on employer coverage; employee eligibility for the law's benefits; entitlement to leave, maintenance of health benefits during leave, and job restoration after leave; notice and certification of the need for FMLA leave; and, protection for employees who request or take FMLA leave. The law also requires employers to keep certain records.

EMPLOYER COVERAGE

FMLA applies to all:

public agencies, including state, local and federal employers, local education agencies (schools), and private-sector employers who employed 50 or more employees in 20 or more workweeks in the current or preceding calendar year and who are engaged in commerce or in any industry or activity affecting commerce including joint employers and successors of covered employers.

EMPLOYEE ELIGIBILITY

To be eligible for FMLA benefits, an employee must:

(1) work for a covered employer;

(2) have worked for the employer for a total of 12 months;

(3) have worked at least 1,250 hours over the previous 12 months; and

(4) work at a location in the United States or in any territory or possession of the United States where at least 50 employees are employed by the employer within 75 miles.

LEAVE ENTITLEMENT

A covered employer must grant an eligible employee up to a total of 12 workweeks of unpaid leave during any 12-month period for one or more of the following reasons:

—for the birth and care of the newborn child of the employee;

—for placement with the employee of a son or daughter for adoption or foster care;

—to care for an immediate family member (spouse, child, or parent) with a serious health condition; or

—to take medical leave when the employee is unable to work because of a serious health condition.

Spouses employed by the same employer are jointly entitled to a combined total of 12 workweeks of family leave for the birth and care of the newborn child, for placement of a child for adoption or foster care, and to care for a parent who has a serious health condition.

Leave for birth and care, or placement for adoption or foster care must conclude within 12 months of the birth or placement.

Under some circumstances, employees may take FMLA leave intermittently—which means taking leave in blocks of time, or by reducing their normal weekly or daily work schedule.

If FMLA leave is for birth and care or placement for adoption or foster care, use of intermittent leave is subject to the employer's approval.

FMLA leave may be taken intermittently whenever medically necessary to care for a seriously ill family member, or because the employee is seriously ill and unable to work.

Also, subject to certain conditions, employees or employers may choose to use accrued paid leave (such as sick or vacation leave) to cover some or all of the FMLA leave.

The employer is responsible for designating if an employee's use of paid leave counts as FMLA leave, based on information from the employee.

"Serious health condition" means an illness, injury, impairment, or physical or mental condition that involves either:

any period of incapacity or treatment connected with inpatient care (i.e., an overnight stay) in a hospital, hospice, or residential medical-care facility, and any period of incapacity or subsequent treatment in connection with such inpatient care; or continuing treatment by a health care provider which includes any period of incapacity (i.e., inability to work, attend school or perform other regular daily activities) due to:

(1) A health condition (including treatment therefor, or recovery therefrom) lasting more than three consecutive days, and any subsequent treatment or period of incapacity relating to the same condition, that also includes:

treatment two or more times by or under the supervision of a health care provider; or

one treatment by a health care provider with a continuing regimen of treatment; or

(2) Pregnancy or prenatal care. A visit to the health care provider is not necessary for each absence; or

(3) A chronic serious health condition which continues over an extended period of time, requires periodic visits to a health care provider, and may involve occasional episodes of incapacity (e.g., asthma, diabetes). A visit to a health care provider is not necessary for each absence; or

(4) A permanent or long-term condition for which treatment may not be effective (e.g., Alzheimer's, a severe stroke, terminal cancer). Only supervision by a health care provider is required, rather than active treatment; or

(5) Any absences to receive multiple treatments for restorative surgery or for a condition which would likely result in a period of incapacity of more than three days if not treated (e.g., chemotherapy or radiation treatments for cancer).

"Health care provider" means:

doctors of medicine or osteopathy authorized to practice medicine or surgery by the state in which the doctors practice; or podiatrists, dentists, clinical psychologists, optometrists and chiropractors (limited to manual manipulation of the spine to correct a subluxation as demonstrated by X-ray to exist) authorized to practice, and performing within the scope of their practice, under state law; or nurse practitioners, nurse-midwives and clinical social workers authorized to practice, and performing within the scope of their practice, as defined under state law; or Christian Science practitioners listed with the First Church of Christ, Scientist in Boston, Massachusetts; or any health care provider recognized by the employer or the employer's group health plan benefits manager.

MAINTENANCE OF HEALTH BENEFITS

A covered employer is required to maintain group health insurance coverage for an employee on FMLA leave whenever such insurance was provided before the leave was taken and on the same terms as if the employee had continued to work. If applicable, arrangements will need to be made for employees to pay their share of health insurance premiums while on leave.

In some instances, the employer may recover premiums it paid to maintain health coverage for an employee who fails to return to work from FMLA leave.

JOB RESTORATION

Upon return from FMLA leave, an employee must be restored to the employee's original job, or to an equivalent job with equivalent pay, benefits, and other terms and conditions of employment.

In addition, an employee's use of FMLA leave cannot result in the loss of any employment benefit that the employee earned or was entitled to before using FMLA leave, nor be counted against the employee under a "no fault" attendance policy.

Under specified and limited circumstances where restoration to employment will cause substantial and grievous economic injury to its operations, an employer may refuse to reinstate certain highly paid "key" employees after using FMLA leave during which health coverage was maintained. In order to do so, the employer must:

—notify the employee of his/her status as a "key" employee in response to the employee's notice of intent to take FMLA leave;

—notify the employee as soon as the employer decides it will deny job restoration, and explain the reasons for this decision;

—offer the employee a reasonable opportunity to return to work from FMLA leave after giving this notice; and

—make a final determination as to whether reinstatement will be denied at the end of the leave period if the employee then requests restoration.

A "key" employee is a salaried "eligible" employee who is among the highest paid 10 percent of employees within 75 miles of the work site.

NOTICE AND CERTIFICATION

Employees seeking to use FMLA leave are required to provide 30-day advance notice of the need to take FMLA leave when the need is foreseeable and such notice is practicable.

Employers may also require employees to provide:

—medical certification supporting the need for leave due to a serious health condition affecting the employee or an immediate family member;

—second or third medical opinions (at the employer's expense) and periodic recertification; and

—periodic reports during FMLA leave regarding the employee's status and intent to return to work.

When intermittent leave is needed to care for an immediate family member or the employee's own illness, and is for planned medical treatment, the employee must try to schedule treatment so as not to unduly disrupt the employer's operation.

Covered employers must post a notice approved by the Secretary of Labor explaining rights and responsibilities under FMLA. An employer that willfully violates this posting requirement may be subject to a fine of up to $100 for each separate offense.

Also, covered employers must inform employees of their rights and responsibilities under FMLA, including giving specific written information on what is required of the employee and what might happen in certain circumstances, such as if the employee fails to return to work after FMLA leave.

UNLAWFUL ACTS

It is unlawful for any employer to interfere with, restrain, or deny the exercise of any right provided by FMLA. It is also unlawful for an employer to discharge or discriminate against any individual for opposing any practice, or because of involvement in any proceeding, related to FMLA.

ENFORCEMENT

The Wage and Hour Division investigates complaints. If violations cannot be satisfactorily resolved, the U.S. Department of Labor may bring action in court to compel compliance. Individuals may also bring a private civil action against an employer for violations.

OTHER PROVISIONS

Special rules apply to employees of local education agencies. Generally, these rules provide for FMLA leave to be taken in blocks of time when intermittent leave is needed or the leave is required near the end of a school term.

Salaried executive, administrative, and professional employees of covered employers who meet the Fair Labor Standards Act (FLSA) criteria for exemption from minimum wage and overtime under Regulations, 29 CFR Part 541, do not lose their FLSA-exempt status by using any unpaid FMLA leave. This special exception to the "salary basis" requirements for FLSA's exemption extends only to "eligible" employees' use of leave required by FMLA.

The FMLA does not affect any other federal or state law which prohibits discrimination, nor supersede any state or local law which provides greater family or medical leave protection. Nor does it affect an employer's obligation to provide greater leave rights under a collective bargaining agreement or employment benefit plan. The FMLA also encourages employers to provide more generous leave rights.

FURTHER INFORMATION

The final rule implementing FMLA is contained in the January 6, 1995, Federal Register. For more information, please contact the nearest office of the Wage and Hour Division, listed in most telephone directories under U.S. Government, Department of Labor.

The Personal Responsibility and Work Opportunity Reconciliation Act of 1996 (110 Stat. 2105)

President Clinton signed the Personal Responsibility and Work Opportunity Reconciliation Act (PRWORA) into law in 1996, replacing the current welfare program, Aid to Families with Dependent Children (AFDC), with Temporary Assistance to Needy Families (TANF). PRWORA's goal is to get recipients employed and off welfare as soon as possible, and the law eliminates the combined focus on education, training, and employment encompassed in the Family Support Act of 1988. PRWORA repealed the JOBS training program and greatly reduced the support services that were offered under previous welfare programs. Critics of the law feel that the goal of TANF has shifted to one of immediate employment rather than long-term self-sufficiency and poverty reduction. The law mandates that a recipient find employment once the state has determined that she is ready to work or after she has received assistance for two years, whichever is earlier. All families receiving benefits are required to work a minimum of 20 hours a week, and two-parent families are required to work at least 35 hours per week. If the family receives support for child care, the recipient's spouse must also engage in work activities for a minimum of 20 hours per week. Each state has the option to exempt a single parent with a child under the age of one year, and assistance is not denied if a single parent with a child under age six cannot work because she is unable to find child care. Lack of adequate child care has been shown to be a primary reason why women leave work and return to welfare.

Supreme Court Decisions

Muller v. State of Oregon, 208 U.S. 412, 1908

In *Muller v. State of Oregon*, the Supreme Court upheld the constitutionality of an Oregon law that prohibited the employment of women in any factory or laundry for more than 10 hours a day. In previous decisions, such as *Lochner v. New York*, the Court had ruled that the liberty to enter into a contract was more important than protective legislation limiting work hours. However in *Muller*, Louis Brandeis argued and was able to successfully convince the Court in his famous "Brandeis Brief" that women were in need of protection from overwork by the Court. The Court upheld the 10-hour workday for women, stating that because women were more fragile and had the special role of motherhood, it was in the public interest to protect women in order to "preserve the strength and vigor of the race," because healthy mothers are essential to "vigorous off-spring." *Muller v. State of Oregon* was used as a precedent to uphold protective legislation barring women from employment and other opportunities for more than six decades.

Radice v. New York, 264 U.S. 292, 1924

In *Radice v. New York,* the Supreme Court followed the precedent of *Muller v. State of Oregon* and upheld the constitutionality of a New York statute that prohibited women from being employed from 10 P.M. to 6 A.M. in restaurants in New York City and Buffalo. The Court ruled that women, who were more delicate, would not get enough sleep and that this would be injurious to them. Though the Court opted for protective legislation in decisions about employment opportunities, the Court had ruled a year earlier, in *Adkins v. Children's Hospital,* that the minimum wage law for women violated liberty of contract in the due process clause of the Fifth Amendment. The judge could see no linkage between wages and women's health or morals and therefore felt protective legislation was not needed.

Goesaert v. Cleary, 335 U.S. 464, 1948

In *Goesaert v. Cleary,* the Supreme Court upheld a Michigan law that allowed women to serve as waitresses in taverns but barred them from the better-paying positions as bartenders, except for the wives and daughters of male bar owners. Though the Court voiced some concern that male bartenders were attempting to have a monopoly on these better-paying jobs, the Court felt that there were moral and social problems with having women serve as bartenders. Presumably, bar owners would protect their own wives and daughters from overwork and issues of morality.

Rosenfeld v. Southern Pacific Co., 293 F. Supp. 1219, 1968

Weeks v. Southern Bell Telephone and Telegraph Co., 408 F2d 228, 1969

Bowe v. Colgate-Palmolive Co., 416 F2d 711, 1969

These three cases from the 1960s all held that single-sex protective laws were invalid under the 1964 Civil Rights Act, Title VII. In

Rosenfeld v. Southern Pacific Co., the Court found in favor of a female employee who had the most seniority and had been refused the opportunity to apply for a position on the grounds that she would not be able to work the hours or lift packages above 25 pounds, as was required by the job. In *Weeks v. Southern Bell*, the Court held that a company policy that disqualified women from positions that required the lifting of boxes weighing more than 35 pounds was illegal under Title VII. And, in *Bowe v. Colgate-Palmolive*, the Court told the company they could have a 35-pound weight-lifting limit but that it had to be applied to all employees, regardless of sex. In each of these cases, the decisions made clear that Title VII had permanently dismantled earlier protective legislation that had denied women access to certain jobs and in other cases provided them with benefits not available to men.

Phillips v. Martin-Marietta Corporation, 400 U.S. 542, 1971

The Supreme Court overruled the lower court's finding in *Phillips v. Martin-Marietta Corporation*. Phillips was denied a job at Martin-Marietta because she had young children. The Supreme Court ruled that the company could not have different hiring policies for men and women; for example, they could not refuse to hire mothers of small children unless they also refused to hire fathers of small children. But the Court left open the possibility that gender might be considered a bona fide occupational qualification if parenting could be shown to have a lesser impact on a man's job performance than on a woman's job performance.

County of Washington v. Gunther, 425 U.S. 161, 1981

In *County of Washington v. Gunther*, the Supreme Court confronted the issue of comparable worth for the first time. Although the decision did not explicitly favor comparable worth comparisons, it leaned in that direction. The case involved female prison guards who claimed sex discrimination under Title VII for being paid 70 percent of the amount male guards were making. The Supreme Court ruled that intentional discrimination was occurring even though the female job duties were not identical to the male job duties, opening the door for Title VII to provide a remedy for pay disparities related to sex discrimination.

California Federal Savings and Loan v. Guerra, 479 U.S. 272, 1987

The Supreme Court upheld a California law requiring leave for new mothers. Writing for the 6–3 majority, Justice Thurgood Marshall said that such legislation "promotes equal employment opportunity" because "it allows women, as well as men, to have families without losing their jobs." The case involved a receptionist that California Federal refused to rehire after she returned from pregnancy leave. Guerra represented the struggle between proponents of "special treatment" for women, who supported the decision, and those that argued that "equal treatment" for women, in the end, would better serve the goal of equal employment opportunities for men and women. This case was unusual in that it supported the idea of special treatment. Most Court cases since, as well as the Pregnancy Discrimination Act of 1978, support the notion of gender-neutral treatment of employees.

Auto Workers v. Johnson Controls, Inc., 499 U.S. 187, 1991

In a landmark case, the Supreme Court found that Title VII as amended by the Pregnancy Discrimination Act forbids sex-specific fetal protection policies. The Court found that decisions about the health and welfare of future children should be left to the parents who conceive and raise them, rather than to employers who hire these parents. Researchers have demonstrated that women have undergone sterilization in order to keep their jobs when fetal protection policies were in place (Faludi 1991).

References

Faludi, Susan. 1991. *Backlash: The Undeclared War against American Women.* New York: Crown.

6

Directory of Organizations

Many scholarly, activist, and government organizations are working on issues related to the work-family field. This chapter provides contact information and a concise overview of the activities and research being conducted by many of the larger organizations and research centers working at a national level to further the understanding of work-family issues or to push for changes in policies affecting work-family.

Administration on Children and Families
Office of Public Affairs, Suite 700
370 L'Enfant Promenade SW
Washington, DC 20447
(202) 401-9215
apublic_affair@acf.dhhs.gov
www.acf.dhhs.gov/index.htm

The Administration on Children and Families (ACF) is a federal government agency under the Department of Health and Human Services. It is responsible for federal programs that promote the economic and social well-being of children, families, and communities. The ACF oversees a large number of programs related to welfare, foster care and adoption, family preservation and support, child abuse, Head Start, child care, child support enforcement, youth, developmental disabilities, and community building.

Alfred P. Sloan Family Center on Parents,
Children and Work
1155 East 60th Street
Chicago, IL 60637

(773) 256-6315
klmdoyle@lily.src.uchicago.edu
www.spc.uchicago.edu/orgs/sloan/

Established in 1997, the Alfred P. Sloan Family Center on Parents, Children and Work draws researchers from a broad array of fields to collaborate on interdisciplinary work-family research. The center focuses on how working families spend their time and resources and how these choices affect the quality of relationships among family members. It conducts both original research and analyzes existing databases. The center's website contains links to working papers and its annual report. In addition to the Sloan Foundation, the center is supported by the University of Chicago and the National Opinion Research Center at the University of Chicago.

Alliance of Work/Life Professionals
515 King Street, Suite 420
Alexandria, VA 22314
(800) 874-9383
ksharbaugh@clarionmr.com
www.awlp.org

Founded in 1996 from the merger of the national Work Family Alliance and the Association of Work/Life Professionals, the Alliance of Work/Life Professionals is a membership organization for professionals who work in the work-life field. The alliance seeks to integrate work and family life and improve the professional standing of those employed in the work-life field. Members are provided with support, information, and opportunities for professional development, including an annual conference. The website includes a resource library, job opportunities, and a schedule of events.

Bright Horizons Family Solutions
One Kendall Square, Building 200
Cambridge, MA 02139
(617) 577-8020
Welcome@brighthorizons.com
www.brighthorizons.com

Bright Horizons Family Solutions is a national provider of worksite child care, backup care, early education, and work-life consulting services. They manage more than 300 family centers for more than 220 employers. They are also involved in supporting programs aimed at children at risk in the neighborhoods where their employees live and work. In addition to providing child care services, Bright Horizons provides consultation services to businesses who are developing work-family programs, including feasibility and needs assessments, strategic planning, outsourcing work-life management, program effectiveness audits, and community investment strategies.

Bronfenbrenner Life Course Center
G21 MVR Hall
Cornell University
Ithaca, NY 14853
(607) 255-5557
blcc@cornell.edu
www.blcc.cornell.edu/

The Bronfenbrenner Life Course Center, housed in Cornell University's College of Human Ecology, consists of three institutes: Cornell Employment and Family Careers Institute (see separate entry below), Cornell Gerontology Research Institute, and the Family Business Research Institute. These institutes conduct multidisciplinary research, educational, and outreach activities related to work and family, social networks, career pathways, self-employment and family business enterprises, retirement and productive aging, health, and housing transitions. Their website includes working papers, reports, issue briefs, events, and links to related resources.

Catalyst
120 Wall Street
New York, NY 10005
(212) 514-7600
info@catalystwomen.org
www.catalystwomen.org

Catalyst is a nonprofit organization engaged in research and advisory activities that support women's advancement in business. Catalyst works with corporations to develop strategies related to the recruitment, retention, and advancement of women. In addition, Catalyst tracks and quantifies women's leadership development and career advancement, as well as issues relating to work-family. It sponsors an award to businesses engaged in providing opportunities for women to advance and provides a speakers' bureau and publications on issues related to women and work. Catalyst's website provides links to related organizations and resources.

Center for Research on Women
Wellesley College
106 Central Street
Wellesley, MA 02481
(781) 283-2500
pbaker@wellesley.edu
www.wellesley.edu/WCW/crwsub.html

Affiliated with Wellesley College, the Center for Research on Women conducts research on women by investigating "the central questions that are shaped by the experiences and perspectives of women." Researchers come from many different disciplines, and knowledge generated by the center is used to shape public policy and promote change. Some of the ongoing projects at the center that relate to work-family issues include the Boston After School Experiences; Aging, Caregiving, and Complementary Therapies; the Early Childhood Connection; and the National Institute on Out-of-School Time.

The Center for the Childcare Workforce
733 15th Street, NW, Suite 1037
Washington, DC 20005-2112
(800) U-R-Worthy; (202) 737-7700
ccw@ccw.org
www.ccw.org

The mission of the Center for the Childcare Workforce is to improve the quality of child care by providing better pay, improved working conditions, and opportunities for professional development for child care staff. Founded in 1978, the center has been involved in research, documentation, advocacy, and training around these issues. Currently, its focus is on the Worthy Wage Network, a broad-based group of people calling for public funds to be targeted to improving child care jobs. The center's website includes information about training programs, publications, and research.

Center for the Ethnography of Everyday Life
University of Michigan
426 Thompson Street
P.O. Box 1248
Ann Arbor, MI 48106
(734) 763-1500
tomf@umich.edu
www.ethno.isr.umich.edu/

The Center for the Ethnography of Everyday Life (CEEL) uses the discipline of cultural anthropology, in addition to other social science disciplines, to study work-family issues. Funded by the Alfred P. Sloan Foundation and housed within the University of Michigan's Institute for Social Research, CEEL focuses on the changes and cultural shifts that middle-class Americans have undergone in the last few decades. CEEL's website includes information about current projects and research, working papers, and links to related sites.

Center for Work and Family
Boston College
Carroll School of Management
140 Commonwealth Avenue
Chestnut Hill, MA 02467
(617) 552-2844
lynchks@bc.edu
www.bc.edu/cwf

Part of the Carroll School of Management at Boston College, the Center for Work and Family focuses on improving the quality of life for working families by encouraging change in the workplace and the community. The center is involved in performing research, working directly with business organizations, and providing information to the community on work-family issues. In conjunction with the Alliance of Work/Life Professionals, the center has established a Work-Life Certificate Program. In addition, the center has formed the Sloan Work-Family Researchers' Electronic Network, which provides a forum for scholars to discuss work-life research as well as access to a large database of resources on work-life topics. The center is also home to the Work and Family Roundtable and the New England Work and Family Association.

Center for Work and the Family
910 Tulare Avenue
Berkeley, CA 94707
(510) 527-0107
cwfseminar@aol.com

The Center for Work and the Family assists in bridging the gap between the needs of families and the needs of employers. It provides psychological education and support services at the workplace. Its in-depth customized programs support employees in work-family challenges while at the same time communicating employee needs to their employers.

Center for Working Families
University of California, Berkeley
2420 Bowditch Street, MC 5670
Berkeley, CA 94720-5670
(510) 642-7737
info@workingfamilies.berkeley.edu
workingfamilies.berkeley.edu

Established in 1998, the Center for Working Families includes Berkeley faculty, graduate students, visiting scholars, and researchers who are doing qualitative and ethnographic research on working families and the concept of "Cultures of Care." "Cultures of Care" is defined as the care that working families receive from relatives, friends, coworkers, and pubic institutions. The center sponsors workshops, research projects, and public lectures and disseminates information through publications and consultations with business, labor, educational, and governmental groups. Its website includes publications and working papers, current events and lecture schedules, information about research projects and fellowships, and links to related sites.

Child Care Action Campaign
330 Seventh Avenue, 14th Floor
New York, NY 10001
(212) 239-0138
info@childcareaction.org
www.childcareaction.org

Initiated in 1983, the goal of the Child Care Action Campaign is to ensure that every American family is able to find quality, affordable child care. The campaign seeks to communicate innovative ideas for improving child care in order to create change and to encourage people to recognize child care as a bottom-line economic issue and a fundamental component of education. The campaign currently focuses on linking child care and school readiness by promoting language development and preliteracy skills in child care settings and encouraging private investment in quality child care.

Children's Defense Fund
25 E Street NW
Washington, DC 20001
(202) 628-8787
cdfinfo@childrensdefense.org
www.childrensdefense.org

The mission of the Children's Defense Fund (CDF) is to provide a voice for children in the United States, especially poor and minority children and those with disabilities. CDF educates policymakers and the public about the needs of children and encourages a preventive, proactive approach to issues such as family relationships, school retention, and health concerns. CDF was founded in 1973. It is a private nonprofit organization funded by corporate and foundation grants and individual donations. Its website contains reports, statistics, news releases, and a list of publications that can be ordered through the CDF.

College and University Work/Family Association
Office of Family Resources
Boston University
985 Commonwealth Avenue
Boston, MA 02215
(617) 353-5954
nsibley@bu.edu
www.cuwfa.org

The primary goal of College and University Work/Family Association (CUWFA) is to assist students at institutions of higher education in balancing their work and study responsibilities with their personal and family needs. CUWFA provides information on and support for work-family issues within the specialized environment of colleges and universities. It maintains a database of campus work-family programs, collects data on policies affecting work-family integration, disseminates information on related research trends, and initiates projects linking research to practice. Its website provides an extensive list of links to other projects and organizations focusing on work and family issues.

Cornell Employment and Family Careers Institute
G21 MVR Hall
Cornell University
Ithaca, NY 14853
(607) 255-8039
pem3@cornell.edu
www.blcc.cornell.edu/cci

The Cornell Employment and Family Careers Institute was established in 1997 with support from the Alfred P. Sloan Foundation. The mission of the institute is to provide education and conduct research and outreach that promotes an understanding of how work and family have changed and how they interact throughout the life course. The institute conducts surveys and ethnographic research to explore issues related to how couples adapt to two career paths while raising a family, how families adapt to major career and family changes, and how organizational practices affect family and work choices. The institute provides educational opportunities for graduate students as well as outreach to employers. Its website includes working papers, issue briefs, fact sheets, and reports on recent publications.

The Council on Contemporary Families
Council on Contemporary Families
208 E. 51st Street, no. 315
New York, NY 10022
(212) 969-8571
epulleybl@aol.com
www.contemporaryfamilies.org

The Council on Contemporary Families (CCF) is a nonprofit organization founded in 1996 by a group of family researchers, mental health and social work practitioners, and activists. CCF's mission is to contribute to the national conversation about what contemporary families need and how these needs can best be met. It sponsors conferences and research on family issues such as divorce, single parenthood, and working mothers to help policymakers and the public more accurately understand the changing nature of today's families and their needs. The website includes an electronic discussion list for members of CCF.

Emory Center for Myth and Ritual in American Life
Emory University
Emory West Suite 413E
1256 Briarcliff Road
Atlanta, GA 30306
(404) 727-3440
marial@learnlink.emory.edu
www.cc.emory.edu/college/MARIAL/

The Emory Center for Myth and Ritual in American Life is supported by a grant from the Alfred P. Sloan Foundation's Program on Dual-Career Working Middle-Class Families. The center focuses its research on the "functions and significance of ritual and myth in dual wage-earner middle-class families in the American South." Its goals are to promote the scholarly study of myth and ritual among working families in the South, to train the next generation of scholars who study middle-class dual-career families, to publicize research findings, and to find ways to use the results of research to promote positive social change. Detailed information about the center's current research projects is available from its website.

Families and Work Institute
330 Seventh Avenue, 14th Floor
New York, NY 10001
(212) 465-2044
afarber@familiesandwork.org
www.familiesandwork.org

Founded in 1989 by Dana Friedman and Ellen Galinsky, Families and Work Institute (FWI) is a nonprofit organization that addresses the changing nature of work and family life. FWI is involved in conducting research to inform policymaking. Every five years, it conducts a large survey of American workers, the National Study of the Changing Workforce, to investigate issues related to productivity and well-being at work and at home. The institute also provides technical assistance to corporations and communities to help improve connections between business goals and work-life needs of employees. FWI holds an annual conference on work-family issues and provides current research results and news on its website.

Family Caregiver Alliance
690 Market Street, Suite 600
San Francisco, CA 94104
(415) 434-3388
info@caregiver.org
www.caregiver.org

The Family Caregiver Alliance (FCA) was founded in 1977 as one of the first community-based nonprofit organizations in the country to address the needs of families and friends providing long-term care at home. FCA serves as an information center and a public voice for caregivers by supporting the needs of caregivers through education, research, and advocacy. Its website provides press releases, legislative updates for California and the country, informational fact sheets, an online support network for caregivers, and links to related websites and organizations.

The Fatherhood Project
Families and Work Institute
330 Seventh Avenue, 14th Floor
New York, NY 10001
(212) 465-2044
jlevine@familiesandwork.org
www.igc.org/fatherhood

The Fatherhood Project is a national research and education program concerned with developing practical ways to support the involvement of fathers in child rearing. The project develops films, books, seminars, and training around fatherhood issues. Founded in 1981 by James Levine, the project supports ongoing research into strategies for creating a workplace that assists fathers in balancing work and family needs. It is also involved in a national training initiative that helps early childhood programs get fathers to participate more in their children's lives and examines state policy in an effort to promote governmental involvement in fostering responsible fatherhood. The project's website includes many useful and practical publications as well as links to other resources related to fatherhood.

Gender, Work, and Family Project
American University Washington College of Law
4801 Massachusetts Avenue NW
Washington, DC 20016
(202) 274-4494
genderwork@wcl.american.edu
www.genderwork.org/

The Gender, Work, and Family Project focuses on the marginalization of working mothers, the majority of whom work part-time in an economy that penalizes part-time work. It has initiated a public education campaign to "explain how work-family conflict reflects gender discrimination" and is interested in forming a network of lawyers and social scientists to work toward passing legislation to change the structure of the paid workplace and the responsibilities of family members. It also supports research that focuses on reconceptualizing how work and family life are studied.

Institute for Women's Policy Research
1707 L Street NW, Suite 750
Washington, DC 20036
(202) 785-5100
iwpr@iwpr.org
www.iwpr.org

The Institute for Women's Policy Research is a nonprofit public policy research organization that focuses on issues that are important to women and their families. The institute's main areas of interest are poverty and welfare, employment and earnings, work-family, the economic and social aspects of health care and domestic violence, and women's civic and political participation. It works with scholars, public interest groups, and policymakers to conduct and disseminate research on policy issues that affect women and families and is affiliated with the graduate programs in women's studies and public policy at George Washington University. Its work-family research interests focus on paid and unpaid family leave, child care, flexible work arrangements, and changing family and work structures. It is also involved in women and employment issues such as pay equity, the wage gap, part-time and contingent work, and women in management.

Kunz Center for the Study of Work and Family
Department of Sociology

University of Cincinnati
P.O. Box 210378
Cincinnati, OH 45221-0378
(513) 556-4733
david.maume@uc.edu
ucaswww.mcm.uc.edu/sociology/kunzctr/

The Kunz Center for the Study of Work and Family is part of the Department of Sociology at the University of Cincinnati. Faculty, students, and other affiliates of the center conduct research on work and family using an interdisciplinary approach and focusing on local, national, and international issues related to work and family. Its website includes a collection of current statistics on work and family, book reviews, and a bulletin board for scholars.

Labor Project for Working Families
2521 Channing Way, no. 5555
Berkeley, CA 94720
(510) 643-7088
lpwf@home.iir.berkeley.edu
laborproject.berkeley.edu

The Labor Project for Working Families was founded in 1992 in California. It has since expanded its scope and serves as a national advocacy and policy center on family issues in the workplace. The project provides assistance and resources to unions and union members for work-family issues such as child care, eldercare, flexible work schedules, family leave, and quality-of-life issues. It publishes a newsletter on work-family topics and houses an extensive database on collective bargaining language related to work-family. It is funded by both union contributions and private foundations.

The MacArthur Foundation Research Network on Successful Pathways through Middle Childhood
Institute for Social Research
University of Michigan
426 Thompson Street
P.O. Box 1248
Ann Arbor MI 48106-1248
(734) 647-0624
dmigut@umich.edu
midchild.soe.umich.edu

The MacArthur Foundation Research Network on Successful Pathways through Middle Childhood is part of the Institute for Social Research at the University of Michigan. Established to explore ways to increase the likelihood that children in their first school years will succeed, the network focuses on children from the time they enter school until early adolescence. The network includes experts in the fields of anthropology, psychology, economics, education, history of childhood, pediatrics, sociology, and urban geography who look at school, family, community, cultural, and children's individual characteristics to determine factors that influence school success. The network plans to use its research results to design and study programs that will promote development and enhance the well-being of children and families. Its website includes information about recent projects.

Mothers and More
National Office
P.O. Box 31
Elmhurst, IL 60126
(630) 941-3553
NationalOffice@mothersandmore.org
www.mothersandmore.org

Formerly known as FEMALE, Mothers and More is an international nonprofit organization supporting mothers who have changed their career paths in order to take care of their children at home. It advocates for employment policies that accommodate flexible work options for working mothers. There are over 180 chapters and almost 8,000 members worldwide. Mothers and More also provides programming and resources that address the "other than mother" areas of women's lives while they are parents. Members are provided with a bimonthly publication focusing on work-family issues and online services such as chats, message boards, and news.

National Center on Fathers and Families
Graduate School of Education
University of Pennsylvania
3440 Market Street
Philadelphia, PA 19104
(215) 573-5500
vgadsden@gse.upenn.edu
www.ncoff.gse.upenn.edu

Established in 1994, the National Center on Fathers and Families seeks to improve the lives of children and the ability of fathers to be involved in their children's lives. The center is involved in research that is practice-focused and multidisciplinary, the goal being to increase the knowledge base on father involvement with families and contribute to policymaking in this area. Funded by the Annie E. Casey, Charles Stewart Mott, Ford, and Hewlett Foundations, the center is located within the Graduate School of Education at the University of Pennsylvania. The website contains a database of resources related to father involvement, working papers and reports, events scheduled throughout the United States, and links to relevant resources.

National Child Care Information Center
243 Church Street NW, Second Floor
Vienna, VA 22180
(800) 616-2242
info@nccic.org
nccic.org

The National Child Care Information Center (NCCIC) was created by the Child Care Bureau within the Department of Health and Human Services to promote comprehensive child care services for children. It provides information about child care to policymakers, child care organizations and providers, businesses, and parents on issues such as funding, current research, and electronic resources. It publishes the *Child Care Bulletin* and serves as a resource to states on current child care activities.

National Coalition for Campus Children's Centers
11 E. Hubbard Street, Suite 5A
Chicago, IL 60611
(800) 813-8207; (312) 431-0013
ncccc@smtp.bmai.com
ericps.crc.uiuc.edu/n4c/n4chome.html

The National Coalition for Campus Children's Centers (NCCCC) is a nonprofit educational membership organization supporting research and programs on college and university early childhood education and services, work-family issues, and the field of early childhood education in general. In addition to producing a newsletter and other publications, the coalition has a website providing links to resources related to childcare and an electronic discussion list.

The National Committee on Pay Equity
1126 Sixteenth Street NW, no. 411
Washington, DC 20036
(202) 331-7343
fairpay@aol.com
www.feminist.com/fairpay

Founded in 1979, the National Committee on Pay Equity is a national membership coalition of more than 180 organizations working to eliminate sex- and race-based wage discrimination. Its goal is to achieve pay equity. To educate the general public about inequities in pay by gender and race, the committee provides leadership, information, and assistance to pay equity advocates, public officials, employers, the media, and the public. It is supported by membership dues and donations. Fact sheets and other publications can be ordered from the website.

National Partnership for Women and Families
1875 Connecticut Avenue NW, Suite 710
Washington, DC 20009
(202) 986-2600
info@nationalpartnership.org
www.nationalpartnership.org

Founded in 1971 as the Women's Legal Defense Fund, the National Partnership for Women and Families (NPWF) is a nonprofit organization that uses public education and advocacy to help women and men meet the dual demands of work and family. NPWF works with business, government, unions, and other organizations to develop solutions to work and family issues. It is also involved in promoting fairness in the workplace and quality healthcare. This group assisted in passing the Pregnancy Discrimination Act of 1978, helped win one of the landmark cases that made sexual harassment illegal in 1977, wrote the first draft of the Family and Medical Leave Act (FMLA) in 1984, and worked with other groups to pass this important law. Currently, this group is working on expanding the coverage of the FMLA to more working people.

New Ways to Work
785 Market Street, Suite 950
San Francisco, CA 94103
(415) 995-9860
in@nww.org
www.nww.org/

New Ways to Work encourages organizations to experiment with work time options such as job sharing, work sharing, time-income trade-offs, and flextime in order to address work and family needs. It has been involved in a number of community-based pilot programs to demonstrate the value of flexible work options. One example, New Ways Workers National, a youth employment program, promotes regular part-time opportunities for high school and college students. The website includes a list of available publications and links to related resources.

Office of Workplace Initiatives
The U.S. General Services Administration
1800 F Street NW, Room 6119
Washington, DC 20405
(202) 208-3965
warren.master@gsa.gov
www.gsa.gov/pbs/owi/owi.htm

The Office of Workplace Initiatives (OWI) falls under the auspices of the U.S. General Services Administration. Its mission is to improve federal government productivity through a variety of means, including assisting the federal government in being a model family-friendly employer. OWI has been involved in setting up on-site child care centers and promoting alternative workplace arrangements such as telecommuting. Its website contains more information about its programs.

Radcliffe Public Policy Center
69 Brattle Street
Cambridge, MA 02138
(617) 496-3478
RPPC@radcliffe.harvard.edu
www.radcliffe.edu/pubpol/

The Radcliffe Public Policy Center is a research center affiliated with the Radcliffe Institute for Advanced Study at Harvard. The center brings together policymakers, scholars, labor and business-people, the media, and grassroots organizations to generate ideas to address public policy concerns. Current projects focus on work and the economy, including the restructuring of work, work-family relations, and gender equity for women and men. Recent publications have included topics such as eldercare, work and family, the Family and Medical Leave Act, and self-sufficiency for poor single mothers.

The Third Path Institute
4918 Cedar Avenue
Philadelphia, PA 19143
(215) 747-8790
info@thirdpath.org
www.thirdpath.org/index.html

The Third Path is a nonprofit, national organization that provides information about ways to redesign work to create more time for family and community life. Using workshops, trainings, books, and academic meetings, the Third Path assists individuals and groups in balancing work and family life. The website provides information about services and links to other work-family related sites.

Wider Opportunities for Women
815 15th Street NW, Suite 916
Washington, DC 20005
(202) 638-3143
info@WOWonline.org.
www.wowonline.org/contact.htm

Founded more than 30 years ago, Wider Opportunities for Women (WOW) is a women's employment organization that works to achieve economic independence and equality for women and girls. WOW focuses on providing education for women with an emphasis on literacy, technical training, and nontraditional skills training. It oversees three projects: the State Organizing Project for Family Economic Self-Sufficiency, which provides technical assistance to activists and state officials in order to implement new policies; Work4Women, which supports women's access to high-wage nontraditional occupations; and Workplace Solutions, a web-based assistance network that helps employers and unions increase the numbers of women in nontraditional jobs.

Women's Bureau
U.S. Department of Labor
200 Constitution Avenue NW
Room S-3002
Washington, DC 20210
(800) 827-5335
www.dol.gov/dol/wb/welcome.html

Established by Congress in 1920, the Women's Bureau is mandated to represent the needs of working women to policymakers. The Women's Bureau identifies issues that are important to working women, investigates ways of addressing these needs, publishes fact sheets on the status of women workers, and provides resources for addressing problems in the workplace. Currently, the bureau is involved in efforts to reach pay equity, increase access for women to high-paying nontraditional jobs, and end pay discrimination. It has been active in work-family issues such as encouraging employer-sponsored child care and the establishment of a Fair Pay Clearinghouse.

Work and Family Connection, Inc.
5197 Beachside Drive
Minnetonka, MN 55343
(800) 487-7898
Info@workfamily.com
www.workfamily.com

Work and Family Connection is a clearinghouse for news and information about work and family issues. It provides some free and some subscription-based information, including extensive links to other resources and 10 years of searchable archives filled with news and information about companies with the best practices in the area of work and family. It also provides an online encyclopedia and hosts a forum where information about work and family is exchanged.

Work and Family Research Group
Department of Management
Bennett S. LeBow College of Business
Drexel University
Philadelphia, PA 19104
(215) 895-1796
parasurs@duvm.ocs.drexel.edu
www.lebow.drexel.edu/workfamily/

The Work and Family Research Group began 12 years ago and consists of faculty and graduate students from Drexel University who are interested in issues related to work-family. The group's leaders include Jeffrey H. Greenhaus and Saroj Parasuraman, who have conducted research and published widely in the field of work-family. The group focuses its research efforts on sources of work-family conflict; entrepreneurship and work-family; social support and work-family; and race, gender, and career experiences. The website includes abstracts of recent books and articles published by members of the group.

7

Selected Print Resources

This chapter contains descriptions of recent books on work-family and related topics and a list of journals that regularly publish articles about work-family issues. The titles were selected to represent a broad range of disciplines and a diversity of methodologies and views on work-family topics.

Books

Bailyn, Lotte. 1993. *Breaking the Mold: Women, Men, and Time in the New Corporate World.* New York: Free Press. 189p. ISBN 0029012813, $25.95.

Bailyn effectively makes the case that in order to be successful, employers need to incorporate the personal needs of employees into current work strategies. The traditional system of favoring employees who dedicate themselves to work above all else is no longer a tenable model when so many women and a growing number of men are finding they are unable to meet the demands of both work and family. Using cases to illustrate successful programs, Bailyn challenges long-held assumptions about career paths, traditional management practices, and the one-size-fits-all definition of work. She questions the assumption that a career needs to be a continuous climb up the corporate ladder and instead suggests that careers can be divided into segments to allow individuals to adjust their investment in work and family life according to the varying demands of each at different points in time. She also challenges the idea that managers need to have tight control over work practices and employee time. Instead, managers need to hold employees accountable for results. Work needs to be organized around tasks and not time, and the perceived relationship between time and both productivity and work commitment needs to questioned.

Barnett, Rosalind C., and Caryl Rivers. 1998. *She Works/He Works: How Two-Income Families Are Happier, Healthier, and Better-Off.* San Francisco: HarperSanFrancisco. 272p. ISBN 067480595X, $15.95.

Based on a study of 300 dual-career couples, Barnett and Rivers challenge the idea that families benefit when one parent stays home. Their study confirms earlier research that indicates that mothers who work outside the home tend to benefit both psychologically and physically. In addition, they found that mothers who work part-time often experience more stress than mothers who work full-time. This result may occur because mothers working part-time often try to "do it all" at home, whereas mothers who work full-time are more likely to share tasks with their husbands and outsource some household duties. Mothers who work part-time are also more likely to receive less rewarding projects at work and are often passed over for promotions and raises. The authors also found that a number of men in dual-earner couples are trading high-pressure jobs for work that will allow them to spend more time with their children. The authors review the literature on child care that indicates that children do not suffer when placed in care outside the home. Barnett and Rivers point out that dual-earner families are better protected from financial problems and fear of job loss and that often these families work in a cooperative style in which everyone pitches in to keep the household running.

Blau, Francine D., and Ronald G. Ehrenberg, eds. 1997. *Gender and Family Issues in the Workplace.* New York: Russell Sage Foundation. 336p. ISBN 0871541173, $42.50.

Blau and Ehrenberg, labor economists from Cornell, have gathered together a group of economists and sociologists in this collected work that investigates what factors have impeded professional women's progress in the workplace and what can be done to promote equity. The authors highlight the role work-family issues play in terms of gender inequality in the workplace, though workplace discrimination is also brought up as a factor.

The book also focuses on family leave policies and other trends in corporate family-friendly benefits, including an investigation of the theory that these benefits serve to reinforce traditional gender roles and undermine true equality for women in the workplace.

Blossfeld, Hans-Peter, and Catherine Hakim, eds. 1997. *Between Equalization and Marginalization: Women Working Part-Time in Europe and the United States of America.* New York: Oxford University Press. 354p. ISBN 0198280866, $85.00.

This book is the product of a collaborative research effort by a group of European sociologists and economists. It includes case studies and cross-national comparisons of part-time work in the United States, Greece, Italy, France, Germany, the Netherlands, Britain, Denmark, and Sweden and an overview of part-time work in central and eastern European countries. Part-time work is defined broadly as anything from working one hour a week to working 35 hours a week. Part-time work has become increasingly common in industrialized countries, where women make up a large percentage of part-time workers, though the levels vary considerably from country to country. Variables such as women's education, family stage, child care availability, and political frameworks such as taxation are connected to women's participation in part-time work as trends are traced longitudinally. The authors challenge the feminist perspective that part-time work hinders equality for women and is often considered marginalized work.

Coltrane, Scott. 1996. *Family Man: Fatherhood, Housework, and Gender Equity.* New York: Oxford University Press. 304p. ISBN 0195082168, $30.00.

Coltrane investigates how parents come to share housework and child care and what factors contribute to fathers becoming nurturing, contributing family men rather than detached providers. In interviews with two groups of dual-income middle- and working-class couples, Coltrane was able to identify 10 variables that make sharing family responsibilities more likely. The degree to which men were able to accept and approve of their wives' employment outside the home appeared to be a key variable in how likely these men were to become involved fathers. Coltrane calls to task those who feel that men need to restore their masculinity and leave children and household duties to women. He disagrees with those who feel there are essential differences between men and women that need to be maintained, and he points out the social benefits to having nurturing fathers. Coltrane is optimistic that more fathers will become "family men," given current social trends, and that American society will move toward greater gender equity, but he also calls attention to the increasing numbers of single-parent families and the lack of support for child care, health care, and education.

Coontz, Stephanie. 1997. *The Way We Really Are: Coming to Terms with America's Changing Families.* New York: Basic Books. 224p. ISBN 0465077870, $23.00.

Coontz, a historian from Evergreen State College, disagrees with what the media has dubbed "traditional" families. The author of *The Way We Never Were*, which challenged long-held myths about the American family throughout history, argues that the "Ozzie and Harriet" family of the 1950s was a short-lived phenomenon brought about by postwar social and economic conditions that made it possible for women to stay home with their children. Current economic and social conditions, rather than an abandonment of responsibility, account for the new families that are emerging. Coontz argues that we should stop idealizing and romanticizing the "traditional" family and instead embrace the diversity of family structures that exist in the United States today. For example, being raised by a single mother is less predictive of a child's welfare than the educational background of the mother. Coontz urges us to recognize the strengths of our new, more diverse families and to engage in activities and policymaking that can support the needs of these families by investing in programs such as income support policies to assist single parents, improved day care, and paid parental leave.

Coontz, Stephanie, ed. 1999. *American Families: A Multicultural Reader.* New York: Routledge. 544p. ISBN 0415915732, $80.00.

Coontz brings together works from a diverse range of authors with the goal of demonstrating the ways different families function. Many of these chapters are excerpted from previously published books and articles. Chapters explore families from different racial or cultural backgrounds such as African American, Latino,

Native American, Vietnamese, Chinese, recent immigrant, lesbian, teenage mother, and other minority groups. Coontz does not cover middle- or upper-income families that have been widely written about and researched in the work-family literature.

Dodson, Lisa. 1998. *Don't Call Us Out of Name: The Untold Lives of Women and Girls in Poor America.* Boston: Beacon Press. 272p. ISBN 0807042080, $24.00.

Dodson, a policy fellow at the Radcliffe Public Policy Institute, uses material from four studies she conducted over the last 10 years, including an in-depth life history study with 50 women who were living in poverty. She uses this material to present a vivid picture of the diverse lives of poor women in the United States. Girls move swiftly into adulthood by taking on major household and child care responsibilities from an early age and then become mothers themselves, often in their teenage years, thinking this will be their path to independence and adulthood. The book discusses how these women manage to find creative strategies to juggle child care and work and provides illustrations of those women who have managed to make it out of poverty. Dodson also makes recommendations for changes in public policy that will increase the prospects for the millions of women and children living below the poverty line.

Drew, Eileen, Ruth Emerek, and Evelyn Mahon. 1998. *Women, Work, and the Family in Europe.* London: Routledge. 248p. ISBN 0415153514, $24.99.

This interdisciplinary collection of 19 chapters focuses on the effects of economic, political, cultural, and demographic changes in Europe on women's work and family roles. Divided into three sections, the first third of the book deals with changes in the family and in state policy that have occurred as more women enter the labor market and the demand accelerates for ways to replace the nonwage labor previously performed in the home by these women. The second section investigates part-time employment, working from home, and other flexible work arrangements and family-friendly employment policies. The third section covers the changing roles of mothers and fathers as they try to fulfill their family roles while pursuing employment opportunities. Most chapters focus on one particular European country, but the authors manage to compare parents from different racial, ethnic, and income groups while connecting their findings to the broader context of all European Union countries.

Dubeck, Paula J., and Kathryn Borman, eds. 1996. *Women and Work: A Handbook.* New York: Garland. 592p. ISBN 0824076478, $80.00.

This book presents an overview of the research on women and work in 150 articles by different authors. Included are sections covering labor force participation, different methodologies and approaches to the topic, women in diverse occupations, factors influencing career choice, legal issues relating to women and work, women's work experiences within different organizations, cross-cultural and international comparisons, and work-family issues. The work-family section includes a historical review, an overview of child care and eldercare research, and the impact of family life on women's work experiences. The authors selected articles that reflect the experiences of women from diverse racial, ethnic, and economic backgrounds.

Frankel, Judith, ed. 1997. *Families of Employed Mothers: An International Perspective.* New York: Garland. 296p. ISBN 0815317549, $52.00.

This edited volume is one of the few works that focuses on lesser-developed countries such as Nigeria, Taiwan, Mexico, and India as well as more developed countries such as the United States, Great Britain, Germany, and Israel. In each of these countries, women are entering the workforce in greater numbers than before, and this shift in roles has greatly affected the functioning of the family unit. Each chapter explores how women's employment has changed family life in a particular country, taking into account the political, social, and economic background of that country. Though each contributing author uses different methodologies to investigate the impact working women have on their families, common themes emerge despite significant differences in cultural and economic circumstances. The challenge of combining household duties with paid employment; the impact women's participation in the labor force has on marital relations, household division of labor, and child development; and the effect work has on women's physical and psychological health are explored.

Fried, Mindy. 1998. *Taking Time: Parental Leave Policy and Corporate Culture.* Philadelphia: Temple University Press. 256p. ISBN 1566396476, $16.95.

Fried spent one year as a participant observer in a large financial services company that was known for providing generous work-life benefits. She wanted to find out why, even in a company that offered liberal family-friendly benefits, employees failed to take advantage of these options. Fried discovered that corporate culture, with its emphasis and reward structure based on employee commitment and "face-time" spent at work, made employees reluctant to take advantage of policies such as parental leave that could damage long-term career opportunities. The corporation she investigated viewed parental leave requests as "taking time" away from the company rather than as "making time" for children. Management attitudes were particularly meaningful in determining whether employees under a particular supervisor were more or less likely to take leave. As a result, taking advantage of family benefits varied widely across this corporation of 27,000 employees. Gender was also a relevant factor, with very few new fathers taking formal parental leave. Instead, new fathers either used vacation time or sometimes increased the time they spent at work. Women in upper management also did not take advantage of formal parental leave policies; nonprofessional women made up the majority of those taking parental leave.

Galinsky, Ellen. 1999. *Ask the Children: What America's Children Really Think about Working Parents.* New York: William Morrow. 391p. ISBN 0688147526, $25.00.

Ellen Galinsky, the president and cofounder of the Families and Work Institute, adds children's voices to the national debate on work-family. Though many studies have shown that having a working mother does not directly harm children, the public debate about working mothers continues. Few studies have asked children how they feel about work-family issues. Galinsky surveyed more than 1,000 children from homes where both parents worked, homes where one parent stayed home and one worked, and homes where a single parent worked or stayed home. Children in grades three through 12 rated their parents in 12 areas that are strongly linked to child development and school success. Galinsky found that having a mother working outside the home was not predictive of how children rated parenting skills. What she did find was that even though the amount of time children and parents spend together is important, most children do not want *more* time with their parents. What children want is to have the time they spend with their parents be less rushed and more devoted to shared activities.

Garey, Anita I. 1999. *Weaving Work and Motherhood.* Philadelphia: Temple University Press. 240p. ISBN 1566397006, $19.95.

Garey, a sociologist at the University of New Hampshire, analyzes the results of an ethnographic study she conducted with a diverse group of 37 female hospital workers with children. She interviewed nursing directors, administrators, nurses, nurse's aides, clerical workers, and janitorial staff who worked at a large private hospital to explore how these women managed to integrate their work and mothering roles. Garey challenges assumptions that women are either "career-oriented" or "home-oriented" and suggests that many women are instead finding ways to integrate or "weave" their two identities together. She reframes the work-family equation by pointing to the work and family structures that make it difficult for women to combine both, rather than assuming there is something inherent in women that draws them toward one or the other domain.

Gerson, Kathleen. 1993. *No Man's Land: Men's Changing Commitments to Family and Work.* New York: Basic Books. 368p. ISBN 0465063160, $25.00.

Gerson, a New York University sociology professor, places her research in the context of the changing economy and the dramatic movement of women into the workforce to examine men's roles as fathers. She interviewed 138 men in their thirties and forties to discover why some men remain traditional, uninvolved breadwinner-fathers, others abandon the responsibility of fatherhood altogether, and still others become much more involved in fatherhood than men of previous generations. The striking fact is that there does not seem to be a large shift from one category, such as uninvolved breadwinner-father to the category of involved father, but rather that there are three very diverse paths that men are continuing to choose, with little change predicted for the future. Opportunity and cultural and economic changes in these men's lives seemed to be the overriding variables affecting which category of father they might wind up in, rather than values regarding masculinity or gender socialization. Gerson identifies public policies that could be implemented to support men in becoming more involved fathers and equal parents.

Googins, Bradley K. 1991. *Work/Family Conflicts: Private Lives, Public Responses.* New York: Auburn House. 328p. ISBN 0865690030, $22.50.

Googins's book provides a comprehensive overview of the field of work and family until 1990. He also provides a historical overview of the relationship between work and family in the United States from colonial times to the present. But the major focus of the book is to provide findings from some of the first large work-family surveys conducted in major corporations. Googins explores work and family conflicts within the context of family, government, and corporate responses and responsibilities. He asserts that the failure of government and corporations to respond adequately to work-family needs has resulted in families having to bear most of the burden of coping with the added stresses created by changing social demographics. Googins demonstrates why corporations would benefit from addressing work-family issues and why the government should become more involved in areas such as child care, parental leave, and health care.

Harrington, Mona. 1999. *Care and Equality: Inventing a New Family Politics.* New York: Alfred A. Knopf. 206p. ISBN 0415928222, $15.95.

Harrington, a lawyer, calls our attention to the problem of women being prevented from achieving true equality in the workplace because there is still an ingrained societal dependence, in large part, on women's presence and unpaid labor at home. Private sector options for child care and eldercare are inadequate and insufficient, and retaining high-quality caretaking staff is impossible because of low wages and lack of support and education for caretakers. This crisis in caretaking needs to be addressed by the government and employers. Harrington rephrases the issue by defining it as a problem of morals and ethics that affects all social classes. Parents want to spend more time with their families, but the current system of work does not enable parents to compete effectively in the workplace and have time for caretaking. Harrington asserts that care needs to be adopted as a national priority and that new and innovative initiatives need to be developed to support working parents and their families.

Hochschild, Arlie R. 1989. *Second Shift: Working Parents and the Revolution at Home.* New York: Viking. 260p. ISBN 0670824631, $18.95.

Hochschild, a sociologist at the University of California at Berkeley, conducted extensive interviews with 50 dual-career couples from working-class to upper-class backgrounds. She found that most men are not sharing the load with their wives in terms of child rearing, cooking, cleaning, grocery shopping, or other household duties. The result is that most wives who are working full-time come home to a "second shift" of household and child care duties. Hochschild cites studies demonstrating that women have 15 fewer hours of leisure time each week than their husbands and that over the course of a year, they work an extra month of 24-hour days. Hochschild labels this inequality in home responsibilities the "stalled revolution" and asserts that men and women are stuck in following traditional "gender strategies" that prevent progress. Though more recent studies provide evidence that at least some men are starting to increase their load at home, Hochschild found that in the couples she studied, only 20 percent split household and child rearing duties equally. She suggests that the United States adopt more profamily policies such as providing tax breaks to companies that encourage job sharing, part-time work, and flextime for both mothers and fathers.

Hochschild, Arlie R. 1997. *The Time Bind: When Work Becomes Home and Home Becomes Work.* New York: Henry Holt. 316p. ISBN 0805044701, $22.50.

Hochschild analyzes the results of a rich ethnographic study she conducted during the early 1990s at the corporate headquarters and production facility of a Fortune 500 company. Her goal was to discover why employees were not taking advantage of generous family-friendly benefits being offered by the corporation she called "Americo." She discovered that the workplace has adopted a lot of the communal characteristics of home life and that home life has become more bureaucratized and task-driven. She suggests that Americans are caught in a "time bind": the more time they spend at work, the more stressful their life at home becomes, and the more stressful their life at home becomes, the longer they stay at work. Staying at work allows Americans to avoid the unpleasantness of mounting household duties and unfulfilling caretaking responsibilities. Hochschild argues that Americans are making the wrong choices in terms of how they allocate their time and that family relationships and children are suffering as a result.

Hood, Jane E. 1993. *Men, Work, and Family.* Newbury Park, CA: Sage. 272p. ISBN 0803938918, $26.00.

The chapters in this edited volume use quantitative and qualitative sociological methodologies to explore men's experiences with combining work and family roles. Fathers from different racial, ethnic, income, and family structures are covered as the researchers focus on work-family issues such as role strain, household labor, and caregiving. Studies on men from Japan and Sweden are also included. The book calls attention to the expanded role many fathers are playing as caregivers while underlining the limitations of and lack of change in the workplace with regard to men's increasing responsibilities in the home. The book draws attention to the larger social structural influences on work and family life and suggests practical steps policymakers and business leaders might take to support men in their expanding role within the family.

Jones, Jacqueline. 1985. *Labor of Love, Labor of Sorrow: Black Women, Work and the Family from Slavery to the Present.* New York: Basic Books. 448p. ISBN 0465037569, $25.95.

Jones, a historian at Brandeis University, provides an historical survey of black women and their work in the household and in the workplace from slavery to the present time. Using a variety of historical techniques and making use of oral histories, letters, fiction, and demographic data, Jones describes and analyzes black women's experiences. She writes of the ways black women rebelled both individually, by putting their own children first while working for white families, and collectively, by becoming involved in strikes and boycotts and the larger civil rights movement. Jones highlights black women's traditional survival networks, such as the church, which provided the foundation for later civil rights actions. Because there is a dearth of work-family research that focuses on black women's experiences, Jones's book provides both historical analysis as well as some thoughts about the future for this understudied group.

Kanter, Rosabeth Moss. 1977. *Work and Family in the United States: A Critical Review and Agenda for Research and Policy.* New York: Russell Sage Foundation. 120p. ISBN 0871544334, $9.95.

Kanter, a management theorist at the Harvard Business School, opened the door for work-family researchers in 1977 when she published this now classic work. Her thesis was that there was a prevailing "myth" that work and family were separate worlds with their own functions, rules, and territories. For the most part, men were studied in the workplace, and women and family life were studied in the home. As women entered the workforce in greater numbers in the 1970s, researchers did not immediately link their research on work with their research on family life. Soon after Kanter's work was published, sociologists began to study the interconnections between these two key areas of life and how they influenced each other, and the new field of work-family was established.

Landry, Bart. 2000. *Black Working Wives: Pioneers of the American Family Revolution.* Berkeley: University of California Press. 260p. ISBN 0520218264, $24.95.

Landry, a sociologist at the University of Maryland, brings a new perspective to the work-family field by demonstrating that black middle-class women in dual-career families were the first to practice an egalitarian lifestyle that whites did not experience until many decades later. When industrialization during the nineteenth century separated the home and workplace, black women were excluded from the white middle-class model of women staying home with the family and men working outside the home. Prior to the feminist revolution, black women found the route to greater equality in the home through employment in the labor market, even if employment was not necessary for their family's economic survival. Landry uses historical records, demographic data, and biographies to demonstrate how these women set the stage for women from other races to follow suit several decades later.

Lerner, Jacqueline V. 1994. *Working Women and Their Families.* Thousand Oaks, CA: Sage. 128p. ISBN 0803942095, $42.00.

Comprehensively investigating how working mothers impact

their children's development, Lerner uses the life span developmental perspective and the developmental contextual model to support her research. Both theories assume that development is lifelong and that there are multiple determinants of development. In her research, Lerner exposes two myths about mothers: that because of their innate maternal instincts mothers are the best caretakers of their children and that stay-at-home mothers do a better job mothering than their working counterparts.

Levine, James A., and Todd L. Pittinsky. 1998. *Working Fathers: New Strategies for Balancing Work and Family.* San Diego: Harcourt Brace. 288p. ISBN 0156006030, $13.00.

Levine, the director of the Fatherhood Project at the Families and Work Institute, and Pittinsky, a professor at the Harvard Business School, combine scholarly research with practical advice on the neglected topic of fathers who are trying to balance work and family demands. Much of their research is culled from seminars and studies conducted for major corporations in the United States. The authors point to studies showing that fathers experience just as much stress as mothers do from trying to combine work and family roles. They also point to research that suggests that good fathers make better employees. They provide a laundry list of practical ways corporations can better accommodate "working fathers," a term that has yet to enter the popular lexicon.

Levine, Suzanne Braun. 2000. *Father Courage: What Happens When Men Put Family First.* New York: Harcourt. 288p. ISBN 0151003823, $24.00.

Levine, a founder of *Ms.* magazine and a former editor of the *Columbia Journalism Review,* interviewed men from diverse backgrounds about their roles as fathers. Uniformly, men spoke of wanting to be more involved parents than their own fathers had been. Levine investigates the problems men face when they try to become more involved in child rearing and family responsibilities. Men tend to have less support from the workplace, where it is rare to find a culture that supports leaving early for a soccer game or taking paternity leave. In addition, some women are unwilling to relinquish their primary parent role and hamper their husbands' efforts to play an active role in day-to-day caretaking duties. Levine views men's desire to embrace fatherhood as the unfinished business of the women's movement. Now that women have somewhat successfully entered the workplace, the time is ripe for men to become a more integrated part of family life.

Lilly, Teri Ann, Marcie Pitt-Catsouphes, and Bradley K. Googins. 1997. *Work-Family Research: An Annotated Bibliography.* Westport, CT: Greenwood Press. 336p. ISBN 0313303223, $78.75.

Compiled by researchers at the Center for Work and Family at Boston College, this book provides a comprehensive annotated bibliography of the research literature on work-family. The authors divide the field into nine sections, including women and work, work-family issues as structural and developmental concepts, work and family roles, work-family experiences among different population groups, dependent care, work-family and human resources departments, flexible and part-time work, workplace policies, and linkages to corporate strategies. The bibliography is now available and kept up to date online at the center's website: www.bc.edu/bc_org/avp/csom/cwf/.

Mintz, Steven, and Susan Kellogg. 1988. *Domestic Revolutions: A Social History of American Family Life.* New York: Free Press. 400p. ISBN 0029212901, $27.95.

Mintz, a historian, and Kellogg, an anthropologist, have written a comprehensive survey of the research on the history of the American family from colonial times to the present. The authors provide a general account of family life in the United States while attending to the diversity of family experiences by providing an extensive review of the research on African-American and Native American family life. Working-class families during industrialization are also covered in detail. Mintz and Kellogg argue that American families have undergone a series of "domestic revolutions" that have profoundly influenced their structure and characteristics. Changes in family size, women's roles, attitudes toward love and marriage, shifting views of childhood, and changes in the social and economic functions of the family are explored.

Moen, Phyllis. 1992. *Women's Two Roles: A Contemporary Dilemma.* Westport, CT: Greenwood. 192p. ISBN 0865691983, $59.95.

Moen's research was inspired by Alva Myrdal and Viola Klein's classic study, *Women's Two Roles: Home and Work,* which suggested that women leave the labor force to raise their young children and resume work when their children enter school. Moen sees women today as having more options. She advocates making work more flexible for parents with young children so that they can work reduced hours without losing their seniority. Drawing together a large amount of research on women's home and work roles, Moen argues for restructuring work and rethinking how society sequences education, work, and retirement so that men and women might have more time at home when their children are young. She ultimately views work and family decisions as having no single solution and reviews research literature that supports the idea that a mother's *attitude* about being employed may have more influence on her child's development than whether or not she works outside the home.

Neal, Margaret B., Nancy J. Chapman, Berit Ingersoll-Dayton, and Arthur C. Emlen. 1993. *Balancing Work and Caregiving for Children, Adults and Elders.* Newbury Park, CA: Sage. 292p. ISBN 0803942818, $49.95.

This collection provides a thorough overview of the research on caregiving within the work-family context, as well as an analysis of a large empirical study of 10,000 employees. The authors, approaching the issue from different disciplines, examine the characteristics, demands, resources, and sources of stress for each category of caregiver. They view dependent care as a family, community, and corporate concern, and they provide a detailed analysis of the research on the impact of family caregiving on work responsibilities. Drawing strong connections between caregiving demands and employee absenteeism and stress, the authors call for corporations and the government to implement policies and programs to support individuals who are both employed and are providing caregiving to one or more family members. In addition, they present a number of policy recommendations that would provide more support for dependent care providers.

Nippert-Eng, Christena E. 1996. *Home and Work: Negotiating Boundaries through Everyday Life.* Chicago: University of Chicago Press. 304p. ISBN 0226581462, $16.95.

Using a qualitative methodology, Nippert-Eng explores the cultural and structural constraints that influence boundary setting between work and home. Interviewing machinists, personnel administrators, and scientists working in a research laboratory, she identified a continuum of types ranging from those who completely segmented their work and home life to those that greatly integrated the two domains. She found that segmentors, who were more likely to be machinists, alternated between two distinct "selves" depending on whether they were at work or at home. Integrators, who were more likely to be scientists and professionals, made little distinction between work and home in terms of social contacts and friends, physical items such as calendars and clothing, the time and place of work activities, and alcohol and coffee consumption. Nippert-Eng also found that where one fell on the continuum of segmentation and integration was not entirely a matter of choice. Pressure from family members or from colleagues and supervisors greatly influenced boundary-setting behavior. Nippert-Eng suggests there are negatives associated with either approach. Segmentors have less discretion at work and find it difficult to make the transition between work and home, whereas integrators suffer from long, unpredictable work hours and work-based interruptions at home.

Parasuraman, Saroj, and Jeffrey H. Greenhaus, eds. 1997. *Integrating Work and Family: Challenges and Choices for a Changing World.* Westport, CT: Quorum. 272p. ISBN 1567200389, $65.00.

This collection brings together work from a variety of disciplines, including human resources, law, management, work-family, psychology, and business. Many of the chapters are revised versions of presentations Parasuraman and Greenhaus gave at the College of Business and Administration at Drexel University in 1994. One of the themes of the book is the focus on work-family integration rather than the notion of balance or conflict. The authors also assert that though corporations are more actively pursuing work-family and work-life policies, the workplace cannot be solely responsible for addressing work-family issues. The government, communities, individuals, as well as the employer must all work together to find solutions. This book presents a comprehensive overview of the field of work-family and also highlights key trends such as implementing effective work-life initiatives and the transition from work-family as a "women and daycare" issue to a larger focus on the successful integration of work and life for all employees. Employment law such as the Family and Medical Leave Act, international comparisons, and the evolution of work-family programs are some of the topics covered in this extensive collection that combines frontline reporting with scholarly research.

Parcel, Toby L., and Elizabeth G. Menaghan. 1994. *Parents' Jobs and Children's Lives.* New York: Aldine de Gruyter. 228p. ISBN 0202304833, $43.95.

Parcel and Menaghan move beyond the traditional question about whether mothers' employment negatively affects children and instead focus on the more complex relationships between mothers' *and* fathers' employment conditions and what impact their work may have on their children's lives. Using an interdisciplinary framework, the authors use data from the National Longitudinal Surveys on Youth to assess the relationship between factors such as home environment, family composition, and working conditions of both parents on cognitive and behavioral child outcome measures over time. The authors found that parental characteristics such as self-concept and educational background and family conditions such as size and income level interact to buffer or exacerbate the positive or negative influences of work. Parcel and Menaghan assert that parents' employment influences children's social and developmental outcomes because work conditions affect economic, psychological, and social aspects of the home environment. For example, children whose mothers have jobs high in occupational complexity experience better home environments than children whose mothers' jobs are more routine.

Pitt-Catsouphes, Marcie, and Bradley K. Googins, eds. 1999. **"The Evolving World of Work and Family: New Stakeholders, New Voices."** In *The Annals of the American Academy of Political and Social Science.* Thousand Oaks, CA: Sage. 239p. ISSN 0002-7162.

This volume provides a collection of articles written by many of the key players in the work-family field today. The book focuses on the future of work-family and of research on that subject. The goal is to expand and renew the field by incorporating more diverse theoretical models and embracing new assumptions about work-family and the roles of various stakeholders. The first section is on diverse family structures such as families headed by gays and lesbians, single-parent households, and households that consist of single adults without children. The second section focuses on the changing nature and characteristics of the family in relation to changes in work status such as retirement or job loss. The third section looks at work-family issues at smaller workplaces and nonprofit organizations. The final sections look at transformations within organizations and linking work-family issues to policy change.

Robinson, John P., and Geoffrey Godbey. 1999. *Time for Life: The Surprising Ways Americans Use Their Time.* 2nd ed. University Park: Pennsylvania State University Press. 564p. ISBN 0271019700, $20.00.

Robinson and Godbey use time surveys taken in 1965, 1975, and 1985 from thousands of participants to determine how much time Americans are spending working, attending to family and household responsibilities, taking care of their own personal needs, and performing leisure activities. One of their goals was to determine if Americans were spending more time at work and if there was a significant gender difference in how time was spent. The book provides a comprehensive picture of how Americans use their time, using other research findings to support the authors' conclusions. Their results counter prevailing assumptions, finding that American are spending less time at work than in previous decades and that men's and women's time does not differ to a large degree. Men generally are doing more housework, and women who work outside the home are doing less housework than they were in previous decades. Men and women have more free time but tend to spend their free time watching more television than in past years. Women with small children, not surprisingly, still have less time than all other groups.

Schor, Juliet B. 1992. *The Overworked American: The Unexpected Decline of Leisure.* New York: Basic Books. 336p. ISBN 0465054331, $21.00.

Schor draws on historical materials, statistical evidence, and other sources to put forward the thesis that Americans are overworked both on the job and at home. Workers are putting in longer hours at work every week, and technology has not allowed us to spend less time on housework but instead raised expectations about what should be accomplished. Schor points out that many people now have second jobs, put in more over-time, and take less vacation time. She calls attention to the capi-talist underpinnings of these trends—employers save money on benefits and other costs by paying fewer workers to work longer hours, while other people remain underemployed or unem-ployed. Though some researchers have questioned Schor's analysis, most agree that the issues she raises are important. Schor renews interest in the fight for a shorter workweek and also calls attention to what she calls the "consumerist treadmill," a never-ending cycle that results in workers spending more hours working overtime in order to acquire more possessions. Schor also demonstrates how women in particular have suffered from overwork because they have taken on greater roles in the labor market while still being the primary person responsible for children and housework.

Snarey, John. 1993. *How Fathers Care for the Next Generation: A Four-Decade Study.* Cambridge, MA: Harvard University. 415p. ISBN 067440940X, $37.50.

Snarey, a developmental psychologist, grounds his work in Erik Erikson's concept of generativity—caring for the next generation. Drawing on a four-generation, four-decade-long study tracing parenting and family variables, Snarey provides evidence of how the experience of fatherhood can influence a father's own per-sonal growth as well as the development of his children. Snarey employs both quantitative and qualitative measures to explore connections between the involvement fathers had in their chil-dren's early lives and later educational and occupational mobili-ty. Snarey's study provides evidence that fathers play an impor-tant role in the emotional, intellectual, and physical development of children and that the experience of being a father contributed to healthier psychological development for men in midlife.

Spain, Daphne, and Suzanne M. Bianchi. 1996. *Balancing Act: Motherhood, Marriage, and Employment among American Women.* New York: Russell Sage Foundation. 240p. ISBN 0871548151, $16.95.

Balancing Act uses demographic data from the decennial census and other federal statistics and public opinion data to trace changes in marriage, family structure, and employment for women since 1950. The authors are especially adept at analyzing how work and family changes occur over successive cohorts by breaking apart data, for example, on traits of older women in the workforce versus women just entering the workforce when looking at salaries, types of careers, and other variables. The authors also address racial and ethnic differences for these topics and provide data for some international comparisons. In addition to providing a comprehensive collection of statistics on women, Spain and Bianchi also offer some theoretical perspectives to explain some of the more dramatic changes that have occurred in women's lives.

Strober, Myra H., and Agnes M. K. Chan. 1999. *The Road Winds Uphill All the Way: Gender, Work and Family in the United States and Japan.* Cambridge, MA: MIT Press. 276p. ISBN 0262194155, $35.00.

Strober and Chan surveyed Stanford University and Tokyo University graduating classes of 1981 a decade after their graduation to investigate the economic position of high-achieving women in both countries. They found striking similarities between the two countries, and their study focuses on the difficulties these women experienced in combining family and high-level management or professional work. The gender gap in pay was significant in both countries (0.79 ratio of women's earnings to men for Japan and 0.80 ratio for the United States), and men and women both expected the gender gap to widen during their careers. Both sets of women spent much more time participating in household duties and child rearing than their husbands, though Japanese women experienced more difficulty finding child care, and in the United States the more a woman earned, the more her partner shared household responsibilities. The authors conclude with recommendations for helping women successfully combine work and family roles.

Swiss, Deborah J., and Judith P. Walker. 1993. *Women and the Work-Family Dilemma: How Today's Professional Women Are Finding Solutions.* New York: John Wiley and Sons. 253p. ISBN 0471533181, $24.95.

Swiss and Walker surveyed 902 women who had graduated from professional programs in medicine, law, and business at Harvard University. All the women were middle-aged, had achieved a certain status in their respective field, and were trying to balance family needs with their work responsibilities. Swiss and Walker's qualitative study found that successful college-educated women today must deal with both a "glass ceiling," being denied a promotion on the basis of gender, as well as a "maternal wall." They define the maternal wall as a powerful invisible barrier that prevents women from being able to compete successfully in the workplace while trying to fulfill family responsibilities. The women in their study assumed they would "have it all" but soon learned that combining child rearing with a professional career usually meant sacrifices on both sides. Using many anecdotes from their surveys, the authors illustrate the challenges these professional women faced. They also outline some alternative strategies for women such as part-time careers, entrepreneurial work, ways to change corporate attitudes, and new measures of employee performance focused less on overtime and more on performance.

Williams, Joan. 2000. *Unbending Gender: Why Family and Work Conflict and What to Do about It.* Oxford: Oxford University Press. 352p. ISBN 0195094646, $30.00.

Williams, a codirector of the American University Law School's project on gender, work, and family, explores the dilemma of women straddling the worlds of work and family while feeling unfulfilled in both areas. Williams demonstrates that gender bias continues to be common, and strong ideas about who should do what kind of work contribute to both the wage gap and the ability of women to feel satisfied with work and home life. In her book, she suggests that if Americans can work to overcome bias and support innovative work policies such as flexible work time, people can be more productive and fulfilled at work and still have time for family responsibilities. Williams suggests that society needs to acknowledge that family roles are a common part of most employees' lives and that it is time for the workplace to better accommodate working parents.

Journals

The following is a list of journals that frequently cover work-family research topics.

American Psychologist
American Psychological Association
750 1st Street NE

Washington, DC 20002-4242
Phone: (202) 336-5500; (800) 374-2721
Fax: (202) 336-5568
webmaster@apa.org

The monthly journal of the American Psychological Association, *American Psychologist* publishes empirical and theoretical articles.

American Sociological Review
Pennsylvania State University Department of Sociology
206 Oswald Tower
University Park, PA 16802
Phone: (814) 863-3733
Fax: (814) 863-3734
asr@pop.psu.edu

This bimonthly sociology journal covers broad sociological research topics.

Community, Work, and Family
Carfax Publishing Limited
P.O. Box 25
Abingdon, Oxon, OX14 3UE
England
Phone: 44-1235-401000
Fax: 44-1235-401550
enquiries@carfax.co.uk
www.carfax.co.uk

Issued three times a year, this journal covers theory, research, policy, and practice relating to the links between community, work, and family.

Families in Society
Manticore Publishers
11700 W. Lake Park Drive
Milwaukee, WI 53224
Phone: (414) 359-1040
Toll-free: (800) 221-3726
fis@fsanet.org

Families in Society is a bimonthly refereed journal for human service professionals.

Family Relations
National Council on Family Relations
Wayne State University
87 E. Ferry Street
Detroit, MI 48202
Phone: (313) 873-5032; (888) 781-9331
Fax: (313) 871-9383
ncfr3989@ncfr.com
www.iog.wayne.edu/fr

Family Relations is a quarterly interdisciplinary journal of applied family studies.

Gender, Work, and Organisation
Blackwell Publishers Ltd.
108 Cowley Road
Oxford OX4 1JF
England
Phone: 44-1865-791100
Fax: 44-1865-791347
jnlinfo@blackwellpublishers.co.uk
www.blackwellpublishers.co.uk

This quarterly journal publishes theory, research, and applications of gender studies at work.

Gerontologist
Gerontological Society of America
1030 15th Street NW, Suite 250
Washington, DC 20005-1503
Phone: (202) 842-1275
Fax: (202) 842-1150
geron@geron.org
gerontologist@maxwell.syr.edu

This bimonthly, multidisciplinary, peer-reviewed journal presents clinical ideas and applied research in gerontology.

Industrial and Labor Relations Review
Cornell University
201 ILR Research Building
Ithaca, NY 14853-3901

Phone: (607) 255-3295
Fax: (607) 255-8016

Industrial and Labor Relations Review is a quarterly interdisciplinary scholarly journal providing information on industrial and labor relations.

Journal of Family and Economic Issues
Kluwer Academic-Plenum Publishers
Human Sciences Press
233 Spring Street
New York, NY 10013
Phone: (212) 620-8000
Fax: (212) 463-0742
info@plenum.com
http:www.plenum.com

This quarterly journal covers family consumer behavior, household division of labor, and the interrelationship between work and family life.

Journal of Family History
Sage Publications
2455 Teller Road
Thousand Oaks, CA 91320
Phone: (805) 499-0721
Fax (805) 499-9871
libraries@sagepub.com
www.sagepub.com

Journal of Family History is a quarterly focusing on historically based studies on families, kinship, and demography.

Journal of Family Issues
Sage Publications
2455 Teller Road
Thousand Oaks, CA 91320
Phone: (805) 499-0721
Fax: (805) 499-0871
info@sagepub.com

Journal of Family Issues is a bimonthly family studies journal.

Journal of Marriage and the Family
National Council on Family Relations
30 Merrill Hall
University of Maine
Orono, ME 04469
Phone: (207) 581-3103
Fax: (207) 581-3120
nctr3989@ncfr.com

This quarterly journal publishes original research and theory, research interpretations, and critical discussions related to marriage and the family.

Journal of Organizational Behavior
John Wiley and Sons
605 3rd Avenue
New York, NY 10158
Phone: (212) 850-6000
Fax: (212) 850-6049
subinfo@wiley.com

Published seven times a year, this scholarly journal covers recent research and topics on occupational behavior.

Journal of Women and Aging
Haworth Press
P.O. Box 830
Key West, FL 33041-0830
Phone: (305) 744-9913
Fax: (305) 744-9835
getinfo@haworthpressinc.com

Journal of Women and Aging is a quarterly journal aimed at professionals concerned with the health and well-being of older women.

Marriage and Family Review Journal
Haworth Press
10 Alice Street
Binghamton, NY 13904-1580
Toll-free: (800)-HAWORTH
getinfo@haworthpressinc.com

This is a quarterly journal for marriage and family specialists and researchers.

Organizational Dynamics
American Management Association
1601 Broadway
New York, NY 10019-7420
Phone: (212) 586-8100
Fax: (212) 903-8083
cust-serv@amanet.org

This quarterly magazine on organizational behavior is aimed at management executives.

Personnel Psychology
Personnel Psychology
745 Haskins Road, Suite D
Bowling Green, OH 43402
Phone: (419) 352-1562
Fax: (419) 352-2645
www.personnelpsychology.com

This quarterly journal features research on industrial psychology, employees, and the workplace.

Sex Roles
Plenum Publishing
Graduate School
City University of New York
33 W. 42nd Street
New York, NY 10036
Phone: (212) 642-2514
Fax: (212) 642-1987
sexroles@email.gc.cuny.edu

This monthly journal contains empirical research on sex roles.

Social Forces
University of North Carolina Press
IRSS
Manning Hall
University of North Carolina
Chapel Hill, NC 27599

Phone: (800) 848-6224
uncpress.unc.edu

Social Forces is a quarterly journal covering sociological research and theory.

Social Problems
University of California Press/Journals
2120 Berkeley Way
Berkeley, CA 94720-0001
Phone: (510) 643-7154
Fax: (510) 642-9917
journal@ucop.edu
journal@garnet.berkeley.edu
www.ucpress.edu/journals/sp/

This quarterly sociology journal addresses social issues.

Social Work
National Association of Social Workers
750 1st Street NE, Suite 700
Washington, DC 20002-4241
Phone: (202) 408-8600
Fax: (202) 336-8312
press@naswda.org

Social Work is the bimonthly journal of the National Association of Social Workers.

Sociological Forum
Plenum Publishing
233 Spring Street
New York, NY 10013-1578
Phone: (212) 620-8000
Fax: (212) 463-0742
info@plenum.com

This quarterly journal covers all areas of sociology.

Work and Occupations
Sage Publications
2455 Teller Road
Thousand Oaks, CA 91320
Phone: (805) 499-0721

Fax: (805) 499-0871
info@sagepub.com

This quarterly sociology journal publishes articles on work, occupations, employment, and labor relations.

Work and Stress
Taylor and Francis
325 Chestnut Street
Philadelphia, PA 19106
Phone: (215) 625-8900
Toll-free: (800) 821-8312
Fax: (215) 625-2940
info@taylorandfrancis.com

Work and Stress is a quarterly journal on employment, stress, health, and safety.

8

Selected Nonprint Resources

This chapter provides descriptions of videos that focus on work-family issues and websites of organizations involved in work-family research and activism.

Videos

A Balancing Act: Family and Work in the '90s
Date: 1993
Length: 25 minutes
Cost: $225.00
Source: Lucerne Media
           37 Ground Pine Road
           Morris Plains, NJ 07950
Phone: (201) 538-1401
Fax: (201) 538-0855

This video investigates new alternatives, such as flextime and job sharing, for people balancing career and family.

Balancing Home and Career
Length: 25 minutes
Date: 1991
Cost: $495.00
Source: Excellence in Training Corporation
           11358 Aurora Ave.
           Des Moines, IA 50322
Phone: (515) 276-6569
Fax: (515) 276-9476

A training program is provided in this video that demonstrates how various people handle the issue of combining family and work.

Careers for the Twenty-first Century:
Women in Non-Traditional Roles
Length: Five programs with varying run times
Date: 1992
Cost: $495.00
Source: Takeoff Multimedia
6611 Clayton Road
St. Louis, MO 63144
Phone: (314) 863-0700
Fax: (314) 863-1612

Women from twenty-two nontraditional professions discuss their careers.

A Century of Women: Work and Family
Length: 95 minutes
Date: 1994
Cost: $17.99 (from Amazon.com)
Source: Turner Home Entertainment Company
P.O. Box 105366
Atlanta, GA 35366
Phone: (404) 827-3066
Fax: (404) 827-3266

This is the first in a series of three videos documenting the history of women in the twentieth century. Jane Fonda narrates this video on work-family issues. The other two videos in the series cover "Sexuality and Social Justice" and "Image and Popular Culture."

Cherry v. Coudert Brothers: The Mommy Track
Length: 50 minutes
Date: 1998
Cost: $34.95
Source: Courtroom Television Network (Court TV)
600 Third Avenue
New York, NY 10016
Phone: (800) 888-4580

This documentary covers the trial of *Cherry versus Coudert Brothers,*

...vho sued for being fired after

...kers Library
...E. 40th Street
...New York, NY 10016
...e: (212) 808-4980
...ax: (212) 808-4983

This video illustrates the love-hate relationship women have with the task of cleaning the family's clothes.

Daddy's Girls

Length: 25 minutes
Date: 1994
Cost: $195.00
Source: Filmmakers Library
124 E. 40th Street
New York, NY 10016
Phone: (212) 808-4980
Fax: (212) 808-4983

This film explores the lives of several women whose relationships to their fathers have been pivotal in their lives. It discusses the roles fathers play in their daughter's lives.

Day Care Dilemma

Length: 45 minutes
Date: 1991
Cost: $19.95
Source: Cambridge Educational
P.O. Box 2153
Charleston, WV 25328
Phone: (304) 744-9323
Fax: (304) 744-9351

In discussing the issues parents should consider when choosing a day care arrangement, the film considers location, safety, type of setting, and standards.

Day Care Grows Up
Length: 55 minutes
Date: 1991
Cost: $159.00
Source: Films for the Humanities and Sciences
P.O. Box 2053
Princeton, NJ 08543
Phone: (609) 275-1400
Fax: (609) 275-3767

This video explores the new measures being taken to increase the quality of child care in the United States.

Did I Say Hairdressing? I Meant Astrophysics
Length: 15 minutes
Date: 1998
Cost: $150.00
Source: Filmmakers Library
124 E. 40th Street
New York, NY 10016
Phone: (212) 808-4980
Fax: (212) 808-4983

This is an animated video that demonstrates why women are underrepresented in science, engineering, and technology. The film encourages young women to consider training in these fields.

The Double Burden: Three Generations of Working Mothers
Length: 57 minutes
Date: 1992
Cost: $250.00
Source: New Day Films Library
22D Hollywood Avenue
Hohokus, NJ 07423
Phone: (201) 652-6590
Fax: (201) 652-1973

In this documentary, interviews are conducted with members of three diverse families in which the grandmother, mother, and daughter all hold jobs to support the family. Historical footage is also shown.

The Double Shift
Length: 47 minutes
Date: 1997
Cost: $149.00
Source: Films for the Humanities and Sciences
P.O. Box 2053
Princeton, NJ 08543
Phone: (609) 275-1400
Fax: (609) 275-3767

Susan Sarandon narrates this documentary on equality for employed women around the world. The video focuses on opportunity, pay, career and family, value placed on traditional activities, exploitation, self-employed women, and househusbands.

Economic Equity: Realities, Responsibilities, and Rewards.
Length: 120 minutes
Date: 1997
Cost: unavailable
Source: Women's Bureau
United States Department of Labor
200 Constitution Avenue NW, S3311
Washington, DC 20210
Phone: (800) 827-5335

A video of the national working women's summit hosted by the Women's Bureau in 1997 on equal pay for equal work by women, "Economic Equity" includes introductory remarks by Vice President Albert Gore, Labor Secretary Alexis M. Herman, and Women's Bureau director-designate Ida L. Castro.

Families in the Balance
Length: 23 minutes
Date: 1989
Cost: $49.00
Source: Cornell University
Audio Visual Resource Center
8 Business and Technology Park
Ithaca, NY 14850
Phone: (607) 255-2091
Fax: (607) 255-9946

This video explores the daily lives of four American families as they try to balance work and family and includes interviews with child development experts and policymakers.

Fatherhood U.S.A.: Dedicated Not Deadbeat and Juggling Family and Work
Length: 56 minutes
Date: 1998
Cost: $57.90
Source: Families and Work Institute
330 Seventh Avenue, 14th Floor
New York, NY 10001
Phone: (212) 465-2044
Fax: (212) 465-8637

A two-part PBS documentary hosted by former U.S. senator Bill Bradley, the video looks at fathers actively involved in child-rearing activities and balancing work and family responsibilities.

The Glass Ceiling
Length: 30 minutes
Date: 1997
Cost: rental: $10.00 (must be member)
Source: The Society of Women Engineers
120 Wall Street, 11th Floor
New York, NY 10005-3902
Phone: (212) 509-9577

This is a videotape of an in-service program designed to facilitate discussion about gender discrimination against women engineers.

Hard Hats
Length: 15 minutes
Date: 1998
Cost: $29.95
Source: CBS Video
60 Minutes
524 West 57th Street
New York, NY 10019
Phone: (800) 848-3256

The video explores the lives of women who work in the construction industry and discusses why they became construction workers and the obstacles they face at work. It was originally aired on *60 Minutes* on 27 September 1998.

Living with Elderly Parents
Length: information not available
Date: 1990
Cost: $45.00
Source: Meridian Education Corporation
Library Filmstrip Center
236 E. Front Street
Bloomington, IL 61701
Phone: (309) 827-5455
Fax: (309) 829-8521

Using interviews with both adult children and their elderly parents, this video looks at people who are "parenting their parent."

Not Just a Job: Career Planning for Women
Length: 35 minutes
Date: 1991
Cost: $250.00
Source: Cambridge Documentary Films
P.O. Box 385
Cambridge, MA 02138
Phone: (617) 354-3677
Fax: (617) 492-7653

In this video, eight women from diverse backgrounds discuss their interests and skills in a career development workshop.

Parenting on One Income
Length: 28 minutes
Date: 1999
Cost: $24.95
Source: KTCA-TV (Television station: Saint Paul, MN)
PBS Adult Learning Satellite
Right on the Money
P.O. Box 55742
Indianapolis, IN 46205
Phone: (888) MONEY79

From the series *Right on the Money,* hosted by Chris Farrell, this video profiles a couple who is exploring the option of living on one income and also provides tips from a stay-at-home father.

**Parents with Careers: Practical Ways to
Balance Career and Family**
Length: 32 minutes
Date: 1990
Cost: $149.00
Source: Cambridge Educational
P.O. Box 2153
Charleston, WV 25328
Phone: (304) 744-9323
Fax: (304) 744-9351

This video teaches coping techniques to two-career families who are trying to effectively balance their home life and careers.

Taking on the Boy's Club: Women in the Workplace
Length: 36 minutes
Date: 1998
Cost: $89.95
Source: Films for the Humanities and Sciences
P.O. Box 2053
Princeton, NJ 08543
Phone: (609) 275-1400
Fax: (609) 275-3767

Part 1 is a segment from the television program *20/20* about sexism in the workplace and was originally broadcast in 1992. Part 2, filmed by ABC News, covers sexual harassment in the U.S. military and other organizations.

There's No Such Thing as Women's Work
Length: 30 minutes
Date: 1987
Cost: $39.95
Source: National Women's History Project
7738 Bell Road
Windsor, CA 95492
Phone: (707) 838-6000
Fax: (707) 838-0478

Newsreels, photographs, and cartoons show women's changing influence on the workforce in the United States.

Through the Glass Ceiling
Length: 17 minutes
Date: 1996
Cost: $195.00
Source: Filmmakers Library
124 E. 40th Street
New York, NY 10016
Phone: (212) 808-4980
Fax: (212) 808-4983

This animated video uses humor to discuss women's equality issues in the workplace.

When Mom Has to Work
Length: 23 minutes
Date: 1988
Cost: $295.00
Source: Professional Research
1560 Sherman Street, Suite 100
Evanston, IL 60201
Phone: (708) 328-6700
Fax: (708) 328-6706

This video discusses why women have to work and asserts that women should be able to have a family and a job without feeling guilty.

Women and the American Family
Length: 28 minutes
Date: 1987
Cost: $29.95
Source: Video Knowledge
29 Bramble Lane
Melville, NY 11747
Phone: (516) 367-4250
Fax: (516) 367-1006

The role of women in the family, both historically and in the future, is reviewed.

Women's Work
Length: 30 minutes
Date: 1991
Cost: $39.95
Source: Great Plains National
1800 N. 33rd Street
P.O. Box 80669
Lincoln, NE 68583
Phone: (402) 472-2007
Fax: (402) 472-4076

Women employed in technical careers discuss the challenges they have had to overcome.

Work and Family Stress: A Question of Balance
Length: 60 minutes
Date: 1986
Cost: $400.00
Source: University of Southern Maine
3 Baily Hall
Gorham, ME 04038
Phone: (207) 780-4200
Fax: (207) 780-5621

Using dramatization and a panel discussion, this video looks at issues that affect parents who are trying to balance work and family life.

Working Solutions: Work vs. the Family
Length: 30 minutes
Date: 1993
Cost: $100.00
Source: PBS Video
1320 Braddock Place
Alexandria, VA 22314
Phone: (800) 344-3337

This video is one of a four-part series on work. It focuses on the problems faced by working parents in finding good daycare and balancing work-family demands and provides examples of model family-friendly corporate programs.

Working with Care
Length: 14 minutes
Date: 1998
Cost: $150.00
Source: Filmmakers Library
124 E. 40th Street
New York, NY 10016
Phone: (212) 808-4980
Fax: (212) 808-4983

This is an animated video that suggests if an employer assists with the family needs of an employee, it's an investment that will pay off.

Web Resources

This selective list of websites provides access to the most useful and comprehensive information about work-family issues on the Internet. Many of these sites provide extensive annotated links to other work-family sites on the web.

Alliance of Work/Life Professionals
www.awlp.org

This website includes a resource library, job opportunities, and upcoming events and conferences.

Center for Working Families
workingfamilies.berkeley.edu

This site offers publications and working papers, current events and lectures, information about research projects and fellowships, and links to related sites.

College and University Work/Family Association
www.cuwfa.org

This website provides an extensive list of links to other work-family related projects and organizations.

ElderWeb
www.elderweb.com

A comprehensive resource for professionals and family members looking for information on eldercare issues and services, this site includes thousands of reviewed links related to eldercare services, finances, housing, and health, as well as information on policy, research, and statistics.

Family Caregiver Alliance
www.caregiver.org

In addition to press releases, legislative updates for California and the country, and informational fact sheets, this site features an online support network for caregivers and links to related websites and organizations.

National Center on Fathers and Families
www.ncoff.gse.upenn.edu

This website contains a database of resources related to fathers' involvement with their children, working papers and reports, events scheduled throughout the United States, and links to relevant resources.

National Coalition for Campus Children's Centers
ericps.crc.uiuc.edu/n4c/n4chome.html

This site provides an extensive list of links to resources related to child care.

The Sloan Work-Family Researchers' Electronic Network
www.bc.edu/bc_org/avp/csom/cwf/wfnetwork.html

Created for work-family researchers, this network is designed to facilitate researchers' access to work-family studies. It attempts to track emergent research trends and is also engaged in proposing new research agendas. This website includes access to an extensive research literature database, several work-family discussion forums, and a research newsletter. Other offerings include an extensive list of links to other work-family organizations and websites and a collection of course syllabi. The network is supported by the Alfred P. Sloan Foundation and is managed by the Center for Work and Family at Boston College.

Work and Family Clearinghouse
National Resource and Information Center at the Women's

Bureau of the U.S. Department of Labor
www.dol.gov/dol/wb/public/programs/NRICmain.htm

The Work and Family Clearinghouse is a computerized database and resource center with information on women's employment issues that affect work and family life. This site contains the "Working Women Count Honor Roll Report" and the "Working Women Count Executive Summary," which include profiles of companies that are attempting to make balancing work and fam ily easier for working parents.

Work and Family Connection
www.workfamily.com

Work and Family Connection is a clearinghouse for news and information about work and family issues. It provides some free and some subscription-based information, including extensive links to other resources and 10 years of searchable archives filled with news and information about companies with the best practices in the area of work and family. It has also compiled an online encyclopedia and hosts a forum where information about work and family is exchanged.

Work-Family Listserv
www.la.psu.edu/lsir/workfam/

This listserv, moderated by Robert Drago from the Labor and Industrial Relations department at Pennsylvania State University, distributes current news and research information to more than 400 researchers, activists, and policymakers.

Glossary

Many of the terms listed below were developed since the 1960s to describe new events and issues, such as the "mommy track" or "family-friendly" benefits, that emerged from the changing relationship between work and family as middle- and upper-income women entered the workforce in growing numbers. Other words listed below are not specific to the field of work-family but emerge from a variety of social science disciplines to describe social issues such as the "feminization of poverty" and the "glass ceiling" phenomenon.

activities of daily living (ADLs)   Activities that the elderly or disabled might have trouble performing, such as getting in or out of bed, dressing, bathing, or using the toilet. The inability to perform one or more ADLs is often used as an eligibility criterion for long-term care services.

adoption credit   A benefit provided by employers to cover the medical, legal, and travel costs related to adoption. It usually ranges from $1,000 to $10,000 and provides equity for adoptive parents.

adult day care   Community-based group programs designed to meet the needs of functionally or cognitively impaired adults. Adult day care centers provide a homelike setting for individuals who, for their own safety and well-being, can no longer be left at home alone.

alternative work schedules   Flexible work schedules, such as coming in early and leaving early, or compressed work schedules, which often refers to fitting a five-day workweek into four longer days.

assisted living facilities (ALF)   Residential apartment complexes that cater to older adults by providing built-in care services. These residential settings maximize independence but do not provide skilled nursing care. Most ALFs do not accept public financing and rely on private payments from residents or their families.

caregiver Usually refers to informal, unpaid assistance for the physical and emotional needs of another person. Family members or friends frequently provide this type of care. In the child care field, however, the term *caregiver* refers to people who are paid for providing child care services.

comparable worth discrimination This occurs when the setting of wages is influenced by the gender that dominates a particular field. For example, jobs traditionally held by women, such as schoolteacher or nurse, may have lower salaries than jobs traditionally held by men, such as truck driver or electrician, regardless of any objective criteria that could be used for valuing the content and skill requirements for those jobs.

contagion Process by which someone's subjective experiences in one arena, such as work, arouse a set of feelings in another arena, such as family, and affect the dynamics of life in that arena.

corporate citizenship The belief that companies need to take active responsibility for their employees' lives and that corporations have social responsibilities even when meeting those responsibilities may cost money.

cult of domesticity A belief originating in the mid-nineteenth century with the rise of the middle class that the role of women was to stay at home and be responsible for child care and domestic activities. This new ideal of womanhood stated that for women to be considered good and proper, they must strive to cultivate piety, purity, domesticity, and submissiveness.

daddy stress Because fathers are spending more time attending to family and household responsibilities but still work in an environment that provides little support for family needs, they experience stress trying to balance these two demands on their time and emotional energy.

daddy track Used by researchers to discuss men who opt for a slower track at work—less overtime, out-of-town travel, and involvement in work responsibilities that interfere too much with family responsibilities. Men who opt for this track at work often experience fewer rewards such as salary increases and promotions.

dependent care A generic term for child care, eldercare, and care of the disabled.

dependent care assistance program An employee benefit that allows employers to offer employees with caregiving expenses the ability to pay for these caregiving services with pretax dollars.

face time The amount of actual time spent being physically present in the workplace. Work-family researchers argue that "face time" is often not a useful measure of productivity or loyalty. They suggest that tasks completed or actual work accomplished, rather than physical presence, should be used to evaluate employee productivity.

Family and Medical Leave Act   Passed in 1993, this law provides for unpaid leave for the birth, adoption, or foster placement of a child; an employee's own serious health condition; or the serious health condition of an immediate family member. This law currently covers only employers with 50 or more employees.

family friendly   Benefits offered by employers that support the family, such as parental leave, child sick time, or flexible work options. This term is also used to refer to workplace cultures or attitudes that are more supportive and flexible with regard to assisting employees in meeting their family needs.

family work   Unpaid work, such as household chores and child care, that was traditionally done by stay-at-home mothers.

father friendly   Benefits that support fatherhood or a workplace culture that is supportive and flexible with regard to fathers meeting the needs of their families.

feminization of poverty   Over time, the gap has widened between the number of women living in poverty, which has increased, and the number of men living in poverty, which has decreased. Women now make up 80 percent of the single-parent families that live in poverty, and because women live longer and have smaller retirement funds, a large percentage of older women are impoverished.

glass ceiling   First used by the *Wall Street Journal* in 1986, the term describes the invisible barriers that stand between women and their rise up the corporate ladder or to higher management positions in any organization.

glass escalator   Men working in predominantly female occupations or departments within a corporation are more likely to be promoted than are women with equal experience.

home care   Provides a range of services in the home from medical support to assistance with activities of daily living to housekeeping. This support allows many elders and people with disabilities to remain in their own homes without having to rely as much on their relatives.

homemaker services   Services delivered to the home that do not include hands-on care, such as shopping, laundry, cleaning, meal preparation, and transportation assistance.

househusband   A stay-at-home husband or male equivalent of a housewife, with the equivalent stigma sometimes attached. Responsible for providing unpaid child care and attending to household responsibilities and cleaning.

ideal worker   Traditionally defined as a man who was able to put in long hours at work while being supported at home by a wife who took care of all the household and caregiving responsibilities. Many work-family researchers argue that the notion of the ideal worker needs to shift because so many women are now in the workforce. They argue that productivity and worker loyalty need to be measured by actual work accomplished rather than number of hours present in the workplace or by the gender and family responsibilities of a particular worker.

job share Formally defined as two people who are employed in one full-time position. The two employees share full responsibility for the job, and if one of the employees cannot cover his or her hours, the other employee is expected to step in. Usually, employees who job share work alternate days or split days, but arrangements vary.

latchkey children Children under the age of 12 who care for themselves while their parents are at work. Between 3 and 5 million children are estimated to be latchkey children in the United States.

meeting macho policies This phrase refers to employers who call meetings at 7:00 A.M. or 5:00 P.M., when employees who have family responsibilities experience conflict between mandatory family responsibilities, such as dropping their children off at school, and their work responsibilities.

new familism A recent trend that includes a variety of phenomena involving families spending more time together, such as women who are leaving the workforce or switching to part-time jobs in order to spend more time with their children or men choosing to be stay-at-home fathers or staggering their work schedules in order to spend more time caring for their children.

occupational segregation Refers to the concentration of women in occupations in which most of the employees are women (such as nursing) and the concentration of men in occupations that employ mostly men (such as engineering). Almost half of all employed women today work in occupations that are more than 75 percent female. Jobs that are traditionally filled by women tend to be lower paying.

part-time work Any amount of time spent in the labor force that is less than that of a full-time employee in that particular occupation. The amount of time involved in part-time work varies widely from one hour a week to 35 hours a week.

pay equity A tool for eliminating sex and race discrimination in the wage-setting system by using race- and gender-neutral criteria to set wages. Many women and people of color remain segregated in clerical, teaching, and service jobs that have been historically undervalued and continue to be underpaid because of the gender and race of the majority of people who hold these positions.

presenteeism The opposite of absenteeism. Involves employees who want to be viewed favorably by the organization working excessive hours or remaining at work into the evening in order to be seen, regardless of whether they are accomplishing a significant amount of work.

reentry woman   Women who have been out of the paid labor market in order to raise children and then reenter the workforce when their children are older.

sandwich generation   Couples who delay having children and then face the challenge of dealing with aging parents at the same time that they are coping with the emotional and economic demands of young children. This term is often used to refer to women because they are more likely to be the day-to-day caretakers for elderly relatives and also more likely to be the primary caretakers for children.

self-care children   See latchkey children

separate spheres   This is also called "doctrine of two spheres." The belief that men should support the family by working outside the home and women should stay home and take care of children and perform domestic chores. In the United States, this belief originated in the middle of the nineteenth century, when the common belief was that women were inferior to men both physically and mentally.

sequencing   A fluid work pattern in which people, usually mothers, move in and out of paid employment in response to child care demands. Often women devote more time to their jobs before they have children and when their children are older.

shared care   Shared care is a term used to describe family structures in which parents put a high priority on being the primary caretakers of their children while staying actively engaged with work. Different families achieve shared care in different ways—some rely on extended families or limited daycare, some telecommute or work back-to-back shifts, and some reduce work hours or job share.

spillover   Experiences in one arena moderate or exacerbate experiences in another arena. For example, if someone has a stressful job but a supportive marriage, the marriage lessens the amount of stress that person feels at work.

stalled revolution   Used by Arlie Hochschild and other work-family researchers to describe the phenomenon of employed wives continuing to have primary responsibility for child care and household duties.

sticky floor   The inability of women to rise above low-level positions in organizations. These jobs are usually monotonous and low-paying. Some researchers argue that the sticky floor is an even more serious situation than the glass ceiling, which prevents women in middle-management positions from rising to the top of an organization.

tag-teaming   Also called "two-shift families," refers to primarily low- and middle-income couples who work different shifts in order to save money on child care expenses and have one parent on child care duty at all times. Almost 20 percent of two-parent, two-income households in the United States are tag-team families, according to the U.S. Census

Bureau. Research has shown that tag-teaming couples can experience more marital problems than couples with more traditional schedules.

telecommuting A work arrangement that allows an employee to work at a location outside the workplace, usually from home, under specified conditions. Various technologies such as the phone, fax machine, or computer are used to keep the employee connected to customers, colleagues, and supervisors.

30/40 A work week that was compressed to 30 hours for 40 hours' worth of pay. Some manufacturing companies and some companies in the health care industry have adopted this plan, which enables employees to have more time to deal with family and other personal responsibilities.

two-shift families See tag-teaming

work-family A field of study that incorporates a variety of social science disciplines to explore the interrelationship between work responsibilities and family responsibilities and how these two areas of life affect one another.

work-life A term that encompasses not only work-family issues but any personal demands or interests employees have outside their time at work. Work-life benefits accommodate the needs of individuals who have family responsibilities as well as providing employees who do not have immediate family needs with, for example, flexible schedules so that they can take a class or care for a sick friend.

work-family backlash People who do not have children sometimes react negatively to the increase in family-friendly benefits and policies being offered at work.

work-family conflict The assumption that there is an incompatibility between the demands of the work role and the demands of the family role. One common form of conflict occurs when the time demands of one role make it difficult to meet the time demands of another role or when one schedule directly interferes with another. Another form of conflict between these two domains is when stress in one domain "spills over" into the other domain, or when behaviors used in one domain, such as emotional sensitivity useful in family interactions, may not be accepted in another domain.

working father This term draws attention to the fact that many employed men have dual roles, just as their counterparts, "working mothers," have dual roles. This term is not widely used except by researchers and activists.

Index

L eslie F. Stebbins holds a B.A. from the University of Michigan and an M.S. in Library Science from Simmons College. She currently works as a librarian at Brandeis University where she teaches research seminars on work-family and other topics in sociology and women's studies. She also serves on the Brandeis University Committee on Work/Life Issues. In addition to paid employment, she and her husband share parenting responsibilities for their two children.